PLATO, DERRIDA, AND WRITING

Jasper Neel

Southern Illinois University Press

Carbondale and Edwardsville

Library of Congress Cataloging-in-Publication Data

Neel, Jasper P.
    Plato, Derrida, and writing/Jasper Neel.
        p.   cm.
    Bibliography: p.
    Includes index.
    ISBN 0-8093-1440-1
    1. Authorship—Philosophy.   2. Plato.   3. Derrida, Jacques.
I. Title.
PN175.N44 1988   87-28439
808′.001—dc19   CIP

The paper used in this publication meets the minimum requirements
    of American National Standard for Information Sciences—
    Permanence of Paper for Printed Library Materials, ANSI
    Z39.48-1984.   ∞ ™

93   92   91   90   5   4   3   2

For Faye, who is my soul mate

CONTENTS

RENVOI

Risks, Rules, and Assumptions

> Speculative philosophy thus proscribed the preface as empty
> form and as signifying precipitation; it prescribes it, on the
> other hand, insofar as it is in the preface that meaning
> *announces itself.*
>
> Derrida, *Dissemination*

This is, as Derrida has shown all too well in the "Outwork"
to *Dissemination,* the end, the postface, the unglued outside of
the inside to come, the fourth text. I will call it a "Renvoi," a
term that carries into English the following play of meaning:
sending back, returning, sending away; adjournment; reflection
of light; a copy editor's caret; reverberation of sound; countermotion; even a rugby kickout from the twenty-five-yard line;
and (alas!) a rising in the stomach, a belch, some uncomfortable
hot air.

And so I send this back to Plato and Derrida, neither of whom,
I am sure, feels or ever felt the least need of it. Like every writer,
though, I must find a place, and the place I have found, like
that found by all my predecessors, makes me send back, reflect,
repeat, kick off, adjourn, mark empty spots for words left out,
listen for what I missed, attempt a countermotion, and occa-
sionally even expel hot air, at times from an overfullness, at
times from a gnawing void. What I send back is this:

Proclaiming writing as a *process* rather than a *product* has become something akin to a mantra for those in composition studies
during the last fifteen years, so much so that Lester Faigley
("Competing") divides process theory into three "schools."
Nowadays, all composition textbooks, no matter how prescrip-
tive, no matter how obviously current-traditional, *all* of them
claim to be "process based." This book is an attempt to study
what writing as process might actually mean. However solip-
sistic, even narcissistic, it may seem, this book is about itself.
That admission is, I realize, a dangerous one to make in the
third paragraph of a book, when readers have committed only
a few moments of their time and thus have few reasons for
completing that book, but since I intend to ignore the advice of
both Plato and Derrida, the two writers to whose texts I have
attached my own, high risk is the mode I have chosen from the
outset, and there seems little point in hedging.

Plato says not to write at all. Or, if I must, to do it as a sort
of diversion from which the best of myself and my thoughts
should be excluded (*Phaedrus*, sec. 276). However revealing,
however embarrassing it may prove to be, this book represents
(in the full Derridean play of that term) both the best of my
thoughts and the best of myself.

Derrida, on the other hand, says, "Never tell what you're
doing, and, pretending to tell, do something else that immediately crypts, adds, entrenches itself" ("Living On · Border
Lines," pp. 175–76). He also says, "A text is not a text unless it
hides from the first comer, from the first glance, the law of its
composition and the rules of its game. A text remains, moreover,
forever imperceptible. Its law and its rules are not, however,
harbored in the inaccessibility of a secret; it is simply that they
can never be booked, in the *present*, into anything that could
rigorously be called a perception" (*Dissemination*, p. 63). I intend
not only to tell what I am doing, but also to do what I am telling.
And I intend to expose the rules of my text at every point.

I am attempting to demonstrate and to justify five assumptions: (1) Plato's statements about writing (and rhetoric too for
that matter) have been taken seriously for too long. It's time for
someone to show just how deceitful those statements are. (2)
Because Jacques Derrida (whether for good or ill) has become
such an influential figure among Western intellectuals, and because of the importance Derrida attaches to writing, it's time for

someone to make a systematic study of the Derridean canon in order to articulate the theory of writing that informs that canon. (3) Because so many empirical studies of writing are already underway, it's time for someone to undertake a purely theoretical study, one that neither attempts to escape reconditeness nor justifies itself by attempting to emulate social science. Such a study requires the writer to foreground the gaps, dilemmas, and contradictions that all writers encounter when they attempt to insert a new text into the written discourses of the West. (4) Writing must be "saved" from philosophy before it can receive attention as a legitimate field of study. "Saving" writing from philosophy requires liberation from both Plato and Derrida. (5) Those who conceive of writing as a process already inhabit (whether consciously or not) a poststructuralist frame of reference and unavoidably invite deconstruction into their pedagogy.

Three rules govern my text: (1) The way to neutralize an old, strong text—a text so entrenched in the canonized literature of the West that its persistence is assured—is to attack it directly on its own grounds, then show the most obvious way to rehabilitate it, and finally expose the deceptiveness of that rehabilitation. (2) The way to use new texts—texts still under heavy and bitter attack, texts whose place (if any) in the canonized literature of the West remains uncertain—is to inhabit their voices in the most friendly and supportive manner possible, then turn those voices against themselves to reveal their most secret inadequacies, and finally retain the voices while remembering the inadequacies. (3) Since writing has been silenced by philosophy ever since Plato, the only way for writing to operate now without denigrating itself at every moment is to force the self-canceling voice of philosophy into one text. This self-cancellation will in turn clear a space in which writing can operate without being forever prejudged as inferior.

The assumptions that I attempt to justify and the rules governing my text appear in a two-part process. The first part of the process attempts to unwork the fabric of Plato's *Phaedrus*. Before writing as process can even begin, the most powerful voice of the West, the voice that defines itself in writing and then attempts to extract itself from writing by branding writing as trivial play, must be silenced. Silencing this voice requires both revealing its impossibility, which is the goal of chapters 1, 2, and 3, and exposing the destructiveness of attempting to rehabilitate that voice, which is the goal of chapter 4. The second part of the process articulates the theory of writing that informs Jacques Derrida's readings of Western metaphysics. If, as I believe, process writing can never be anything other than (self-)deconstructive, articulating Derrida's notions about the role of writing in the formation of the West is essential. Articulating these notions occurs in three steps. Drawing on those texts published by Derrida between 1967 and 1980, chapter 5 sets out his theory of writing. As a way of supporting chapter 5 and drawing on the same Derridean texts, chapter 6 defines nine terms that appear frequently in Derrida's analyses and that inform his theory of writing. Chapter 7, however, reverses the ground of chapters 5 and 6. Because Derridean analysis calls not only other theoretical positions into question but also its own, chapter 7 turns deconstruction against itself, revealing both the impossibility of its foundation and the inadequacy of its reading strategies.

Tearing down *Phaedrus* only to set it up again coupled with setting up deconstruction only to tear it down again will, no doubt, seem like an odd way to proceed. (I console myself with the knowledge that it is not nearly so odd as Plato's attacks on writing *in writing* or Derrida's attempts to reveal that *writing precedes and enables speaking*.) The temptation is to omit chapters 4 and 7. This would allow the destruction of Plato as a writing theorist, a destruction devoutly to be wished by those of us who work in composition studies, and it would leave Derrida ascendant, a quite attractive ascendency because Derrida repeatedly argues that writing is the truth of the West. But giving in to this temptation would both oversimplify Plato, by suppressing the full sophistication of his attack, and conceal the full canniness of deconstruction, which automatically calls its own position in question.

A second reason—this one even more important than the first—also prevents my giving in to this temptation. Doing so would leave my own text squarely inside the discourses of science and philosophy. I would have formulated a thesis (Plato is deceitful in writing *Phaedrus* and wrong about writing), discovered a methodology (deconstruction allows an unworking of *Phaedrus*), discovered evidence (by applying the methodology in support of the thesis), and reached a conclusion (Plato is wrong and Derrida is right). Thus, I would have concealed my own process of writing by pretending to have written a scientific or philosophical text instead of a purely rhetorical one. But this would be the easy way out, and it would still leave composition studies at an impasse.

The final step, and hence the only real risk, is to offer sophistry as the mode of operating in a post-Platonic, poststructuralist world. My purpose is to attempt to clear a place in intellectual history where the act of writing is neither shameful (as Plato would have it) nor philosophical (as Derrida would have it). This requires me to admit from the beginning that the success of my text depends on my ability to discover and to use the available means of persuasion. I will argue for a new sort of writing, a rhetorical writing that quite self-consciously admits its own rhetoricity and carefully delineates the ethical ramifications of its operation at all times. While it is true that I end up much closer to Derrida than to Plato, I also recognize my absolute need for Plato; without him deconstruction would overwhelm me, blinding me both to its own rhetoricity and to the rhetoricity of life in general. For the strong discourse I advocate in chapter 8 to occur, the writer and the speaker must escape the binary opposition between idealism and deconstruction and begin to write—an act that encompasses and exceeds both Plato and Derrida. Protagoras and Gorgias reveal the way by anticipating deconstruction, undermining Platonism, and using rhetoric to show how one recognizes a good decision and helps it prevail.

Like every other writer, I am indebted to more people than I can hope to thank. I must, however, thank the following: the National Endowment for the Humanities, which gave me a summer research stipend with which I began the reading that led to this book; Professors Geoffrey H. Hartman and J. Hillis Miller, who took the time to introduce me to modern critical theory, who invited me to join their seminars, and who encouraged me to seek a relationship between critical theory and composition theory; Dean William C. Moran, who encouraged me to become a scholar and found the time and money to make that possible; Professor Sharon Crowley, who showed me how to end this book when I had begun to despair that it would ever end and to whom I owe the idea for chapter 8; Professor James Mellard, who helped me know what sort of book to write and who read my manuscript carefully, helping me see how to shape and present it to the world; Mr. Curtis L. Clark, who edited the manuscript with insight and grace; Ms. Cheryl Fuller, who typed (and retyped!) the manuscript so many times and whose patience and preciseness made the task of production so easy for me; and especially Faye Richardson Neel, who gave me the confidence to write the book in the first place.

PLATO,
DERRIDA,
AND WRITING

1.
PLATO'S
(SOUL)
WRITING

However uncomfortable it may make us, Plato undeniably condemns writing. No amount of interpreting can get around the fact that the following passages, in their praise of dialectic, attack writing. In the "Seventh Letter," Plato writes:

Any serious student of serious realities will shrink from making truth the helpless object of men's ill-will by committing it to writing. In a word, the conclusion to be drawn is this; when one sees a written composition, whether it be on law by a legislator or on any other subject, one can be sure, if the writer is a serious man, that his book does not represent his most serious thoughts; they remain stored up in the noblest region of his personality. If he is really serious in what he has set down in writing "then surely" not the gods but men "have robbed him of his wits." (sec. 344)[1]

In *Phaedrus* Plato's Socrates recounts the Egyptian myth of the origin of writing:

In the region of Naucratis in Egypt there dwelt one of the old gods of the country, the god to whom the bird called Ibis is sacred, his own name being Theuth. He it was that invented number and calculation, geometry and astronomy, not to speak of draughts and dice, and above all writing. Now the king of the whole country at that time was Thamus, who dwelt in the great city of Upper Egypt which the Greeks call Egyptian Thebes, while Thamus they call Ammon. To him came Theuth, and revealed his arts, saying that they ought to be passed on to the Egyptians in general. . . . [b]ut when it came to writing Theuth said, "Here, O King, is a branch of learning that will make the people of Egypt wiser and improve their memories: my discovery provides a recipe for memory and wisdom." But the king answered and said, "O man full of arts, to one it is given to create the things of art, and to another to judge what measure of harm and of profit they have for those that shall employ them. And so it is that you, by reason of your tender regard for the writing that is your offspring, have declared the very opposite of its true effect. If men learn this, it will implant forgetfulness in their souls: they will cease to exercise memory because they rely on that which is written, calling things to remembrance no longer from within themselves, but by means of external marks; what you have discovered is a recipe not for memory, but for reminder. And it is no true wisdom that you offer your disciples, but only its semblance; for by telling them of many things without teaching them you will make them seem to know much, while for the most part they know nothing; and as men filled, not with wisdom, but with the conceit of wisdom, they will be a burden to their fellows." (Hackforth, secs. 274d–275b)

After telling the myth, Socrates then explains what it means:

Anyone who leaves behind him a written manual, and likewise anyone who takes it over from him, on the supposition that such writing will provide something reliable and permanent, must be exceedingly simple-minded; he must really be ignorant of Ammon's utterance, if he imagines that written words can do anything more than remind one who knows that which the writing is concerned with. (Hackforth, sec. 275c)

Yes, of course, there are numerous ways to explain these diatribes. In the "Seventh Letter," for example, Plato is disavowing a book by Dionysius in which Dionysius sets out to explain Platonic philosophy; and it is in fact true that Plato's writings take the form of dialogues, not treatises. Or, since *Phaedrus* is an attack on the sophists, the attacks on writing are against sophistic writing (the "bastard" "knack" of manipulating mass opinion) and in defense of Platonic writing, which seeks the truth and "is written on the soul of the hearer" (sec. 276a). But something about these explanations doesn't quite satisfy or the passages would not appear and reappear so often.

When Plato's Socrates says that "nothing worth serious attention has ever been written in prose or verse" (sec. 277d), he effectively excludes writing from the highest forms of thinking, understanding, and communicating. But as we know all too well, Plato had to have writing to condemn it. He could stand under the plane tree beside the Ilissus and shout as loudly as he liked; the only way we "hear" him today is in writing. And writing, for those of us who now call ourselves composition specialists or writing theorists, has become sanctified:

> Until writing, most kinds of thoughts we are used to thinking today simply could not be thought. (Ong, *Rhetoric*, p. 2)

> Why write? One important reason is that unless we do there are mental acts we cannot perform, thoughts we cannot think, inquiries we cannot engage in. (Young and Sullivan, p. 225)

> Writing is hard work. But writing is also opportunity: to convey something about yourself, to communicate ideas to people beyond your immediate vicinity, to learn something you didn't know. (Trimmer and Sommers, p. 6)

> Writing is one way of making meaning from experience for ourselves and for others . . . [I]t serves as the most available and the most compelling way because its outcome as visible language is satisfying as a permanent record of thought and feeling. (Lauer, Montague, Lunsford, and Emig, p. 6)

> Writing is also a way of finding out what we know and what we need to learn. Spoken words disappear as soon as they are spoken; but writing freezes our thoughts, makes

them visible and permanent so we can examine and test their quality. (Raymond, p. 2)

Writing forces us to explore and thereby to enlarge our capacity to think and feel and perceive. (Kane, p. xii)

Writing is the making of meaning, first, last, and always. (Knoblauch and Brannon, p. 60)

Writing is a way to end up thinking something you couldn't have started out thinking. Writing is, in fact, a transaction with words whereby you *free* yourself from what you presently think, feel, and perceive. You make available to yourself something better than what you'd be stuck with if you'd actually succeeded in making your meaning clear at the start. (Elbow, p. 15)

And I could go on. These are merely the first eight books on writing I pulled off the shelf nearest my desk.

So what do we do? We could simply ignore Plato. Theoretically, at least, we could. But in practice we can't. He crops up in *CCC* and *College English* as well as the standard rhetoric and critical theory journals all the time, and every graduate student who decides to pursue composition or rhetorical theory is obliged to read him.[2] *The Bedford Bibliography for Teachers of Writing*, for example, lists *Phaedrus* first among ancient texts writing teachers should know (p. 11).

Since ignoring Plato is a theoretical rather than a practical possibility, we have found several other ways to account for his attack. Perhaps he wasn't attacking writing as an enterprise so much as cautioning us not to become tape recorders, which is what happens to Phaedrus, who likes Lysias's speech so much he sets out not to think about it or learn from it but to memorize it parrotlike the same way teenagers pick up the latest slang. Perhaps Plato was condemning the hieroglyphic writing used in Egypt rather than Greek alphabetic writing, which is the ancestor of modern Western writing. After all, one of the main points of Plato's attack is that writing resembles painting (and while that is true of hieroglyphics, it really isn't true of alphabetic writing). What is more, Plato set the crucial myth condemning writing in Egypt, not Greece. Perhaps Plato was attacking only the part of writing that figured prominently in the sophist's elementary curriculum, where writing was used almost exclusively for rote learning. Thus the attack is merely one more way to ridicule sophistic education and not really an attack on the phenomenon of writing per se.[3]

Good cases can be made for all those defenses. Best of all, they allow us to have Plato and writing too, for they allow us to argue that, though he seems to condemn writing, in fact he merely cautions us to be careful with it and teaches us how to use it. But finally, we don't believe ourselves. There simply is no avoiding the fact that Plato not only condemns rhetoric as either a "bastard" "knack" or a still nascent art,[4] he also condemns writing as bad for us, as antithetical to dialectic, and as nothing more than an inferior amusement for the truly wise (secs. 277b–278c). As a result, we merely read Plato and pass over him to Aristotle, whose *Rhetoric* can serve as the foundation for our own composition theories and pedagogical practices. Everyone seems willing to accept a modern world so changed since Plato's time as to render his ideas, great though they were, inappropriate in a world so thoroughly committed to print as ours is. After all, in Plato's Athens it was pretty easy to talk to anybody who was anybody; the number of interesting people to exchange discourse with was quite small and everybody was together in one place, unlike today's world with its labyrinthine, worldwide systems of communication.

But if the study of writing is to become a legitimate discipline, it must explain itself ontologically and epistemologically, and an attack like the one mounted by Plato (*especially* the one by Plato, because of his role in the definition of Western thought and his position as the first major writing theoretician) simply cannot go unanswered. We can hope he didn't mean it and say he didn't mean it as much as we like. Sooner or later we must take him on. He's wrong about writing, and his error is compounded because he uses writing to make his case.

So far as I know no one has decided to attack him by dismantling his text and showing that it doesn't work. In fact, *Phaedrus* is reducible to an aporia—a set of gaps, dead ends, complexities, and contradictions so entangled as to render the text if not void at least so undecidable as to be disregardable. All one has to do is listen to the "conversation," keeping a careful record of all its strands, and then follow a few strands to their ends (or to the places where they become so entangled with other strands as to be invisible). Once one unravels a few of the strands, enough of *Phaedrus* will be undone for us to see Plato behind the tapestry with a pen in his hand, in silence, attempting the greatest theft of all time, the theft of writing. Rather than using writing, he tries to use it up, leaving nothing for those who follow. Plato uses the most powerful system available to humanity, the system of writing, to steal the most powerful voice of Western civilization, the voice of Socrates, and then he tries to negate the system itself, leaving himself with both the voice of authority and absolute control of a system that after him will be corrupted, unable to regain a position of authority, unable to begin the search for truth.

To accomplish this feat, however, Plato must write a text that escapes the normal sequence of history and operates itself with no outside control, a text that presents itself as a completed structure with no origin at all, a text that is free from the normal diseases of all things human. He can't do that. It is, however, a tribute to his power as a writer that almost no one in the last twenty-three centuries has wanted to be like Lysias. Once an argument can be labeled "mere sophistry," it can be rejected out of hand; no further attack is necessary. Dangerous as it may be to do so, I hereby admit that everything after this sentence is sophistry. Plato has had writing long enough. It's time to free writing from his tyranny. However ridiculous one might find the questions I pose to *Phaedrus*, none of them will be as ridiculous as Plato's attacks on writing (in writing!). The stakes are quite high here, having to do with no less important an issue than who gets to speak and what counts as thinking.

The first two questions are: (1) What is the sequence of events, both of *Phaedrus* in history and inside *Phaedrus* itself? (2) Whose voice speaks where?

I. Sequence

> Every bit of writing is imagined as mass which occupies scarce space. It is the duty of writing, therefore, to admit no other writing, to keep all other writing out.
>
> Edward Said, *Beginnings*

The reader has at least three choices of where to situate *Phaedrus* historically: the Socratic world sometime around 410

B.C., the Platonic world sometime around 367 B.C., and the post-Platonic world, which could be any time after the middle of the fourth century B.C.[5] One can describe the text's circumstances in 410 with some certainty and comfort, those in 367 with a good deal less certainty and comfort, and those after Plato's death hardly at all.

410 B.C.   Socrates, who is about sixty, meets with Phaedrus, who is in his late thirties, and they discuss a speech written by Lysias, who is in his middle thirties. Socrates teaches Phaedrus many things, including the nature of love, the sanity of madness, the principles of true rhetoric, and the inferior value of writing. At the end of their discussion, Socrates sends Phaedrus to tell Lysias and the speech writers, Homer and the poets, and Solon and the politicians what he has learned about love, madness, rhetoric, and writing; Socrates agrees to carry the same information to Isocrates, who is in his late twenties and, according to Socrates, has the potential to become a "lover of wisdom," the highest accolade available to mortals. Socrates, who bitterly opposes the philosophical position of the sophists, regards Lysias and others like him as rogues who maliciously dupe ignorant people out of both their money and the possibility of improving their souls.

Even situated in 410, however, the dialogue exposes itself as something other than literal, as a text that means in ways different from what it says, because Solon has been dead for about 150 years and Homer for about twice that. Thus, Phaedrus is not to speak to them directly. Even read as a document situated firmly in 410, therefore, *Phaedrus* in its own words questions its place in history and in fact becomes a document written "out of time," by which I mean it is a document that simply refuses to have a place in time. This is true, as I will attempt to show below, because Plato is mounting an effort to destroy time by using writing to kill all the voices of the past while at the same time using it to preclude its use in the future. After Plato, there will be nothing but continuing repetitions of Plato. It was a dangerous gamble that succeeded.[6]

367 B.C.   Plato writes a fictional dialogue in which all the events described in the previous two paragraphs take place. With one major difference—none of the events described in those paragraphs actually took place. At least they never took

place literally. Figuratively, perhaps, Plato has made up a dialogue that, with a change here and there, could have taken place.
(In other words, Plato puts nothing in Socrates' mouth that
Socrates absolutely could not have said even though he did not
say exactly this—though one cannot help wondering whether
Plato has not stretched Phaedrus's pliability and simple-mind-
edness a little.) In many ways the Platonic world of 367 parallels
the Socratic world of 410. Plato, like Socrates, is attempting to
be a teacher who uses dialectic to teach true philosophy. The
sophists are as strong in 367 as they were in 410, and still they
are concerned primarily with practical rhetoric and skeptical of
humanity's ability to discover and communicate truth. Except
for Isocrates, however, who in the world of 367 is approximately
seventy, all the characters in *Phaedrus* (except, of course, Plato,
who would have been eighteen or nineteen in 410 and whose
role in *Phaedrus* exists only in its absence) are dead.

The problems with sequence become much more difficult here
because every word has the capability, even the probability, of
meaning something different from what it says. Every statement
that could have been pinned down in 410 becomes much more
problematic in 367, at which time it cannot occur literally and
thus occurs only as a replacement for a voice that could have
spoken in 367 but chose to replace itself with already dead voices
from four decades before. And at this point the text begins to
complicate itself in a variety of ways as we hear a voice that is
the replacement of a voice—the dead Socrates replaces the living
Plato.

When we reflect for a moment, however, we realize that the
replacement itself has been appropriated, for the Socrates we
hear is the Platonic Socrates created after Socrates' death. Thus,
a pattern begins that repeats itself constantly in *Phaedrus*. What
speaks is a replacement of the actual speaker, yet the replacement
has always already been appropriated by the voice it supposedly
replaces. In other words, Plato replaces Plato. He does this by
giving up his voice to Socrates, but when we read from the
situation of 367, we realize that there isn't a Socratic voice for
Plato to take over except for the fictional one Plato himself made
up. Plato's maneuver in 367 is really an attempt to hide his own
voice. Perhaps Plato's most brilliant insight was to realize how
difficult disputing his texts would be if he removed himself from

them by taking on the role of recording secretary for the martyred, authoritatively dead Socrates.

AFTER 348 B.C.   Whether Cicero in the first century B.C., Schleiermacher in the nineteenth century A.D., or a current graduate student in composition theory, any reader after Plato's death must construct some frame of reference within which to read *Phaedrus*.[7] The possibilities are too open-ended even to guess at, but several generalizations about sequence expose the uncertainty of the text. First, we cannot read the text in 410, even though that is surely the simplest place to situate it. Not one single word of the text occurred in 410. Oddly enough, however, we cannot completely extricate it from 410 either, because the text is so persistent in claiming to be nothing more than the recording of a conversation under a plane tree beside the Ilissus near the end of the fifth century B.C. Second, we cannot read the text in 367 because—except for Plato, who effaces himself completely, and Isocrates, who has gone through a time warp that aged him more than forty years—no one in the world of 367 appears in the text. Third, we must content ourselves with a strange sort of floating time frame because we are reading a text that, after claiming not to be written at all, claims to have been written for fifth-century Greek society (which very oddly includes not only Solon and Homer but a plethora of divinities), when in fact it was first revealed to fourth-century Greek society and clearly aimed at all posterity.

This text, modest though it *seems* to be, not only explains how to discover the truth but also explains the *only* way the discovery can be communicated. As a result of the floating time frame, every statement must be interrogated with at least three questions: (1) Are you merely the recreation of a statement (ironic or otherwise) that could have been made in 410? (2) Because you were written in 367 and attributed both to a time and a speaker not your own, should I distrust what you seem to be saying in all innocence and honesty in 410? (3) If after twenty-three centuries I can figure out how you want me to read you, should I do it? Complicated though these questions are, the answers they generate are even more complicated because they reveal Plato's attempt to steal discourse from Western society.

Two examples will suffice. After listening to Phaedrus read Lysias's speech, Socrates begins to tease him and finally calls the speech a poorly done "piece of youthful exhibitionism." When Phaedrus demands a better speech, Socrates demurs: "My good Phaedrus, it would be ludicrous for a layman like myself to extemporize on a subject which has been already treated by a good writer." A few lines later, however, Socrates agrees to make the speech: "I'll speak with my face covered. In that way I shall get through the speech most quickly, and I shan't be put out by catching your eye and feeling ashamed" (sec. 237a).

I'd like to interrogate these two statements a bit, and I'll treat them in Plato's order. First, "My good Phaedrus, it would be ludicrous for a layman like myself to extemporize on a subject which has been already treated by a good writer." Question 1: Are you merely the recreation of a statement (ironic or otherwise) that could have been made in 410? The answer, of course, is yes. One cannot help enjoying the jovial banter between the two men as Socrates draws Phaedrus into admitting he has a copy of Lysias's speech under his cloak, teases him about the "glow" and "ecstasy" with which he reads the speech, and then coyly waits to be forced to say what he really thinks of the speech. And Phaedrus is as fully involved in the play as Socrates. He uses trite clichés, jokingly threatens violence, and finally threatens never to give Socrates another speech unless Socrates agrees immediately to attempt making a better speech than the one by Lysias. The willing reader can become an eavesdropper on a delightful, ancient conversation.

In the Socratic world of 410 (fictional though it is) is the statement ironic? Almost certainly. "Layman" (other translators say "amateur" or "untaught man") does not mean someone who knows only a little of a profession (well, it means that on the surface, but the surface disappears immediately); quite the contrary, it means someone who has not had his thinking process corrupted by nihilism and "rhetoric." When it comes to sophistic education in rhetoric and writing, being a layman is, in the Socratic frame of reference, a very good thing. The phrase "a good writer," rather than being a compliment, is an insult, because a "good" writer is someone "who has devoted his time to twisting words this way and that, pasting them together and pulling them apart" (sec. 278d) for the sole purposes of manipulating and deceiving an audience, giving it false wisdom instead of true wisdom, and making it into "a burden on society" (sec. 275b). Thus a "good writer" is by definition a "bad person." The word *ludicrous* removes itself from the statement entirely because no one of any time period at all believes it would be ludicrous for Socrates to attempt to make a better speech than Lysias. (The key ambiguity, of course, is the word *better*. Does it mean truer? More persuasive? Both?).

Question 2: Because you were written in 367 and attributed both to a time and a speaker not your own, should I distrust what you seem to be saying in all innocence and honesty in 410? Having discovered the irony of the text situated in 410, the reader is satisfied and tempted to stop. Going further seems both impolite and ill-tempered. If we are to save writing, however, we have no choice but to attack the authority who would demean it and take it from us. When we shift to 367, we lose the convivial, jovial discussion under the plane tree beside the river. The games Socrates and Phaedrus play are no longer their own. Now we have a man sitting in silence, fabricating a conversation, and writing with a motive. The shift highlights the word *extemporize* ("it would be ludicrous for a layman like myself to extemporize") because there is nothing at all extemporaneous about the Platonic Socrates' speeches. They never existed as speeches but were writing (the thing that is not speech, that is the death of speech) from the very beginning. As a result, Plato has the chance to think through what Socrates will "say," revise and rearrange it as much as he likes, and ensure that every statement works exactly as he wants it to, both in the individual "speech" and in the "dialogue" as a whole (I use quotation marks because there is neither speech nor dialogue in this *written* text). In fact, Plato can craft each "speech" carefully so that it *looks* like speech. It is easy to forget that speech cannot be seen. But why is Plato so reluctant to speak himself? Why does he always pretend not to be there? What is he hiding? And above all, why is he so careful as a writer to write what "looks" like speech?

His motive is very much in question. Surely it is not to entertain (entertaining though *Phaedrus* is) and surely it is not to ridicule Lysias, who is dead and beyond embarrassment or improvement. When one shifts to 367, in fact, the statement under interrogation "disappears." One cannot see it anymore because behind it the man holding the pen is not concerned with the witty banter of two dead men but rather with the project of defining what counts as thinking. If we let ourselves be delighted by the wordplay and conviviality, we become the Phaedrus of

367, little more than a yes-man taking orders. Plato, master writer that he is, has manipulated us without our realizing it, for we cannot refuse to be drawn into the delight of the 410 discussion without feeling like, and seeming to others like, nitpicking spoilsports. That is the evil of *Phaedrus*: its delightful surface turns those who look for the man with the pen into meanspirited cavilers. But there was a man with a pen, and his motive was not to ridicule Lysias or enlighten Phaedrus or even give us a pleasant afternoon's read.

Question 3: If after twenty-three centuries I can figure out how you want me to read you, should I do it? *Phaedrus* is a dialogue, not a treatise. Its constantly repeated intent is to encourage dialectic over rhetoric, writing, and reading. If it succeeds, Platonism becomes to history what Socrates is to Phaedrus—the intelligence to which one addresses all questions. And both the history of discourse and the history of philosophy stop because they can now be written only as a dialogue with Platonism. This leaves us a choice: either give the moral high ground to Plato in order to have rhetoric and writing as corrupted forms of audience manipulation (in effect, this is what Aristotle does in his *Rhetoric*),[8] or attempt to show that Plato cannot condemn writing in writing and at the same time exempt his own text from the condemnation. If we choose the latter, if we refuse to read Plato's text as it asks to be read, we are outside Platonism and run the risk of appearing incapable of thought because Platonism has already defined itself *as* thought. Thus our attack, rather than threatening Platonism, threatens thought.

Plato has built himself a formidable position indeed. He has used writing, the one possible means to invent his specialized kind of "thinking," and then denied that means to all who follow him. Thus we see the statement "My good Phaedrus, it would be ludicrous for a layman like me . . ." not as the ironically witty banter of 410 or even as Plato's suspect attempt to hide himself in 367; we see the statement as one thread in a tapestry behind which a man mounts projects no less ambitious than defining the truth and appropriating the means whereby truth is communicated while seeming to do neither—in fact, while seeming not to be there at all.

Now for the other quote: "I'll speak with my face covered. In that way I shall get through the speech most quickly, and I shan't be put out by catching your eye and feeling ashamed." With the text situated in 410, the reader cannot help being attracted to this Socrates who plays so splendidly at speaking. Even now I smile as I think of him winking and hiding his face, full of life, joy, and play. The passage is charming—disarming even the severest critic. But, alas, the answer to the first question (Are you merely the recreation of a statement that could have been made in 410?) is, no. And the answer to the second question (Should I distrust what you seem to be saying in all innocence and honesty?) is, yes.

Plato has created a Socrates who is a charming prisoner of the sequence of time in 410. Plato's Socrates does not know what is coming. But *Plato* knows, because he has moved into the one medium that allows both the creation of fictional time and sequence and the manipulation of the things inside that fictional creation. One who can only speak is a prisoner of uncontrollable sequence. One who writes, on the other hand, invents history first, then controls it, and finally determines its sequence. When the reader looks behind the scene beside the Ilissus to Plato alone in his study, Socrates' first speech becomes no speech at all. It is merely the place that Plato will later fill with the only speech he wants us to hear (see!).

This is so in two ways. First, in having his Socrates disavow the first speech before making it ("I'll speak with my face covered"), make fun of the speech while giving it (sec. 237a), and condemn the speech as "silly and more than a little blasphemous" (sec. 242d) after it is over, Plato, even in the act of giving it, takes the speech away from the reader because even the fictional Socrates of 410 does not believe what he says, as he makes abundantly clear. In effect, Plato's Socrates gives a speech while at the same time announcing its death. Second, the speech exists only as the temporary replacement of the permanent replacement to come, for the man with the pen is creating a place for the only "real" speech he wishes to leave for us. Plato, the writer who can look back over his composition and remake it any way he likes, knows, as he refuses to let his Socrates know, that a second speech is coming, and it is the second speech that the reader is supposed to hear (see). But in order to make this second speech into speech (and to keep it from being writing), Plato must create a time, a place, and a speaker. And that is what he is up to in both the written speech of Lysias and the "extemporaneous" first speech of Socrates. In effect, Plato has made his own monologue appear as dialogue; removed himself entirely from the apparent dialogue so as to put any potential opponents at a serious disadvantage because they must go through this wonderful, lovable Socrates to get at him; and then, without the reader's ever noticing, turned the dialogue back into monologue by silencing all the voices around his messages about the nature of love, the soul, the good, and the means of communicating about them.

Now for the third question: If I can figure out how you want me to read you, should I do it? The answer: Only if you wish to give your voice to Plato, who will do to you exactly what he does to Lysias, Phaedrus, even Socrates—usurp your right to speak and take from you the only means you have of reestablishing your own voice: writing.

II. Control

> Our present problem is the intricate relationship of the so-called real author with his various official versions of himself.
> Wayne C. Booth, *The Rhetoric of Fiction*

Plato clearly gains much by writing before his own time and out of Socrates' mouth. But once one undoes the first knot in the tapestry by asking the questions Who wrote what when? and Where am I when I read? it is quickly apparent that *Phaedrus* is writing; thus, however much it may try to hide its writtenness and deny validity to writing, *Phaedrus* is subject to the same interrogation as any other written text.

Plato's text would have us believe that no one is in control, that it is a disinterested movement toward truth set in operation and kept in motion by the power of dialectic as exercised by the superior philosopher, Socrates. Plato himself, for example, is absent everywhere. No surviving manuscript even has his name on it, yet never in history has anyone seriously questioned Plato's authorship (De Vries, p. 3). Even in the nineteenth century, when the authorship of almost every ancient manuscript was questioned, no one ever successfully advanced an argument about *Phaedrus*. One of the curious things about reading *Phaedrus* is that Plato seems present everywhere, as he had to be, but everywhere one looks, he vanishes. Stating "Plato says that . . ."

is exceedingly dangerous because whatever Plato "says" floats out of the dialogue as a whole and can never be pinned down to the example of a specific utterance because Plato is intentionally, carefully absent from every specific statement.[9] As a result, there is not a single direct statement in the entire *Phaedrus*.

Because all the apparent speakers and writers were dead before *Phaedrus* existed, we can be sure that no one with a name in or on the text ever actually said or wrote any of it. The image from the frontispiece of Matthew Paris's *Prognostica Socratis Basilei*, made famous in Derrida's *La carte postale: De Socrate à Freud et au-delà*, is inescapable.[10] In the picture (see fig. 1), Socrates sits at a writing desk, pen in hand, head cocked as if listening, his name (beginning with a capital letter) elaborately written over his head. A much smaller Plato stands on tiptoe behind him, his right index finger prodding Socrates' back, his left raised in the manner of a nitpicking school teacher. Plato, whose name begins with a small letter, is frowning and straining his eyes as if to see whether Socrates has written what he was told. Derrida describes the scene like this:

> Une révélation apocalyptique: Socrate écrivant, écrivant devant Platon, je l'avais toujours su, c'était resté comme le négatif d'une photographie à développer depuis vingt-cinq siècles—en moi bien sûr. Suffisait d'écrire ça en pleine lumière. Le révélateur est là, à moins que je en sache encore rien déchiffrer de cette image, et c'est en effet le plus probable. Socrate, celui qui écrit—assis, plié, scribe ou copiste docile, le secrétaire de Platon, quoi. Il est devant Platon, non, Platon est *derrière* lui, plus petit (pourquoi plus petit?) mais debout. Du doigt tendu il a l'air d'indiquer, de désigner, de montrer la voie ou de donner un ordre—ou de dicter, autoritaire, magistral, impérieux. Méchant presque, tu ne trouves pas, et volontairement. (pp. 13–14)

> (An apocalyptic revelation: Socrates writing, writing in front of Plato, I had always known it, it had remained like a photography negative to develop for twenty-five centuries—in me, of course. Sufficient to write that in full light. The developer is there, unless I don't yet know how

Fig. 1. Plato Watching Socrates Read. From *Prognostica Socratis Basilei*, by Matthew Paris. MS. Ashmole 309, folio 31 verso, reproduced by permission of the Bodleian Library, Oxford.

to decipher anything of this image, and this is, in fact the most probable. Socrates, the one who is writing—seated, bent over, docile scribe or copyist, the secretary of Plato, what? He is in front of Plato, no, Plato is behind him, smaller (why smaller?), but standing. With an extended finger, he seems to indicate, to point out, to show the way, or to give an order—or to dictate, authoritarian, magisterial, imperial. Almost naughty [wicked], don't you think, and intentionally.) (my translation)

This picture raises the question of control in an absolutely unanswerable way. Plato, as I have already argued, is absent everywhere in *Phaedrus*. He "exists" there one might almost say because of his everywhere-apparent absence. But Plato is not the only one absent from *Phaedrus*. Socrates, too, is absent, for he is dead. Whatever he might have said is always already lost to us. The absence of Socrates coupled with the absence of Plato makes for some exceedingly curious and baffling reading circumstances. Both Socrates and Plato live in Socrates' death; both are present through his absence. Socrates, "he who does not write,"[11] must die and vacate his voice for it to exist, for since he limits himself to speaking, his voice in living lives only as it passes out of existence. Thus he can live *for us* only after his death, after his voice ceases to sound and has been usurped by another, by the Platonic Socrates, who, though not a writer either, is written and only written. Plato, on the other hand, he who *says* he does not write ("If I thought . . . any adequate . . . written account could be given to the world . . . what more glorious life-work could I have undertaken than to put into writing . . . ?" [sec. 341d]; "No intelligent man will ever dare to commit his thoughts to . . . written characters" [sec. 343a]), must lose his voice in order to have the already lost voice of Socrates.[12] Socrates' voice lives in the death of Plato's voice, which lives in the death of Socrates' voice. Whichever voice one hears, the other man is speaking. Or at least so it seems.

The play of absent authors (speakers) is part of the fabric of the text itself. Socrates' first speech again serves as a good example. To begin with, Plato has made Socrates reluctant to give the speech. The reluctance is, from Plato's perspective as weaver of the tapestry, a deception, of course. There is never any doubt that Socrates will give the speech if for no other reason than that

Plato must create a place in speaking for Socrates' second speech to exist so it will not appear to be writing. But quite apart from Plato's role in *Phaedrus*, the authorship of the second speech shifts constantly. To begin with, the author is a sort of Socrates-against-his-will: he speaks with his head covered because he is so ashamed of what he is saying. In other words, even in the fictional world of 410 the speech is not given by Socrates but by his antiself, his *sophistical* self, the adept rhetorician who can represent "evil as in fact good." Socrates as a sophist is a problem I will deal with later; for now let it suffice that the speaker of Socrates' first speech is clearly an adept sophist who says convincingly what he does not think no matter how frequently he calls attention to his discomfort in that role.

But Socrates-as-sophist is just the beginning. Soon he becomes Socrates-as-medium. First, there is the invocation of the muse, but it is a very odd invocation because the Greek words call themselves into question. The Greek that is usually translated as something like "Come, O Muses" loses its parodic feel in English; in Greek there is at least the possibility (if not the certainty) of self-parody. Then Socrates uses one of his strange ("fanciful," "playful," "strained") etymologies linking the muses talents to the "tuneful race of Ligurians."[13] In fact, however, the invocation says, I am not an invocation, just as the speech itself throughout says, I am not a speech. Everything about the speech is a sort of now-you-see-me-now-you-don't self-removal. Given the parodic invocation, the reader cannot help but question Socrates' contentions in midspeech ("I am inspired"; "The nymphs take possession of me" [sec. 238]) that he has become nothing more than a medium. One cannot help thinking Socrates peeks out from under his head cover to wink as he says this, and one feels exactly the same at the end of the speech when Socrates repeats his contention that he is nothing more than a medium ("These nymphs, to whose influence you meant to expose me all along, will drive me positively beside myself" [sec. 241d]). While one can surely believe that someone is putting words in Socrates' mouth, the someone is not a muse of Ligurian ancestry.

The complexities of the origin of the speech do not, however, stop with Socrates-as-sophist or Socrates-as-pretend-medium. They include Socrates-as-manipulated-friend, for Socrates claims four times that the speech really belongs to Phaedrus, who has forced him to give it: at the beginning, "Help me in the tale which this fine gentleman is forcing me to tell" (sec. 237a); in the middle, "*You* [Phaedrus] are responsible for this" (sec. 238d); and twice after the speech is over, "In that speech of yours, which came out of my lips because you put a spell on them" (sec. 242) and "You must realize that the previous speech was the work of Phaedrus, son of Pythocles" (sec. 244a).

There is, however, yet another turn, for we learn that the speech was not really by Socrates-as-sophist or Socrates-as-pretend-medium or Phaedrus; it was by *Lysias* of all people. At the end of his second speech, Socrates apologizes to the God of Love for making the first speech and then reveals the true author of the first speech: "If in the beginning Phaedrus and I uttered aught that offended thy ears, lay it to the account of Lysias the true begetter of that speech . . ." (sec. 257a). In other words, Plato gets to write a sophistical speech contending the opposite of what he believes by putting the speech in the mouth of a dead Socrates and then through a series of shifts and sleight-of-hand maneuvers gets away with attributing the speech to Lysias, the arch-sophist. Socrates is off the hook, and Plato smiles in his study as he looks at the twice-defeated Lysias, whose rhetorical and writing skills were opened to ridicule in his written speech and whose limitations as a thinker were revealed in Socrates' first speech, which, it turns out, was really by Lysias himself. Lysias exposes himself to ridicule.

But wait! This isn't speaking, it's writing. The text is always there for one more interpretation. If Plato takes himself out of the dialogue entirely and gives all the positions to dead people, then he can't stay around to stop the continuing circle of interpretation. If by writing his speech on love and thereby prompting Phaedrus to force Socrates to compete with him, Lysias is really the author of Socrates' first speech, by extension of the same logic, isn't Lysias also the author of Socrates' *second* speech because without Lysias's written speech, Socrates would not have been forced to give his first speech and thus would have had no reason or occasion to give the second speech as a penance for the first? Therefore doesn't Socrates' long second speech, including its explanation of the soul and the good, come indirectly from the arch-sophist Lysias, and by extension doesn't knowledge of the good come from sophistry compounded?

III. Beginning and Ending

> As a problem, beginnings seem to have a sort of detachable
> abstraction, but unlike an idea about which one thinks at some
> distance from it, a beginning is already a project under way.
> Edward Said, *Beginnings*

> Endings, then, are faked, as are all other parts of a narrative
> structure that impose metaphor on the metonymic sequence.
> Frank Kermode, "Sensing Endings"

The question of Lysias's role in *Phaedrus* brings me to the
ultimate question of sequence, beginning and ending. The dialogue "begins" because of Lysias's written speech. Not surprisingly, however, Lysias's role in Plato's text is at least as problematic
as Socrates'. Indeed, Lysias himself is present through a sort of
triple absence: (1) He, like Socrates and Phaedrus, must be absent
(dead in history) for Plato to take over his voice. (2) He must be
absent from the discussion under the plane tree for Phaedrus to
take his voice by reading his speech and then for Socrates to
destroy his voice twice by showing in one speech that Lysias
failed to say what he intended to say and then in a second speech
that what Lysias intended to say should not be said anyway
because this intended message is wrong. (3) Almost certainly,
Lysias never wrote the speech. Plato did.[14] In other words, Plato
has inserted himself into the now-past year 410 in order to preempt
a voice he will himself preempt later. He has done this by pretending not to have composed a speech by Lysias (here he
preempts Lysias's voice by writing "before Lysias has a chance
to") and then pretending not to have composed two speeches
by Socrates that destroy the forged speech by Lysias (here he
preempts Lysias a second time, except that the Lysias he preempts
is himself).

At the risk of redundancy and tedium, I'll say that another
way: Plato takes over Socrates' voice in *Phaedrus* in order to
destroy the sophistic writing of Lysias, but because Plato himself
already wrote the sophistical writing of Lysias, what happens
is that Plato gives up his own voice to the dead Socrates in order
to destroy his own writing (the forged speech by Lysias), which
was written in the first place to be destroyed. A fairly good case,

it seems, could be made that vast stretches of *Phaedrus* (of which the written speech by Lysias and the two long speeches on love by Socrates are good examples) are in fact either absolute silence or a doubled voice saying exactly opposite things at the same time. The text demands that one ask, Where did this speech begin and where does it end? Then the text tries to provide its own answer, but once the questioning has begun, the text loses control of the process.

Perhaps a slightly simplified, somewhat artificial record of the layering of sequence and control revealed up to now will make this idea clearer (again the point of departure is Socrates' first speech, that sophistical transition—and place making—between the sophistry that appears in the written speech attributed to Lysias on one hand and the philosophy that presents itself as speaking in the long discourse by Plato's Socrates on the other):

1. Socrates gives a speech that he does not believe, praising the nonlover over the lover.
2. In giving the speech, Socrates undercuts it by making it a self-parody, a sort of humorous antithesis of itself.
3. Socrates attributes this speech, which cannot be his own if he is not to be a sophist, to a variety of origins, including nymphs and even Phaedrus, but finally, in a somewhat surprising reversal, attributes it to Lysias, whose writing caused the speech to occur *and provided its content*.[15]
4. Thus Socrates' first speech, which is the occasion and necessity of his second speech, really belongs to Lysias, whose written "speech," the only self-proclaimed piece of writing in the entire "dialogue," jars the reader from the fictional world of 410, allowing a brief glimpse of Plato in 367 *writing* "behind the scene."
5. Suddenly one is aware that Lysias's writing has become Plato's for Plato forged Lysias's writing as a way to begin (without seeming to begin) his own form of writing, which denies that it is writing by pretending to be dialogue and which even denies the validity of writing as a medium.
6. Plato has caught not the sophists but himself, because the "true" "speaking" in *Phaedrus* comes not from itself but from the false writing of Lysias (which is doubly false because Lysias never wrote it). Is it possible that Plato has caught himself so thoroughly that his text shows how

the true comes from the false, how philosophy finds its occasion in sophistry, how knowledge of the good requires nihilistic audience manipulation to know itself, and how speaking comes from writing?

7. In effacing himself so as to seem not to write and in sacrificing writing to the primacy and purity of speaking, has Plato lost himself in a variety of other selves so thoroughly that he has effaced himself entirely? Clearly he has tried to set sequence in sequence and take control of control in order to remove himself from sequence and make his text not a text but an act of final control. But to do this he needs writing, and if we read his text as writing, instead of its opposite, which it claims to be, Plato loses control and becomes part of sequence like everyone else.

The play of contradictory forces is no less violent at the end of *Phaedrus,* where Socrates agrees to carry a message to his "still young . . . favorite," Isocrates, whose future he predicts like this:

> It seems to me that his natural powers give him a superiority over anything that Lysias has achieved in literature, and also that in point of character he is of a nobler composition; hence it would not surprise me if with advancing years he made all his literary predecessors look like very small-fry—that is, supposing him to persist in the actual type of writing in which he engages at present—still more so, if he should become dissatisfied with such work, and a sublimer impulse lead him to do greater things. For that mind of his, Phaedrus, contains an innate tincture of philosophy. (Hackforth, secs. 279a–b)

Several times before this quote, which comes only a few lines before the end of the dialogue, the reader has caught a glimpse of Plato behind the tapestry. Here, his full figure, sitting alone in his study, *writing,* is visible. Sequence becomes an aporia, for the "young" Isocrates of 410 (Isocrates was twenty-six in 410) is not young at all. He is sixty-nine. Thus Socrates predicts an already-known future. And in that future, Isocrates has indeed become the most influential writer and educator of his time.[16] But he *is* a writer *and* a sophist. Whatever tincture of innate Platonic philosophy marked his mind has long since been washed clean. And suddenly *Phaedrus* reveals itself not as an attack on Lysias but as an attack on Isocrates, Plato's principal rival as an educator in mid-fourth-century Athens. Thus Plato's manipulation of his reader is finally revealed: in order to attack a rival, who is both a rhetorician and a writer, Plato creates a fictional dialogue, sets it forty-three years in the past, when both he and his rival were young, puts his argument in the mouth of the martyred Socrates, and excoriates rhetoric, writing, and sophistry.

To do this, however, the one device Plato *must* have is writing, and the one strategy he must use is sophistical rhetoric. The *only* way he can speak in his own absence, speak with someone else's voice, and speak out of his own time is in writing. The only way he can speak with Lysias's voice is to use sophistry. As Derrida says, "In writing what he does not speak, what he would never say and, in truth, would probably never even think, the author of the written speech is already entrenched in the posture of the sophist: the man of non-presence and of non-truth" (*Dissemination*, p. 68). In order to attack writing and sophistry, Plato becomes a writer and a sophist. This is disingenuous. But Plato is playing for much higher stakes than dominance of mid-fourth-century Athens. He has set out to define thought for humanity, and his strategy is more than disingenuousness; it is vicious, for he uses rhetoric and writing to define and then occupy the moral high ground, and then he tries to destroy the means he has used so that no one else can use that means again, not in 367 B.C., not ever. What Platonism offers in *Phaedrus* is not dialectic. What Platonism offers in *Phaedrus* is a continuous repetition of Platonism. Plato wants to use writing, rhetoric, and sophistry to destroy themselves. What he must leave behind to do so, however, is writing. Fortunately, he cannot use it and use it up. With writing, one *must* have one's cake and eat it too!

Phaedrus ends *before* it begins, for it ends with a compliment to the Isocrates of the year 410, but it is sent out to the world of the year 367 (and after). Thus only at the end, with Isocrates—the most influential sophist and writer of his age—in full view can one begin to read *Phaedrus*, because only when the Platonic Socrates predicts the future are we forced to realize that this future is already past. And only then can we *begin* to read—by which I mean *re*read. But here at the end, when the text should end, it begins *as a text*, for only texts repeat themselves exactly as before while revealing themselves to "say" something quite different from what they said the first time. The Platonic Socrates is wrong, or naïve, or manipulated by the writer behind the scene when he says, "You might suppose that they [written words] understand what they are saying, but if you ask them what they mean by anything they simply return the same answer over and over again" (sec. 275d). Reread texts do not say the same thing over and over again. And as we "begin" to (re)read *Phaedrus*, having finally reached the end where true beginning begins, we can "begin" to see the absences through which the text exists and Plato—the most influential writer and sophist of all time—is caught stealing writing from us.

IV. Repetition and Replacement: Composition as De-composition

> He who writes with the alphabet no longer even imitates. No doubt because he also, in a sense, imitates perfectly. He has a better chance of reproducing the voice, because phonetic writing decomposes it better and transforms it into abstract, spatial elements. This *de-composition* of the voice is here both what best conserves it and what best corrupts it. What imitates it perfectly because it no longer imitates it at all. For imitation affirms and sharpens its essence in effacing itself. Its essence is its nonessence. And no dialectic can encompass this self-inadequation. A perfect imitation is no longer an imitation. If one eliminates the tiny difference that, in separating the imitator from the imitated, by that very fact refers to it, one would render the imitator absolutely different: the imitator would become another being no longer referring to the imitated.
>
> Derrida, *Dissemination*

Phaedrus operates through repetition and replacement. It operates, in fact, as only writing can, for only a writer—working alone with plenty of time for revision, research, and rewriting—could produce something so apparently like dialogue yet so utterly dependent on other texts. (Speech made visual does not look like itself. It must be changed, made to differ from itself in order to be seen as itself.)[17] Three examples will show what I mean: Plato's treatment of Isocrates, who "appears(!)" to be absent until the last few lines; his treatment of Lysias, who appears to be present throughout the dialogue; and his use of the epitaph on the tomb of Midas the Phrygian, which is the consummate example of nonsequential sequence.

EXAMPLE 1: ISOCRATES, OR THE ABSENCE OF PRESENCE. "Now before arriving at the end of *Phaedrus*," says Gerrit J. De Vries, "the reader will have been struck by many allusions to Isocrates" (p. 16). The number of allusions to the writings of Isocrates in *Phaedrus* is so great that Ronna Burger calls it a "hidden dialogue with Isocrates which runs through the *Phaedrus*" (p. 152, n. 24). The very fabric of *Phaedrus* depends on the writing of Isocrates; indeed *Phaedrus* repeats that writing.[18]

Only in writing could Plato spread before himself the writing of his principal rival, find the exact passages he wanted, and integrate them into his own text. It is a cruelly successful procedure, so successful as to be comic in the way Swift's treatment of his rivals is comic in *Tale of a Tub*. By keeping Isocrates hidden throughout the dialogue (a hiding is an act of obscuring what is present), Plato can use the Isocratic sophistry that he must have to write at all. By exposing him at the end of the dialogue, Plato tries to destroy both Isocrates and his sophistry. The noble future Socrates predicts can only be, to use De Vries's phrase, a "bitter taunt" (p. 18). Isocrates lives in the already-completed future that Socrates predicts, a future that has shown him to be a writer and a sophist, not a Socratic philosopher.[19]

By creating a dialogue that pretends to occur in 410 and that predicts a possible future that has already not been fulfilled at the moment of its prediction, Plato reduces Isocrates to nothing more than a failed mind that once had promise. But the very fabric of Plato's text consists of, indeed could not have been woven without, the written sophistry of Isocrates. In fact, Plato's treatment of Isocrates is a miniature of the Platonic strategy throughout *Phaedrus:* appropriate a medium belonging to others while pretending not to use it, and then use it to build your own position; once your own position is established, call attention to the medium as corrupt and inadequate and try to remove it from history, denying it to both the past and the future. Plato uses writing as repetition in which the repetition attempts not to repeat what it imitates but to overthrow and negate it. Plato uses Isocrates' future and after he has used that future for his own ends attempts to deny that future the right to occur.

By its very nature, writing is replacement. Something has to

come before it. And anything not original, anything in fact derivative or repetitive or imitative, cannot be finally authoritative.
It is a place in the sequence of discourse; thus, it "always owes
its motion to something else" (sec. 245c). *Phaedrus,* like all writing, is a place in a sequence. But Plato's strategy is to use writing
and then call attention to its inadequacy in an attempt to separate
his writing from writing, just as he tries to separate his sophistry
from sophistry.

EXAMPLE 2: LYSIAS, OR THE PRESENCE OF ABSENCE.
"Just let me see what it is you are holding in your left hand
under your cloak; I strongly suspect it is the actual speech. If I
am right you can make up your mind to this, that, much as I
love you, I have no intention of letting you use me to rehearse
on *when I might have Lysias himself"* (sec. 228d; italics mine).

Even without Harold Bloom we can see that written texts must
repeat prior written texts, even if the second text tries to subvert
what it repeats by making the predecessor text seem to depend
on its successor. Even without Jacques Derrida we can see that
the one thing above all others denied to writing is absolute origin.
Plato's need for Isocrates and sophistry in general is evidence
enough for that. And *Phaedrus* carries within itself the revelation
of its own circularity. Lysias, whose writing originates the discourse, has already been replaced by Plato's forgery.[20] Thus in
addition to beginning at the end when Isocrates is finally brought
on stage, thereby allowing the reader to know how to begin
*re*reading, the text of *Phaedrus* begins before it begins.

Before writing *Phaedrus,* Plato wrote the speech by Lysias that
he would later situate inside his own dialogue as its raison d'être;
thus, the first text, Lysias's speech, is forever part of *Phaedrus,*
the text that includes it and gives it life, while at the same time
Lysias's speech is excluded from *Phaedrus,* the text that seizes it
as an occasion to kill it and live in its place. This, however, is
just the beginning of the circle, for no sooner has the replacement
of Lysias's writing appeared than it is replaced by Socrates' first
speech, which is then replaced by his second speech. Then after
the long second speech, the dialogue shifts from the subjects of
discourse (e.g., love, the soul, and so forth) to the techniques
of discourse (e.g., rhetoric and writing), and Plato replaces sophistic rhetoric with "true" rhetoric and sophistic writing with
"true" writing. But since his own dialogue exists through audience manipulation (sophistic rhetoric), through saying what

he does not believe or even have occasion to think (sophistic thinking), and above all, through writing, Plato has taken a position through which he can use sophistry in all its forms and at the same time destroy it. He wants to eat his cake and *not* have it.

Because his text is in writing, however, writing itself over-throws him. Plato wants writing to go one way, from himself to the reader, and he succeeds brilliantly because he almost manages to use writing not to write but to speak and not to speak his own voice but someone else's. Fortunately, just as Socrates can "have Lysias himself" through *his* writing, we can "have Plato himself" through his writing though we must strug-gle mightily to do so for he has hidden himself more thoroughly and made his writing more nearly not his own than any writer in history.

The chain of displacements works as follows: Plato forges[21] a text by Lysias and uses it as the beginning for his own text, which presents itself as speech, not writing, and which attempts to destroy writing. Once the Lysias text is in place, Plato sup-plants it with a speech (written) by Socrates (himself a displace-ment of Plato) and then immediately supplants that first speech with a second speech, which is presented as an oral statement of true philosophy. Then, still speaking with the voice of true philosophy that he assumed in his second speech, Socrates dis-mantles sophistic rhetoric as nothing more than a preliminary art that has not yet found itself. Finally, to destroy writing, Plato uses Egyptian folk tradition to fabricate a myth (Iversen, p. 172) and then supplants Socrates' voice with that of the King of the Egyptian gods, Ammon. Thus God condemns writing and si-lences the voice of its creator-defender: we never hear Theuth's reply.

But wait! This is still writing. We can still go back and "hear" the origin of this myth. As soon as Socrates finishes the myth, Phaedrus says, "Yes, Socrates, you can easily invent tales of Egypt or any other country." Socrates' response humiliates Phae-drus and finally destroys whatever resistance he may have had: "There was a tradition in the temple of Dodona that oaks and rocks first gave prophetic utterances. The men of old, unlike in their simplicity to young philosophy, deemed that if they heard the truth even from 'oak or rock,' it was enough for them; whereas you seem to consider not whether a thing is or is not true, but who the speaker is and from what country the tale comes" (Jowett, secs. 275c–d). But note well what has happened here. Plato has invented a myth and given it to his Socrates. The myth effectively removes writing in ink as a moral possibility. Then Plato's Phaedrus points out that the myth is a brand-new invention. Finally, Plato's Socrates turns on his Phaedrus, rebukes him for trying to link truth with its speaker or origin (a rebuke that Plato's Phaedrus accepts abashedly), and condemns writing as the opposite of knowledge.

It is dazzling to watch Plato's genius at play. He uses writing to know and define truth; then he uses it to convey the knowledge of his definition. At the same time, he uses writing to say that truth is separable from and superior to its knower and that it cannot be found in writing. It is a brilliant rhetorical ploy: use a medium against itself so as to debase it and impede its use by all followers. That way, only you can have it in its pristine form.

EXAMPLE 3: MIDAS, OR CONTINUOUS SELF-REVERSAL.
A girl of bronze on Midas' tomb I stand,
As long as water flows and trees grow tall,
Remaining here on his lamented tomb,
I'll tell to all who pass "Here Midas lies."
(sec. 264d)

Socrates notes that "it is of no consequence what order these lines are spoken in" (sec. 264d). And this is writing. Wherever one enters it, there is something before and something after that makes it meaningful. Plato attempts to write from outside writing, to establish an eternal dialectic with himself, a dialectic that always already existed. The writing he would allow is located in the place that we know by its absence, the soul (sec. 276a). Fortunately for us and for writing, he has failed, for he is above all else a writer.

If there were a marker on *Phaedrus,* it would say, "Plato lies here" in both senses of the verb, for he must become a sophist to destroy sophistry, and he must become a writer to destroy writing. Plato has sown "his seed in the black fluid called ink," and in doing so he has produced "discourses which cannot defend themselves." In speaking of writers, Plato's Socrates says, "If any of them had knowledge of the truth when he wrote, and can defend what he has written by submitting to an interrogation on the subject and make it evident as soon as he speaks how comparatively inferior are his writings, such a one should take his title not from what he has written but from what has been the object of his serious pursuit" (sec. 278c). By commencing this interrogation of writing, the invisible Plato is attempting to free one written text, his own, from all interrogation. He does this by using his text as the voice of the interrogation of writing. It's high time we pulled the tapestry down and revealed Plato in the game with the rest of us where writing tells him what he thinks he knows, not the other way around.

△

2.
THE STRUCTURE OF ORIGIN AND THE ORIGIN OF STRUCTURE

This is not an essay. It's an example based on the epitaph of Midas the Phrygian that I quoted in ending my last chapter. Like the epitaph, whose four lines "mean" the same thing no matter how they are arranged, my four vignettes can be arranged in any order you like. You see, Plato's Socrates is wrong when he says, "Any discourse ought to be constructed like a living creature, with its own body, as it were; it must not lack either head or feet; it must have a middle and extremities so composed as to suit each other and the whole work" (Hackforth, secs. 264c–d). Actually, it's the other way around: any living creature ought to be constructed like a discourse, with its own language as it were; it must not lack either a preexisting sign system or group of sign users; it must have an infinite series of differences so that it can come to know itself through differing from itself and thus be whole by being part.[1]

I. A Vignette in Which the Critical Edifice Divides Without Collecting

Reason, thus, unveils itself. Reason . . . is the *logos* which is produced in history. It traverses Being with itself in sight, in sight of appearing to itself, that is, to state itself and hear itself as *logos*. It is speech as auto-affection: hearing oneself speak. It emerges from itself in order to take hold of itself within itself, in the "living present" of its self presence. In emerging from itself, hearing oneself speak constitutes itself as the history of reason through the detour of *writing*.

Derrida, *Writing and Difference*

What is *Phaedrus* about? Love? Rhetoric? Philosophy? All three? Something else? More importantly, is *Phaedrus* itself "constructed like a living creature" with head, feet, middle, and extremities all suited to each other and to the body as a whole? Not surprisingly, from the very beginning, the answers have been yes and no. First, no.

Even in antiquity the structure of *Phaedrus* was already under attack (De Vries, p. 22). Diogenes Laertius accounts for the failure of *Phaedrus*'s structure on the basis of popular notions that *Phaedrus* was Plato's first written work and thus suffers from the excesses of "the freshness of youth" (p. 311); Olympidorus then repeats Diogenes' story as fact.[2] Centuries later Schleiermacher, who assigns *Phaedrus* "die früheste Stelle unter allen Werken des Platon" ("the earliest place among all of Plato's works"), accounts for the failure the same way and proves that *Phaedrus* was written by a young and inexperienced writer by explaining that an experienced writer would have known better than to condemn writing (pp. 55–82; my translation).[3] Then in a "through the looking glass" sort of reversal, Hans Raeder, responding to the fact that "einige haben sogar den *Phaedrus* für die allererste Schrift Platons gehalten" ("a few have even thought *Phaedrus* the very first thing Plato wrote") (p. 245; my translation), argues that *Phaedrus* was clearly written at the *end* of Plato's life after advancing age had destroyed his ability to write (pp. 245–79). The assumption that *Phaedrus* is poorly constructed remains the same; only the explanations change.

And change! Paul Shorey, for example, by calling *Phaedrus* "Gothic," tries to say as politely as possible that *Phaedrus* is an eclectic grab bag of ideas, as compared, for example, to the "classic architecture" of the *Symposium* or the "architectural unity of the *Republic*" (*What*, p. 198; *Unity*, p. 79). Both Gerrit De Vries and Walter Hamilton fault the disproportionate length of Socrates' second speech, but each blushes while doing so because of the greatness of the speech itself. Hamilton says of the speech's length, "In view of the fact that the speech marks one of the highest points in Plato's achievement as artist and poet we can hardly regret this" (p. 10), while De Vries says, "The length may, however, be excused—if an excuse is thought to be needed for this piece of passionate writing—by its central position in the work, both in a literal and in a figurative sense" (p. 23, n. 1).

Thus, Hamilton and De Vries, without intending to do so I suspect, have given Plato carte blanche. Because of his greatness as a writer he is exempt from his own rules of writing. The earlier attackers, on the other hand, neither felt obliged to spend much time "proving" what seemed obvious to them—that *Phaedrus* does not meet its own criterion for structure—nor felt obliged to discover the way *Phaedrus* does in fact meet its own requirements for structure no matter how difficult such a discovery might prove to be—a difficulty that leads me to the other side of the argument, Yes, *Phaedrus* does have sound structure.

This side of the argument, too, is a position taken since antiquity. Hermias and Iamblichus both defend the structure of *Phaedrus,* and the twentieth century offers an extraordinary variety of explanations of how Plato adheres to his own rules. Such explanations, which lead to increasingly sophisticated and complex interpretations, are not surprising given the power of the New Criticism, which includes as primary tenets both organic wholeness and protection of the traditional canon. However objective the New Criticism may have pretended to be, it was not in the habit of measuring canonized texts against critical principles and then throwing out those texts that failed to measure up. Rather, it consistently demonstrated how even the most recalcitrant texts in the canon conformed to New Critical principles. With neither disregarding such an important Platonic text as *Phaedrus* nor retaining it despite its violation of principles of structure as an option, the recent spate of explanations showing how *Phaedrus* has structure was inevitable.

Early in the century, Alfred E. Taylor rejects out of hand any possibility that *Phaedrus* is about love, for if it were, it would be "hard to see how its elaborate discussion of the possibility of applying a scientific psychology of the emotions to the creation of a genuine art of persuasion, or its examination of the defects of Lysias as a writer, can be anything but the purest irrelevance" (p. 300). In other words, if one works from the assumption that Plato was incapable of writing a poorly constructed text, it quickly becomes apparent that the text cannot include anything that digresses from the main subject; thus, there are no digressions even if digressions appear to be there. After that maneuver, suddenly "in structure the dialogue is of the simplest type."

In midcentury, Werner Jaeger builds on Taylor and shows how everything in *Phaedrus* grows out of Lysias's speech, which is a written speech about love and thus introduces the ideas of speechmaking, writing, and love all three (pp. 183–88). In other words, since the three major ideas in *Phaedrus* are all there, it is unified in being about all three. Also at midcentury, but with a different explanation entirely, Helmbold and Holther argue that *Phaedrus* is doubly unified (doubly unified?): first by the idea of dialectic, which is "employed as much as expounded," thus offering a union between rhetoric and love, and second by "the prevailing tone, which is that of light irony" (De Vries, p. 23). In other words, if there are two competing ideas, we should just see the work as a metadialectic in which these two ideas make up the dialectic. If that doesn't work, we should check to see if the tone remains consistent; if it does, the actual content becomes unified by the consistent concealed smile of "light irony."

And these are just the beginning of the competing explanations of how *Phaedrus* has structural unity. Also at midcentury, in the preface to his translation of Plato's text, Reginold Hackforth gives up on "attempting to recapitulate and mediate between the views of modern scholars" on structure, which he calls "infinite." Then Hackforth states "baldly and somewhat dogmatically" his own three-part explanation of how *Phaedrus* is unified through its purposes:

> (1) To vindicate the pursuit of philosophy, in the meaning given to that word by Socrates and Plato, as the true culture of the soul, by contrast with the false claims of contemporary rhetoric to provide that culture. This I regard as the most important purpose.

> (2) To make proposals for a reformed rhetoric, which should subserve the ends of philosophy and adopt its method.

> (3) To announce a special method of philosophy—the "dialectic" method of Collection and Division—and to exemplify this both positively (in the two speeches of Socrates) and negatively (in the speech of Lysias).

"Although the first or dominant purpose," Hackforth goes on to admit, "is most clearly discerned and most directly pursued in the middle part of the work (the second discourse of Socrates), it is present throughout, and is what gives the dialogue its unity. Once this is seen, or rather felt, by the reader, he will no longer think it necessary or helpful to ask whether the main subject is Love or Rhetoric" (p. 9).

Obviously, as Hackforth would have it, the dialogue is unified in its attempt to vindicate philosophy, right? Well, not quite. As recently as 1984, Donald C. Stewart could quote Hackforth's explanation to say that "Hackforth pretty well settles the question about the unity of the subject in *Phaedrus*." But Stewart sees Hackforth as arguing that *Phaedrus* is about *rhetoric*, not philosophy (p. 118). Whether Hackforth means *Phaedrus* is about philosophy or rhetoric, however, he certainly did not settle the question.[4] In 1969, for example, De Vries argues that one should not expect "strict" thematic unity from a Platonic dialogue, but that "there is always a centre" to which the numerous themes "are subordinated." In this case, De Vries says, "the central thema is the persuasive use of words. The aim of the dialogue is to show its foundation. Its means is beauty, its condition (unlike current rhetoric's) is knowledge. Eros is the striving after knowledge and after beauty. So the main subthemes of the dialogue are intertwined" (pp. 22–23). In other words, there is thematic unity even though one should not expect it.

In 1973, Hamilton seems to agree with Stewart's pronouncement of closure: "There can be such a thing as a scientific or philosophic rhetoric or art of persuasion, and the main purpose of the *Phaedrus* is to establish the true principles of that rhetoric." Hamilton goes on to say that these true principles must be based on knowledge of truth, which can be attained only through the inspiration of love. Thus, Socrates' second speech is both an example of philosophic rhetoric and "an exposition of the experience on which that rhetoric . . . must be founded." This, says Hamilton, leads us back to the common subject of all three speeches, love, and shows that philosophic rhetoric can grow only from love. OK so far, but Hamilton cannot let the question rest, for he then turns to *Phaedrus*'s final few pages on writing, which reopen the whole question of structural unity, leading Hamilton to admit that Socrates' second speech is disproportionately long and elaborate and that "the severity of Plato's depreciation of writing" may have resulted from his own knowledge that "the poet in him has got the better of the philosopher." In other words, because it is in writing, which lures the gifted writer Plato to excess, *Phaedrus* is not structurally unified after all; then again, because Plato points out that writing "is a poor second-best, a kind of pastime with which the philosopher may amuse himself in his less serious moments," the section on writing and the disproportionate length of Socrates' second speech negate each other, leaving *Phaedrus* (you guessed it) structurally whole (pp. 8–11).

Then in a book-length study in 1980, Burger raises the issue of structure yet again. She, too, finds *Phaedrus* structurally whole, but for reasons different from all the others. Burger's book, which argues that *Phaedrus* is a defense of philosophic writing through an attack on sophistic writing, discovers a single metaphoric pattern unifying all the apparently separate parts of *Phaedrus:*

> In this analysis, the white horse, lover of honor and true opinion, provides the same link between the restraining charioteer and the dark horse, friend of *hubris* and pride, as Socrates' first speech provides between the speech of Lysias, representing the nonloving silence of the ideas, and Socrates' recantation, praising the divine madness of *eros.*
>
> If, however, Socrates' recantation provides the poetic image for the unity of the three speeches on *eros,* it does so only in the context of praising divine madness; but precisely because the madness of *eros* can only be a divine blessing through its transformation to philosophic *eros,* the uncovering of the true whole, which would reveal the three love-speeches as parts, must await the critical examination displaying that alienation from the madness of *eros* which Socrates' mythic hymn cannot acknowledge. (p. 45)

In other words, the parts of *Phaedrus* having to do with analysis of rhetoric and writing are part of the work as a whole because without them the reader would never have the analytical tools to see that the three separate speeches are really three parts of a whole just as the two horses and the charioteer are three parts of a whole. Thus, *Phaedrus* is whole because it carries within itself a commentary explaining how to see its wholeness.

Now there is one very odd thing about all these defenses of structural unity (and there is no doubt that defenders of unity have predominated during the last fifty years).[5] What is there about *Phaedrus* that makes the repeated, increasingly elaborate defenses of its unity necessary? For there to be so many answers, some of them exceedingly complex, there must be a question. The obvious answer, of course, is that everyone who has read *Phaedrus* has had the feeling that the focus of the dialogue shifts around a bit (not to mention the fact that nearly every first reader has surely found Socrates' second speech a bit longish). My hunch, however, is that Plato would not care whether we find *Phaedrus* poorly or well structured. Either way, he still holds the position of authority, for it is the famous Socratic dictum against which we are judging discourse. Plato wants to write the rules much more than he wants to play the game. And if that is true, we must declare the question of *Phaedrus*'s structure void and turn instead to the dictum on structure itself. If we want to remove *Phaedrus* as a hallowed text in the history of writing and rhetorical theory (as I do), we must study it as an origin, not a structure. Even if an incontrovertible case that *Phaedrus* is poorly structured could be made, the case itself would merely reconfirm *Phaedrus* as the authority by which case making is judged. If its doctrine is left intact, the attack on writing stands. The way to get rid of *Phaedrus* is not to demonstrate how it fails to conform to its own rules. The way to get rid of *Phaedrus* is to show what a deceitful text it is.

Accustomed as we are to living in a post-Platonic (indeed post-Aristotelian, poststructuralist, highly sequential, electronic) world, almost no one would dispute Socrates' dictum on structure. Anyone who did so would be dismissed as a knave or a fool. What is at risk in *Phaedrus,* however, is not the relative importance or unimportance of structure: what is at risk is the act of thinking, for Plato is defining thinking. His pronouncement on structure in discourse, indeed, everything he says about discourse, is really the replacement of a treatise on thinking, a treatise that is all the more powerful and persuasive (as well as *much* more difficult to attack) because it seems to be absent.

Plato is much too clever a writer to argue his point directly. He knows all too well how dangerous that would be. In fact, his Socrates explains the idea that any sequential argument begets and includes its antithesis. After Socrates completes his first speech, Phaedrus says, "I thought you were only half way . . ." and Socrates replies, "I've already said enough about both types; simply take the opposites of all the bad qualities I attributed to the first and confer them on the second" (sec. 242a). In order to avoid the trap of being undone by his own argument, Plato does the same thing with his argument he has done with himself— he displaces it.

Plato's strategy is never to bring the act of "thinking" into his writing, because he cannot possibly do so without using metaphor and thus treating "thinking" through some sort of replacement.[6] But because treating "thinking" through a replacement (e.g., "thinking is like . . .") would position "thinking" as something that emerges from writing instead of as something that originates writing, Plato constantly disguises the fact that *Phaedrus,* which can only exist through the rhetorical, sophistical strategies of writing, is itself a metaphor for thinking. In other words, *Phaedrus* the written text defines "thinking" by replacing "thinking" with itself. Thus when *Phaedrus* gives the rules for itself, without ever doing so directly, it has given the rules for thinking. Writing then becomes the absence, or series of absences, that allows itself to be filled up with thinking, for without writing there is no thinking of the sort embodied in *Phaedrus,* which absolutely never could happen as conversation. Nobody talks or ever has talked like the "speakers" in *Phaedrus.* Plato's attack on writing implies some position outside writing where writing itself can be seen whole, evaluated, and regulated. That, of course, is the place Plato has claimed for himself. He attempts to be the one person in history outside writing, able to judge it and pronounce its rules while at the same time condemning it. Plato wants his metaphors to work in only one direction: he tells us the truth through an explanation (e.g., "discourse ought to be constructed like a living creature"). He does not want his metaphors to work like the metaphors he bequeaths to everyone else where each metaphor is the replacement of another metaphor and where writing, rather than being the disclosure of "truth," is the repetition of itself. Plato's writing, as he would have it, escapes the curse he places on all other writing and tells us the "truth." But Plato exempts only one set of texts, his own, from the curse he places on writing.

More importantly, the epitaph on Midas's tomb and Socrates' dictum on structure for which the epitaph serves as example reveal the way Plato has built his position and made it nearly invulnerable while seeming to have no position at all. There are four maneuvers in his strategy: (1) replace one thing with another: in order to have *Phaedrus* as a discourse, Plato must write it down, thus replacing speaking with writing; (2) use the replacement to define the thing it replaces: through the written text Plato explains the principles of a true rhetoric, which is a rhetoric of spoken dialectic; (3) attack the replacement as inferior and corrupt: having described "true" rhetoric, Plato condemns writing as "nothing worth serious attention"; and (4) pretend the original is available in its pristine, uncorrupted form: the lover's discourse inscribed on the soul never reveals itself as something that came into possibility only through the detour of writing.

When the god Ammon makes his famous attack on writing, he says, "Those who acquire it will cease to exercise their memory and become forgetful; they will rely on writing to bring things to their remembrance by external signs instead of on their own internal resources" (sec. 275). But the process, and the *only* process, through which *Phaedrus* could come into existence was exactly this sort of externalizing of private discourse. Plato operates in a world of writing in which what one knows emerges through the recursive, nonsequential externalizing of discourse, discourse that then remains available for limitless modification. At the same time, he valorizes a world in which knowledge is an entirely internal phenomenon that, rather than being created, is gradually recognized through oral discourse with a lover. It is a fundamental problem of Platonism that knowledge comes to know itself through the detour of writing while claiming it was always already there as a mystical reintuiting of itself.

All the business about structure is nothing but a red herring. Structure is nothing more than the residue of writing. Structure is what remains behind as the trace of the effort to create a place in which knowledge can come to know itself and present itself to the world. I wish I didn't think Plato knew that.

II. A Vignette on the Idea of Structure

Form fascinates when one no longer has the force to
understand force from within itself. That is, to create.
Derrida, Writing and Difference

What, after all, is structure? Couldn't one make a fairly
good case that structure is the end of writing? That structure is
what is visible after writing—the struggling, uncertain, chaotic
process that never finishes finding and remaking itself—has
already left? Where—except from some now vanished, unsatisfactory, incomplete effort—does structure originate? An analysis of structure, after all, assumes a teleological whole, something
closed and complete whose operations and laws can be exposed
and evaluated. A structural study of a still-developing structure
(of writing still being written) could be provisional at best, for
as long as the structure develops it is never what it was or will
be. On the other hand, an analysis of origin, as Derrida has
explained at length in *Writing and Difference*, assumes process;
at any moment of its operation, analysis of origin is positioned
to move to the moment before when things were different. Analyses of origin must finally lead to the before or the beyond of
any "object of study" by constantly diverting attention from any
such "object" toward its possibility. The distinction between
structure and origin is crucial because the one thing the *act of*
writing cannot be is structure. At the moment of structure, writing has ceased to be writing and has become a text to be read
because the writer is what must be gone for the reader to take
over. As long as the writer is still the writer, any analysis of
structure is precluded: what will be the text, the site that will
present itself for excavation as structure, is not yet fully itself.

Obviously any sort of analysis of origin must be haunted by
the idea of structure because such analysis, though always committed to the place before where it now rests, requires the moment, however brief, of recognizing its own point of departure.
An analysis of origin cannot deny existence to the question Origin of what? which demands at least momentary acknowledgement of structure. The idea of structure, on the other hand,
is itself problematically unable to deny existence to the question
Where did this structure come from? which demands at least

momentary acknowledgement that the rules and foundation of the structure came from somewhere else, from the before and the outside of this structure. Each system starts from, yet excludes, the other. Since *Phaedrus* demands to be read as structure and has prepared its defenses for such a reading, no structural reading can reveal its law of composition. And if *Phaedrus* is to set itself up as *the law* of composition, it is only fair to demand the law by which *the law* came to be. When Socrates demands structure in discourse, what he raises are the problems of structure as a means of analysis. I'll give four examples of these problems.

First, structural analysis is problematic because of its effect on the text. The text becomes geometric and spatial. "This geometry is only metaphorical," Derrida admits, "but metaphor is never innocent. It orients research and fixes results. When the spatial model is hit upon, when it functions, critical reflection rests within it. In fact, and even if criticism does not admit this to be so" (*Writing*, pp. 16–17). Thus when Socrates says "any discourse ought to be constructed" and goes on to compare the structure to a living being, he has outlined a geometry of thought. Anything that does not fit inside the space created by that geometry is outside thought. This explains the twenty-three-century struggle over whether *Phaedrus* itself has structure, for *Phaedrus* must be shown to fit within its own geometry in order to be taken seriously. No one has ever said (and Plato does not want anyone to!) *Phaedrus* is both wrong and wrong about itself. Why not reverse its case? (1) Demonstrate that *Phaedrus* is great discourse; (2) admit that it does not have the sort of structure it demands; and thus (3) overthrow the demand for structure? Because Plato has made such a demonstration almost impossible; that's why not. *Phaedrus* orients our research and fixes its results by privileging rules over their embodiment. Since Plato uses discourse to know discourse, demonstrating that his own discourse does not, in fact, know itself would erase the lines of the geometry that orients our research and fixes our thoughts, leaving our research with no way to know itself.

Second, structural analysis is problematic because it is, to use Derrida's term, preformationist. By preformationism Derrida means "the well-known biological doctrine, opposed to epigenesis, according to which the totality of hereditary characteristics is enveloped in the germ, and is already in action in reduced dimensions that nevertheless respect the forms and proportions of the future adult" (*Writing*, p. 23). That Socrates' dictum articulates "preformationism" is unmistakeable. Even the metaphor "constructed like a living creature" makes discourse biological with its complete form bound up in the DNA. The dictum also unquestionably subordinates writing and all discourse to thought. Thinking is defined as structure, system, and organization. Discourse, which is the vehicle for transporting thinking, must be made to fit the thinking that comes to it preformed. Such an idea is rampant in the West and clearly dominates the American composition industry, where patterns-based composition texts (those based on such patterns as comparison-contrast and cause and effect) clearly dominate the market. Thinking is defined as structure; students (whether Plato's or ours) must learn to think; thus, they must be provided structures through which their thinking can emerge and know itself. But the principle that is merely assumed here—assumed without even an attempt at justification—is that the first word spoken or inscribed is like the first cell formed in a living being, with the complete DNA code and all the instructions necessary for the formation and development of the whole organism. Plato must assume the principle that thinking precedes and informs discourse because any attempt to justify the principle would open questions about its origin, an origin that would finally prove to occur in discourse itself.

Third, structural analysis is problematic because it assumes receptivity. It demands a preformed emptiness "waiting, like a girl in love, ready for its future meaning to marry and fecundate it" (Derrida, *Writing*, p. 18). Discourse, and especially written discourse, becomes empty structure waiting helplessly until the moment it is inhabited by meaning. Discourse is the empty, unformed structure that comes to know itself as space with a border, as geometry, once it is filled with thinking.

Finally, structural analysis is problematic because it demands the law of simultaneity, which requires that the work be "simultaneously present in all its parts in order to be global." The structural reader must discover this simultaneity: "Similar to a 'painting in movement,' the book is revealed only in successive fragments. The task of the demanding reader consists in overturning this natural tendency of the book, so that it may present itself in its entirety to the mind's scrutiny. The only complete reading is the one which transforms the book into a simultaneous network of reciprocal relationships. . . ."[7] There is, however, only one way for a speaker to offer a speech so carefully structured that the whole work is simultaneously present in all its parts: write it down and revise it into structure. The disingenuoùsness of a writer demanding such structure from discourse while at the same time denying writing as a mode of attaining that structure cannot be overstated. More importantly, the idea of simultaneity in effect precludes the possibility of "parts" because each part is the embodiment of a wholeness that disallows parts. The idea of simultaneity can lead only to a metalanguage that in effect silences whatever language might have been spoken if it had not been perverted by being forced to seem to serve the thought it in fact creates. Every composition teacher who has taught patterns should be able to see this clearly. What occurs from the assignment of a cause-effect essay is an essay that says, usually in several hundred words, I am a cause-effect essay that explains the causes and effects of something. The apparent "content" of the essay (e.g., the causes and effects of alcoholism or child abuse) vanishes at the moment it appears on paper. The essay is then read as a record of the absence of writing, an absence that leaves behind nothing but structure. The student's goal is not to communicate an idea or opinion; quite the contrary, the student's goal is to demonstrate mastery of the form named cause-effect.

There are a variety of other problems with structural analysis. To begin with, any structure is a "field divested of its forces" (Derrida, *Writing*, p. 5), for the force that will someday die and leave behind a structure must be gone already for the structure to be static and fixable in an unchanging way before the analyst's gaze. Knowledge of the end stifles whatever force might have occurred, because the discourse is already complete in its first word. "How," Derrida asks, "can an organized totality be perceived without reference to its end, or without presuming to know its end, at least" (*Writing*, p. 26)? If the idea preexists its relief in discourse, discourse can never be anything more than a receptacle.

Structure is, however, forever vulnerable to questions of genesis, history, and origin. For example, once one begins to question *Phaedrus* about its origin, both its demand for structure and its privileging of thought over discourse fail. All one has to do is ask Who says so? It doesn't matter where the question is posed because the answer will always be the same, Nobody, because nobody *says* anything in *Phaedrus*. No one thinks Socrates' second speech could be an extemporaneous, oral creation. No one thinks the sort of structure demanded by Socrates' dictum could be achieved in speech. Both emerge only because Plato can write, with the leisure to remake his discourse into the "structure" it will present itself as having always had. Both the idea of structure and the act of Platonic thinking emerge from writing. Plato was creating "thinking," and the only way he could create the kind of thinking he did was in writing, because the sort of disinterested speculation advocated throughout the Platonic canon is impossible in a preliterate culture. Said differently, the force that forms the structure of what calls itself "thinking" after Plato and the force that dies and leaves behind the idea of structure after Plato, is writing, for the origin not only of *Phaedrus*, but also of all Platonism is writing.[8]

One can extend the argument to theory of instruction in writing with the conclusion that the degree to which instruction in writing is instruction in structure is just the degree to which "Platonic" writing (which is the kind of writing actually practiced by Plato before he displaced it) is already dead. It is also just the extent to which writing is a repetition of Platonism, which is nothing more than the reinhabiting of an already existing structure. In a world where instruction in writing is instruction in structure, Plato has succeeded in using writing to kill writing, thus making what we call "invention" into nothing more than reinvention, or repetition of structure. By repeating Plato's structure, we kill our own force.

To (re)read *Phaedrus*, by which I mean to get to the end where structure can be recognized, requires a theory of writing based on *Phaedrus* as writing, which has nothing to do with what *Phaedrus* says about writing. This theory is the opposite of the theory *Phaedrus* tries to trick us with, for *Phaedrus* does not do what it says. A theory of writing based on *Phaedrus* as writing would say these things: (1) Pure speech requires writing. There is no purer speech than Socrates' long second speech, and that speech can come to know itself and remain available in history only through the recursive process of inscription. While a case could be made that this speech has all the hallmarks of structure, including preformationism and simultaneity, the speech got them

only through the recursive, unstructured, nonlinearity of writing. (2) Thinking (at least in the speculative, metaphysical sense
so prized by the West) requires writing to know itself, indeed
must be written, separated from its origin, and located in written
discourse to be recognizable as thinking. (3) Thinking occurs in
isolation, in the silent, lonely "discourse" of writing. "Writing,"
says Derrida, "is the outlet as the descent of meaning outside
itself within itself; metaphor-for-others-aimed-at-others-here-and-
now, metaphor as the possibility of others here-and-now, metaphor as metaphysics in which Being must hide itself if the
other is to appear. Excavation within the other toward the other
in which the same seeks its vein and the true gold of its phenomenon. Submission in which the same can always lose (itself)"
(*Writing*, p. 29).

Plato's attempt to use the force of writing in creating the structure of *Phaedrus* while at the same time denying both the use
and the validity of that force is an attempt to have structure
without origin. But one can discover the origin of this structure,
and it is the sophistical, rhetorical maneuvering available only
to a writer. I wish I didn't think Plato knew this.

III. A Very Odd Vignette

I mean something more drastic and (presumably) absurd,
which is the triumph of having so stationed the precursor, in
one's own work, that particular passages in *his* work seem to
be not presages of one's own advent, but rather to be indebted
to one's own achievement, and even (necessarily) to be
lessened by one's greater splendor.
Harold Bloom, *The Anxiety of Influence*

The act of writing can be deeply expressive of feelings of
violation, ancestor-profanation, forgery, self-exposure.
Geoffrey Hartman, *The Fate of Reading*

Few beginnings are as innocent as "Where have you come
from, my dear Phaedrus, and where are you going?" But, tired
as the saying may be, innocence is known only from experience
when it is already and irretrievably lost. The writer of *Phaedrus*

was not innocent, not by a long shot. If one is not careful, perhaps to the point of rudeness, *Phaedrus* presents itself as having no origin, as merely the inspired conversation of two men, a sort of written tape recording of a conversation in the countryside, merely a segment of the larger whole that contains it, making it innocent and removing the need for an origin. Only if one refuses to read the "dialogue" as spoken, only if one demands at every line that the writer reveal himself, does origin become a problem. Once one begins doing that, however, the problem of origin appears everywhere: with the character Socrates (and it is time we call him what he is in Plato's texts, a character in fiction), with the character Pythagoras (given what we know for certain about him, he cannot be much more than a "character"), and with the pattern of opposing ideas.

SOCRATES AS GOOD-OLE-BOY?   How are we to respond to Socrates' self-descriptions in *Phaedrus*? Look at what he says about himself: Of his ability to judge speeches he says to *Phaedrus*, "Believing that you know more about these things than I do, I followed your example and joined in the ecstasy" (sec. 234). About the "matter" of Lysias's speech he says, "I am such an idiot that I let it pass me by and attended only to the style; the matter I didn't suppose that even Lysias himself could think satisfactory. I submit to your better judgment, Phaedrus, but it seems to me that he has said the same things two or three times over . . ." (sec. 235a). In claiming he can give a better speech than the one by Lysias, he says, "Now I am far too well aware of my own ignorance to suppose that any of these ideas can be my own. The explanation must be that I have been filled from some external source, like a jar from a spring, but I am such a fool that I have forgotten how or from whom" (sec. 235d). When Phaedrus demands a speech to compete with that of Lysias, Socrates says, "It would be ludicrous for a layman like myself to extemporize on a subject which has been already treated by a good writer" (sec. 236). As he begins to advance his position that "true" rhetoric depends on knowledge, he says, "I lay no claim to any proficiency in the art of speaking" (sec. 262). Then he asks Phaedrus to help him remember his speech, "But tell me—I've been so carried out of myself that I've quite forgotten— did I define love at the beginning of my speech?" (sec. 263d). Finally he impugns his own ability to judge writing, "I am an ignoramus, of course, but it seemed to me that the writer showed a fine carelessness by saying whatever occurred to him" (sec. 264b).

What on earth is one to make of all this foot-shuffling, head-scratching, down-home-good-ole-dumb-fella posturing? Who believes Phaedrus knows more or has better judgment about anything than Socrates? Or that Socrates is so dumb he can't pay attention to Lysias's speech, so forgetful he can't remember what he's said in his own speech, or so inexperienced a dialectician he can't compete with Lysias? Or that he is an ignoramus, an idiot, and a fool? Or, above all, that he is a poor speaker who can't come up with anything to say on his own?

Surely what has happened here is that Plato has removed himself from his writing so as to make any attack on his position exceedingly difficult. Then he created the world-champion-of-all-time, plain-dealing, no-ax-to-grind, just-seeking-the-truth-for-its-own-sake, good-ole-honest-fellow to speak his positions for him. There's nothing "wrong" with that strategy, of course.[9] Manipulating one's audience through the creation of a simple, one-of-the-folks ethos is as old as rhetorical strategy itself. But to do so while condemning sophistry, rhetoric, and writing! How gullible does Plato expect us to be? The origin of all Plato's pronouncements in *Phaedrus* is nothing but a rhetorical strategy, and a rhetorical strategy that says what it does not believe into the bargain. And what is worse, the brilliant effectiveness of this rhetorical strategy could only be realized in writing where this consummate writer could continue to tamper with his text until it was certain to situate the audience in exactly the desired position.

PYTHAGORAS, WHERE (WHO? WHAT?) ARE YOU? (Caveat: "As for Pythagoras, of whom we know nothing, the wise reader turns the page when he sees that name" [Shorey, "Platonism," p. 176]). What is the effect of teasing out the Pythagorean origin of so many of Plato's ideas, not only in *Phaedrus* but throughout Plato's writings? There is no doubt that Plato was influenced by the Pythagoreans, a secret brotherhood that included everything from the merely strange to the downright looney (Guthrie, pp. 215, 336). J. A. Philip argues that Pythagoras so profoundly influenced Plato as to deserve much of the credit for Platonism: "We can only conclude that the pythagorizing of the Early Academy was so thoroughgoing as to persuade even a Theophrastus that doctrines characteristic of Plato's thought were not Platonic but Pythagorean" (p. 12). The idea of original origin in Plato comes directly from Pythagoreanism, as do many of the fundamental "Platonic" ideas (the quotation marks are necessary because the ideas are "Platonic" only because Plato managed to write them down in a way that outlived the speaking and quite limited writing of the Pythagoreans). Even Aristotle says Plato's thought, in spite of its own particular qualities, largely depends on Pythagorean theories (*Works*, pp. 1559–62; Philip, p. 37; Rowe, pp. 164, 204–8).

For example, the "Platonic" theory of ideas is, depending on how one reads both Aristotle and modern commentators, somewhere between a minor modification of and a complete redevelopment of the Pythagorean theories that all earthly things imitate cosmic motions and that everything in the cosmos imitates the divine numbers, which themselves constitute primal reality (Gorman, pp. 102, 107; Ross, pp. 160–64). The ideas of reincarnation, immortality and transmigration of the soul, recollection of forgotten truth, and even pure soul as pure motion are all certainly Pythagorean. Even the tripartite psyche of the *Republic* is taken almost wholesale from Pythagoras (Gorman, pp. 26–31, 131–32; Philip, p. 75).

Where Plato's debt to the Pythagoreans really gets interesting for the writing theorist trying to save writing from Plato, however, is the Pythagorean's attitude toward writing, for the Pythagoreans were a secret brotherhood whose ideas and practices were transmitted orally and carefully guarded from public knowledge in order to keep them from falling into the wrong hands. Doesn't that sound a great deal like this from the end of *Phaedrus:* "Once a thing is committed to writing it circulates equally among those who understand the subject and those who have no business with it; a writing cannot distinguish between suitable and unsuitable readers" (sec. 275d)? Not only were the Pythagoreans unwilling to write, this highly secret, carefully oral cult seems to have had a pathological fear that their ideas would not only be misconstrued by "unsuitable" audiences but would be corrupted absolutely if committed to print (Gorman, pp. 196, 202; Jaynes, p. 290; Philip, pp. 8–35; Guthrie, pp. 150–55). And doesn't this belief sound a great deal like the argument from the end of *Phaedrus* that someone in earnest "will not take a pen and write in water or sow his seed in the black fluid called ink, to produce discourses which cannot defend themselves viva voce or give any adequate account of the truth" (sec. 276c)? Dare one say (and I freely admit to thinking it) that all this business about the danger of writing in *Phaedrus* stems at least in part from the hocus pocus of a very, very odd secret cult?

And it gets more bizarre yet. Pythagoras appears to have taught his followers by using cryptic *akousmata* (which loosely translated means "something heard") and *symbola*. These were then formed by his pupils into sacred discourses and handed on orally and in careful secrecy. The brotherhood finally divided into those with a mathematical bent ("mathematici") and those ("acus-matici") who for all the world seem to resemble modern-day Holy Rollers, what with Pythagoras's tendency to teach through a sort of catechistic questioning and highly symbolic metalan-guage (De Vogel, pp. 160–62, 220–21).[10] The acousmatic, prim-itive, magical thought of the Pythagoreans at this point gets too weird for one to know how to deal with it. Anyone interested in a brief introduction to just how weird such thought gets need do no more than read Guthrie's explanation of why the Pytha-goreans were forbidden to eat beans (pp. 184–86)! Of course one cannot dismiss Plato out of hand on the grounds of guilt by association as a result of his ties with the Pythagoreans, but Socrates' second speech, with all the business about inspiration and possession, when read in the light of Pythagoreanism, upon which many of its ideas depend, begins to sound suspiciously like some sort of "sacred discourse" with just enough of the hocus pocus of Pythagoreansim removed for it still to qualify as "thinking." Unquestionably, Plato had to have Pythagoreanism at least as an origin for his own ideas. But how much of that point of origin crept into Plato's text without his knowledge (or permission!)?

OP-POSITIONS.   One other Pythagorean idea bears men-tioning. The Pythagoreans seem to have been extremely con-cerned with the idea of oppositions. Indeed they saw the cosmos as constituted in an oppositional way. The following table was key to their mode of understanding:

The Pythagorean list of opposites

limit	unlimited
odd	even
one	plurality

right	left
male	female
at rest	in motion
straight	crooked
light	darkness
good	evil
square	oblong

All these oppositions grew out of number theory, with One being unity and the Good (something like, perhaps even the origin of, Plato's "idea" of the Good) and the dyad being the evil, cosmic opposite of the One (Gorman, p. 140). In each case, the left concept is privileged over the right, creating a field of oneness and goodness opposed to the field of multiplicity and evil. This tension of forever opposed "ideas" is important to what Plato writes in *Phaedrus* in that it reveals yet another layer in the origin of this written text, for the origin of *Phaedrus* is a pattern of oppositions in which one of the pair is privileged over the other.

There are so many oppositions in *Phaedrus* that it would be impossible to discuss even a small percentage of them. I can, however, demonstrate the pattern with a few of the key oppositions. (1) Lysias's speech exists through the opposition of a nonlover and a lover. (2) Socrates' first speech exists through the same opposition and also through the opposition of a competition with Lysias. At another level the speech exists by opposing what it "says" on one hand to Socrates' true opinions on the other. (3) Socrates' second speech exists through its opposition with his first speech; thus, it exists through the opposition of decency and right thinking against deceitfulness. At another level, the speech exists through the opposition of disease as disease against disease as health. (4) The last section of the dialogue exists through the opposition of dialectical analysis against rhetorical manipulations. (5) *Phaedrus* as a whole exists through a continuing series of oppositions: philosophy-sophistry, truth-probability, speaking-writing, sickness-health, madness-sanity, true rhetoric–false rhetoric, true writing–false writing, and so on.

Plato presents all these oppositions as if they were part of the original law of good versus evil, as if such opposition were Origin itself, requiring no prior medium through which to set the oppositions against each other. And in each case one of the opposing forces is privileged over the other: Socrates' second speech over the first, his first speech over the one by Lysias, philosophy over sophistry, truth over probability, speaking over writing, and so forth.[11] But where is the place or space for all these oppositions to occur? What is the thing outside, or the prior medium that lets opposition know itself? The only possible field for such opposition is writing. For only with writing can opposition be captured, divested of its force, and studied like any other structure as the remains of a once living process. Take sophistry, for example. There was a time when a living, speaking voice could speak sophistry, but Plato has killed that voice in history by using writing to oppose the voice to itself. When Lysias speaks in *Phaedrus* or Socrates speaks like a sophist there, the living, speaking voice of sophistry is already dead because its living voice is dead in Plato's silent text. Worse yet for sophistry's case is its legacy: in appearing to speak for itself in Plato's text, sophistry actually speaks against itself, for its already prejudged opposition in *Phaedrus* is philosophy, which is already privileged to defeat it.

The oppositions in *Phaedrus* are not so much oppositions as techniques whereby one thing takes priority over another. The prior medium in which the oppositions can be constituted is writing; the force that moves the oppositions to structure is rhetorical strategy. The deceit is that in giving rules for rhetoric and writing that effectively preclude both, Plato is trying to steal both the prior medium and its force. He leaves us nothing but his voice and no way to generate a new opposition to that voice without speaking sophistry, which is always already prejudged as deception in an opposition between deception and truth. The opposition presents itself as Origin rather than as something allowed by writing, which is really its origin. I wish I didn't think Plato knew all this.

IV. A Moveable Vignette That Comes Last

This fact about writing is, by the way, typical of all authoritarian regimes; it is what might be called police-state writing: we know, for example, that the content of the word "Order" always indicates repression.

Roland Barthes, *Writing Degree Zone*

As soon as Phaedrus and Socrates arrive at the plane tree beside the Ilissus, Phaedrus asks Socrates if that isn't the spot where Boreas abducted Oreithyia. Socrates replies that the exact spot "so they say," is about a quarter of a mile downstream. Then Phaedrus asks whether Socrates believes the legend. Socrates says he would be in good company if he did not, if he could prove that Oreithyia were merely playing one day and the wind blew her off the rocks to her death. But many other problems would arise if he tried to "explain" that legend, because then he would have to discover plausible explanations for Hippocentaurs, Chimaeras, Gorgons, Pegasuses, and an infinite array of mythic events and figures for which he has no time. "And the reason is," he continues,

> I've not yet succeeded in obeying the Delphic injunction to "know myself," and it seems to me absurd to consider problems about other beings while I am still in ignorance about my own nature. So I let these things alone and acquiesce in the popular attitude towards them; as I've already said I make myself rather than them the object of my investigations, and I try to discover whether I am a more complicated and puffed-up sort of animal than Typho or whether I am a gentler and simpler creature, endowed by heaven with a nature altogether less typhonic. (secs. 229d–230a)

This seems innocent enough: rather than trying to discover plausible explanations for folk myths, Socrates leaves them alone in order to try to understand himself, which is more important and which finally would be the only possible origin for a valid study of such myths. But wait, without such popular folk myths, without the language and the history such myths enable and carry, how is Socrates to understand himself? His strategy for self-knowledge is to treat his "self" as a closed, realized structure, as a knowable entity. That entails two very odd presumptions: First, it requires a system of analysis and a point of view outside the self from which and through which that self can be known. Second, it requires arbitrarily silencing a set of questions in order to use that silence as a foundation to construct a second set of questions whose very vocabulary depends on the silence of the first set. Note well that Socrates explains his self-analysis by using Typho as a sort of benchmark. How easy it is to forget that Typho is one of the monsters that would immediately be called into question were Socrates to allow questions about popular belief. Thus, whatever self-knowledge Socrates reveals in *Phaedrus* depends absolutely on the vocabulary and syntax of an unexamined set of popular beliefs that must never be interrogated for the self-knowledge to occur. The origin of the discourse spoken by Plato's Socrates is an unexamined, unexaminable structure whose interrogation must forever remain silent for the Socratic discourse to proceed.

And what about the rules of that discourse itself? There seem to be three: a definition of terms, a "knowledge of the truth," and an ability to divide and collect. Socrates sets out the first rule at the beginning of his first speech, where he says that "there is one and only one way of beginning if one is to come to a sound conclusion," which is to begin "by agreeing about the use of terms" (sec. 237c). Then Socrates proceeds to define love. First he separates it from its opposite; then he shows how inside itself it is constituted through the opposition of innate, irrational desire for pleasure against acquired, rational desire for excellence. This definition articulated, Socrates can begin his speech. The problem is that this definition does not lead to truth; it leads to falsehood, for it allows Socrates to play the sophist by speaking what he would never think or say. In other words, discourse principle number one not only fails to uncover truth, but it is also absolutely truth neutral in that it leads only to effective discourse. This definition appears again later and raises a new problem, but I'll get to that shortly.

The second rule requires that one know the truth before speaking. Now this is at best problematic. One cannot help sympathizing with Thomas Conley's attack on *Phaedrus* as the self-immolation of rhetoric:

> Plato has Socrates here set conditions for the rehabilitation of rhetoric which guarantee that it would redeem itself only by an act of self-immolation. Once we have understood that, I would contend, we come to see why any conception of rhetoric harmonious with Plato's ought to be scrupulously avoided. . . . Knowledge of the truth as a precondition of legitimate—or "real"—rhetoric is en-

tirely unreasonable. In the first place, rhetoric arises from real questions and problems about matters of particular fact which need to be acted upon *now* (pp. 12, 14).[12]

Rather than arguing with Plato, however, it is better to show how his case cannot be made in rhetoric and writing. The point at which the Platonic edifice collapses is the process of knowing truth. The above explanation of how Plato comes to know himself is a good example. In order to know himself, he must refuse to hear the questions about the system of speaking from which that knowledge emerges. The moment his knowledge appears, it is already structure. But structure, as we know, must originate somewhere. There is no such thing as originless structure. Plato's voice of knowledge is nothing more than the silence of the questions he cannot ask in order to ask the questions he does ask. Whatever the oracle at Delphi may recommend, there is no primary, original discourse, for any discourse is said at the expense of the other discourse(s) that must remain silent. Thus, even using Socrates' own method for knowing knowledge, what one discovers is not knowledge or truth but the discourse that is the other of the discourse that was silenced for this discourse to speak in the first place. As much as Plato would like to have truth precede and validate discourse, even in his own system it emerges *from* discourse and is validated by the ability of one discourse to silence another.

The third rule is the principle of dividing and collecting, a method that in its very nature is opposed to itself, for each of its procedures requires yet undoes the other. The first, collecting, "is to take a synoptic view of many scattered particulars and collect them under a single generic term" (sec. 265d). The second, dividing, is "to divide a genus into species again, observing the natural articulation, not mangling any of the parts, like an unskillful butcher" (sec. 266). Socrates uses his two speeches as an example of this process:

> Take my two speeches just now. Both took irrationality as a generic notion. But just as in a single physical body there are pairs of organs with the same name but distinguished as left and right respectively, so in our two speeches; both postulated madness as a single generic form existing in us, but the first separated the left-hand

part, as it were, and broke it down into further parts and did not give up till it detected among them what may be called a left-hand kind of love, which it very properly reprobated; whereas the second directed our attention to the types of madness on the right-hand side, and, finding there a kind of love which has the same name as the other but is divine. . . ." (sec. 266)

What effect does this method of dividing and collecting have on the dictum on structure ("discourse should be constructed like a living creature")? More generally what effect does it have on the question of "structure as a whole"? There are only two possible answers. The first is probably possible only in theory: Discourse should be constructed like *half* a living being. If we accept Socrates' speeches as two speeches, we have no choice but to revise the dictum on structure along these lines because now we know that each speech was only one side. The second, and probably only really workable answer, is that Socrates gave only one speech. Or, more precisely, Plato *wrote* only one dialogue, and in writing he could make his own voice into a multiplicity of voices. In writing he could generate structure through his own force as a writer, and then reuse that same force to mask itself, seeming to leave behind structure with no need of origin.

This takes me back to the second problem with the first rule—that one must define terms before beginning (leaving aside the problem that one has already "begun" when one defines terms because definitions are never innocent). As Phaedrus and Socrates begin to discuss rhetorical principles, they discover they can speak only in abstractions and need some concrete examples. Socrates says, "Well, by lucky accident the two speeches provide an example of how a speaker who knows the truth can make fun of his hearers and lead them astray" (sec. 262c). A little later in introducing the idea of dividing and collecting, Socrates says of the first rule, "In our recent speech on love we began by defining what love is. That definition may have been good or bad, but at least it enabled the argument to proceed with clearness and consistency" (sec. 265d).

Now this leads to some thorny complications, for it not only makes the definition of love serve as the point of departure for both Socrates' speeches, it makes fairly clear that the two speeches are really one speech, or at least the right and left sides of the same speech. This blurring of what starts where and what includes what raises profoundly troublesome questions about Plato's ability to write *Phaedrus* at all. Does dividing and collecting, a self-contradictory mode of inquiry (is it a singular or plural subject in this sentence?), necessarily require that any speech recognize and carry with it its opposite, the "left-hand" side as it were? Are Socrates' two speeches, which after extensive analysis by Plato's Socrates himself really turn out to be the right and left of the same speech with the same point of departure, are those "two" speeches an example that knowledge exists through the denial of its opposite? Doesn't the pattern of oppositions in *Phaedrus* reveal that sophistry, rhetoric, probability, and writing are absolute necessities for the text's structure, for without them philosophy, dialectic, truth, and speaking have no way of knowing themselves? In order to privilege philosophy, dialectic, truth, and speech, didn't Plato have to become a sophistical rhetorician who could write a text that would probably persuade his readers?[13] I wish I didn't think Plato knew the answers to these questions.

△
3.
"PHYSICIAN, HEAL THYSELF"

Divided, diseased inscription. Writing that opens a gap and continues to know itself as the incomplete border around this gap. Writing that is terminally ill, always dying but never quite dead. This is what Plato leaves us with after *Phaedrus*. Plato would lead us out of this abyss into a realm. He would change our disease into health. But what Plato leaves us *with* is what he himself *leaves*, a divided, diseased inscription. His writing, like ours, is an "idea" of wholeness that knows itself through unclosable openings; a sickness that, after all, is not and can never be death; an inscription that has been left behind, that remains left behind even after what he "says" has fled from it or been driven out. Could it be that we will want to stay behind in the unlimited expanse of the opening, that we will want to live a life of sickness, that we too will want to leave something behind?

I. Openings

> What is offered here is no more than an Introduction to what a History of Writing might be.
>
> Barthes, *Writing Degree Zero*

Phaedrus describes four aspects of discourse: its elements, its process of development, its nature, and its psychological effect on its author. Each stage of the description, however, reveals more than Plato wanted to reveal. We can feel the anger generated by his inability to make writing do what he wanted it to. When he failed, he turned nasty. The desire to escape writing through writing, to limit the opening of the infinity was enormous. But the harder this master writer tried to tame writing in writing, the more certain he was to get caught *inside* writing.

Here are the four aspects of the Platonic Socrates' description of discourse: (1) There are two kinds of words, the ambiguous and the unambiguous. "Well, now," says Socrates, "is not the following assertion obviously true, that there are some words about which we all agree, and others about which we are at variance?" *Phaedrus* requests clarification, and Socrates poses a new question, "When someone utters the word 'iron' or 'silver,' we all have the same object before our minds, haven't we?" Phaedrus agrees and Socrates poses two new questions, "But what about the words 'just' and 'good'? Don't we diverge, and dispute not only with one another but with our own selves?" The "intending student of the art of rhetoric," Socrates concludes, "ought, in the first place, to make a systematic division of words, and get hold of some mark distinguishing the two kinds" (Hackforth, sec. 263b). (2) There are two parts of the composing process, invention and arrangement. Sometimes invention isn't necessary. "Thus, as regards the subject," Socrates says of Lysias's speech,

> do you imagine that anybody could argue that the non-lover should be favored rather than the lover, without praising the wisdom of the one and censuring the folly of the other? That he could dispense with these essential points, and then bring up something different? No, no, surely we must allow such arguments, and forgive the orator for using them, and in that sort of field what merits praise is not invention, but arrangement; but when it comes to nonessential points, that are difficult to invent, we should praise arrangement and invention too. (Hackforth, sec. 236)

(3) Compositions can be judged in two ways, through style and through matter, with each separable from the other: "I let it [the "matter" of Lysias's speech] pass me by and attended only to

the style; the matter I didn't suppose that even Lysias himself could think satisfactory" (sec. 235). (4) Writing, especially if the author is aiming at posterity, is loved in direct proportion to its depreciation by its author; the greater the depreciation, the greater the lust for "immortality in his country . . . equal of the gods," an immortality available only in writing. When Phaedrus says of the politicians, "Those who occupy the positions of greatest power and dignity in our states are ashamed to write speeches or to leave written compositions behind them, because they are afraid that posterity may give them the name of sophists," Socrates replies, "It's a case of Pleasant Bend, Phaedrus. You've forgotten that it is the *long* bend in the Nile which gives rise to that euphemism, and you've forgotten too that the politicians with the highest opinion of themselves are the most passionately anxious to write speeches and leave compositions behind them . . ." (secs. 275b–258).

Strangely enough, we are willing to believe each of these four descriptions because of the power of what we learn through that willingness. In each case, however, the description continues to describe after Plato would stop it. He wants to tell us "just so much," but the writing he must use against his will goes right on meaning long after he would force it into silence.

1. THE ELEMENTS.   Of course no one who thinks about it for long would agree that there are "two kinds of words." *Silver* can be every bit as ambiguous as *just*, *love* as clear as *iron*. Such distinctions about what kinds of words there are or about how words convey meaning can be made only in the gap between past use and future use, only in that place, no place, where the word is no longer its history (the ways it has always been used) and not yet its future (the ways it will be used). Such distinctions exist nowhere but in theory, in a Never-Never-Land where practical use has always just ceased and not quite yet resumed.

What happens to the word *love* in *Phaedrus* is a good example. It enters the dialogue in Lysias's speech where it is known through its deficiency. Lysias (or whoever wrote the speech)[1] explains that nonlove is better than love because nonlove offers more advantages and more happiness. Besides, love is an undesirable state of disease. Love reenters the dialogue in Socrates' first speech as an object of definition and then as an object of description. As a definition, love is known through a pair of oppositions—the opposition of the lover against the nonlover and then the opposition of rational desire for excellence against irrational desire for pleasure. As an object of description, love turns out to be a raging appetite, "'As wolves for lambs, so lovers lust for boys.'"

This presentation of love, however, is complicated because of the parodic nature of the speech itself; when the speech is read as self-parody, love is known through a separation of itself from meaning. Socrates' speech has all the qualities of "a speech," but, of course, it is "a speech" only in that it has no meaning. Socrates reminds us throughout that he does not think what he says; thus, the effect of that speech on the word *love* is to leave it open so that it can be filled by the true definition still to come. At this point, everything actually said about love is already not true.

Love makes its third appearance in Socrates' second speech where it is known both physiologically and mystically. Physiologically, it is a disease. Through mystic revelation, however, this "disease" turns out to be no disease at all but rather the purest form of health. Only by suffering from this "disease" can one's soul regain its lost health and return to heaven. One might say love is not what it is, because it is *a* disease whose effect is the only possible cure for *all* disease; thus, love is fully knowable in its purest form only if it takes no physical form and involves no physical expression.

Plato's use of words, as opposed to what he says about them, reveals that words, rather than being describable things, are openings, gaps, or unfilled places waiting to be filled with (what else?) the other words that will always enter the empty space to fill it up, giving it a border, a content, a "meaning." Of course this system works just so long as no one starts asking about the "other" words that have filled up the emptiness of the word that came to be known by having its emptiness filled with words.

Oddly enough, Plato's theoretical explanation of words turns out to work—for him and for us—because it creates the opening in which we can view "wordness" and come to know the inadequacy of the definition presented in the opening (the inadequacy is not limited to Plato: all who dare to demonstrate a definition in the light of this opening will find their definition inadequate).[2] The power of the definition is the clearing "in words" where words can be exposed and judged. Plato's disadvantage, however, is writing, because *his written* words, like everyone else's, remain forever open, forever receptive to new fillings with other words. Perhaps he was frightened by what he saw there once a space for seeing words had been opened. Brilliant as he was, the one thing he could not do was master the ability of words always to be what they are not, always to be different from what they are, in fact, to depend on what they are not for their essence.[3]

2. THE PROCESS.   Was there ever a time when discourse, whether written or spoken, required *no* invention? A time when the composer's work was limited merely to arrangement? Of course not. But again, Plato's definition draws its power from the opening it creates where discourse can be seen as two processes—finding and shaping. Oddly enough, however, the place where discourse can be found is discourse and the tool with which it is shaped is itself. In an informative and useful piece of scholarship, Janice Lauer has shown how Plato began an argument that continued for centuries: Does invention lead to truth or merely support already made judgments ("Issues," pp. 127–40)? The maddening answer (mine, not Lauer's), of course, is, Yes, both.

Plato's use of invention is an interesting example. When Phaedrus demands that Socrates make a speech to compete with Lysias, Socrates advances his idea that some "fields" of discourse do not allow for invention. In such fields, the best one can do is arrange well. In the debate over whether one should submit to a lover or a nonlover, the inescapable preinvention is that love is a disease, and, like the plague, best avoided. The preinvented idea of love as disease, however, becomes extremely complex at the conclusion of Socrates' second speech, where what was obvious in the field of discourse for his first speech—that love is madness and disease—becomes its even more obvious opposite—that the madness and disease of love offer the only possibility of true sanity and health. In other words, nothing really new has been "invented" for Socrates' second speech. What has happened is that invention itself has been "rearranged" so that what was a discovery, love is a disease, turns out to have been the discovery of its opposite, disease is health. Thus, the division of discourse into invention and arrangement, like the division of words into ambiguous and unambiguous, turns out to be an opening in which the idea of discourse can be discussed. Plato creates a place in discourse where he can expose the two processes that constitute discourse, invention and arrangement.

What Plato seems unwilling to admit, however, is that the two processes found each other. Anyone who was taught formal heuristics can see this readily. Whether Burke's Pentad, the Tagmemic grid, Aristotle's topics, or some other, the heuristic is an endless generator, a sort of perpetual motion machine.[4] A good heuristic never stops until the operator turns it off while it is still humming along, still unfinished finding something new.[5] What sets the process of invention in relief making it recognizable, however, is the need for something to arrange. Arrangement becomes the empty opening in which invention can insert itself and begin to work. But for arrangement actually to occur, invention must end, cease being itself, and become the absent place where invention once was. Invention must become the *remains* of invention on which and in whose place arrangement can now work. Thus arrangement turns out to be dead invention in that it requires invention to know itself, while at the same time invention turns out to be empty arrangement. Empty arrangement, of course, opens the need for invention because of its emptiness.

What Plato the writer must have known, however, is that the two exist as an endless struggle. One does not invent and then arrange. Nor does one arrange things already invented without reinventing. Unless the world has changed in an unimaginable way in the last twenty-three centuries, there is no possible way that all of *Phaedrus* was invented first and then arranged. It is inconceivable that Plato never once did something during arrangement that changed invention and carried him back to the part of the invention that had already been written. Look again at what happens to the invention that love is a disease. In Lysias's speech it appears as just that; thus, the invention is arranged and presented in discourse. In Socrates' first speech, however, the invention is not quite itself in that the speech is the antithesis of itself. Thus, when Socrates mockingly covers his head and says love is a disease, the reader knows some other sort of invention has already overridden the invention that love is disease. Invention, the act completed in Lysias's speech, has become *part of* invention, an ongoing, not yet fully disclosed process. Then Socrates' second speech reverses the invention of love as disease so that disease becomes health. As a result, Lysias's invention, or what Socrates calls "necessary" invention, turns out to be nothing more than the creation of an absent place to be filled by later Platonic invention. Thus invention, which originates in the opening created by the need for something to arrange, is itself the constant holding open of possibility as the inventor unceasingly finds something new and finds that what has already been found can empty itself or reverse itself.

But *Phaedrus* is an act of deception because at every point Plato the author knows what is coming; the inventor of the argument that love is a disease knew when he became the arranger that disease is health. Thus, what is called a "necessary" argument is not only not necessary but already the opposite of the true. Plato must have felt the impossibility of separating discourse into invention and arrangement. He must have known he was clearing an opening in discourse in order to talk about discourse, and he must have known that the one thing that could not fully appear there was discourse itself. But he refuses to admit all that. The only way we know it is to refuse to listen when he tells us about discourse and writing and look at what he does, which negates what he says. Plato apparently was frightened by the constantly reversing, infinitely open process of composition and thus tried to write in talking.

3. THE PRODUCT.   If we believe Socrates' second speech (if the speech even offers itself as something that can be "believed"), we must accept ourselves as not what we are. Though we do have a physical existence and are limited by our mortality, soul is what gives us life, and soul is both originless and immortal. Each of us as a human being is a fundamental, irreconcilable duality of soul and body. And as is true with all Platonic oppositions, one of the pair is privileged over the other. In this case, it is soul over body.

Discourse, too, is an opposition, an opposition between matter and style. And once again, the power of Plato's definition is that it gives us an opening in discourse in which discourse itself can be arraigned. Not surprisingly, with discourse in the light of judgment, especially the light of Platonic judgment, matter is privileged over style, with matter made the business of philosophy and style the business of rhetoric. There is nothing wrong with style, of course, just so long as it comes *after* and remains *subservient to* matter, which alone can be "true." With style, as with all things physical, one must be very careful not to let temporary, essentially unimportant things take precedence over permanent, essentially important things. In time, just as the soul can escape its need for the body and return to heaven, matter can triumph over the need for style, truth needing no vehicle or trappings save its own self-evident self-righteousness.

Plato's trick is to focus our attention on all these aspects of discourse—the nature of words, the process of composing, style versus matter—in order to exempt his own discourse from discourse. *Phaedrus* doesn't have any style! Or more precisely, it presents itself as having no style, as no discourse at all but rather as a dialectical movement toward truth. This movement culminates first with the revelation of pure matter in Socrates' second speech and then, in the discussions of rhetoric and writing after this speech, with the revelation of how one communicates such pure matter. *Phaedrus* is the way we know both the law of matter and the method of its presentation. How astonishingly easy it is to forget that *Phaedrus* too is discourse, and style as well!

But what happens if we refuse to read *Phaedrus* as dialectic? What happens if we call it what it is, writing? Then *Phaedrus* too has a physical existence. It too is the opposition of matter and style. We see *Phaedrus* as a stylistic tour de force so brilliant that the reader never notices the utter impossibility of its position. In fact, the opposition of style to matter is nothing more than another opening in discourse where discourse itself can be discussed. Fortunately for someone trying to save writing from Plato, the opening reveals more than Plato wants to show. If we look carefully, we can see the Platonic strategy of opposing style to matter, then very subtly opposing rhetoric to dialectic, and finally aligning style with rhetoric and matter with dialectic. *Phaedrus* implies that style and rhetoric are the same and that matter precedes and enables them. Plato denies priority to rhetoric, whether written or declaimed, and gives priority to thought, which must be dialectic. He does not want us to notice that his maneuver depends on a style so sophisticated that it seems to be absent. This brings me to the fourth aspect of the description, writing, which Plato is free to devalue because he has exempted his own "product" from writing by making it dialectic, writing's privileged opposite.[6]

4. THE TRAP.   Plato's Socrates claims that writers, especially those who aim at posterity, love writing in direct proportion to their attempts to depreciate it. Few writers in history have been as hard on writing as Plato was, few have written so well as he, and none, I believe, has lusted more mightily after the immortality that writing alone allows. Plato's genius is to depreciate writing, ridicule the vainglorious desires of writers, and do so while seeming not to write himself. He clearly recognized that writing is a forever-open opening. Its words are open spaces always waiting to be filled yet never finally filled up; its process is the forever-incomplete antithesis of itself, as invention and arrangement constantly cancel each other; its embodiment is the Janus-faced operation of matter and style, each emerging from the other.

Plato offers to lead us out of the morass created by writing, rhetoric, sophistry, and discourse in general and into the realm of truth. Like any prophet or witch doctor, indeed like any deceitful rhetorician, he does not want us to know the source of his power, for it is writing. The only possible response to his invitation out of writing into truth, however, is to decline and to remain in the medium where what presents itself as truth could find itself and then present itself as never having been found. Plato did not find his truth in dialectic. That is merely the style through which his matter comes to know itself. The matter itself is knowable and reknowable only in writing, which Plato would have us believe is nothing more than play.

Just before he and Phaedrus leave the shade of the plane tree, Socrates finally dismisses writing as nothing more than amusing play.[7] Writing is, thus, "saved." It is OK for philosophers to spend their idle time amusing themselves and their friends with writing, just so long as no one takes it seriously, just so long as it remains a pleasant (Phaedrus calls it "fine") pastime. This is where Plato makes his biggest gamble. If we accept this devaluation of writing, he has succeeded in escaping from writing. The enormity of the gamble is obvious.

But who really believes writing is a trivial pastime? No one who has ever done it thinks so. And Plato didn't think so either. Dionysius of Helicarnassus and Diogenes Laertius tell us that

Plato worked constantly *revising* (Dionysius calls it "combing and curling") his dialogues. When Plato died, they found a tablet in his house with several *different* beginnings for the *Republic*.[8] And we've got him. Writing for Plato was not play, not by a long shot. It was the most serious possible undertaking a person could embark on. If it were play, what would be the not play, the *serious* thing with which it would be in opposition and through which it could know itself as play? Surely not philosophy, for philosophy as Plato practiced it (one might almost say "invented" it) is above all else writing (try to name a few important philosophers after Plato who operated only orally, who wrote nothing). If anything, writing is play only through its opposition with the impossibility of anything else. Writing is, as they say, the only game in town. Without writing there would be no play, and no anything else that distinguishes the post-Platonic world from its predecessor.

Writing told Plato what he thought he knew. And because writing is an infinite opening, consisting of the gaps made by words that fill themselves with other words, operating through the infinitely antithetical, forever reversing process of invention and arrangement, and presenting itself as the unclosable opening of style and matter, Plato was caught using an instrument that turned out to be using him. He wanted to cure his dis-ease.

II. Physicians, Diseases, Drugs

> There is no such thing as a harmless remedy. The *pharmakon* can never be simply beneficial.
>
> Derrida, *Dissemination*

Phaedrus begins under doctor's orders. Phaedrus meets Socrates because their common friend, Acumenus, a doctor, has recommended a country walk for his health. Socrates agrees that Acumenus is right about the salutary effects of walking and then a few lines later says he will go with Phaedrus even if the walk extends the distance recommended by Herodicus, another doctor famous for recommending long walks (sec. 227). But the real physician in *Phaedrus*, the person who wants to write the prescription and cure the ill of humanity, is Plato. The question we must raise is, Which is worse, the cure or the ill? I think we'd rather be ill than suffer Plato's cure. Before we decide, we'd better look at the state of the patient while still ill and the effect of the drugs if taken. The dialogue itself is filled with diseases and drugs.

Here are just a few of the diseases. When Socrates discovers Phaedrus has a speech by Lysias, he claims his "passion for such speeches amounts to a disease" (sec. 228b). The fourth point in Lysias's speech is that lovers suffer from the disease of madness (sec. 231d). After Lysias's speech, Socrates and Phaedrus agree that a lover is "less healthy" than a nonlover (sec. 236b). In his own first speech, Socrates says the lover has a "diseased mind" (Jowett, sec. 243), and the remainder of the speech is predicated on the idea that a lover is diseased and mad. Socrates' second speech depends even more on the idea of love as madness and disease, except that in this speech disease and madness become their opposites, sanity and health. In this elaborate sequence of reversals, the beautiful love object becomes the physician who cures the madness he caused in the first place and love becomes a sort of "eye infection," allowing the infected one to see himself through his lover's eyes (secs. 252a, 255d). Thus, the cure for disease is disease itself.

There is, however, a drug loose, wandering around in *Phaedrus*, a drug that is not altogether trustworthy for it may cause dis-ease as much as ease. Plato must have it to be who he is and to do what he does. Plato is addicted, with an addiction so intense that periodic doses of this drug alone keep him feeling good; indeed, one might say that doses of this drug are the only things keeping him alive at all. But the drug is a problem. The Greek word for it is *pharmakon*.[9] In English it becomes "spell," "charm," "recipe," and "specific." The thing itself is writing.

Plato's drug of choice, his pharmakon, is obviously writing. His addiction is complete and incurable, for he wrote all his life until his death. Like any addict, he loved and hated his addiction. He loved what it allowed him to do, yet he hated what it did to him. Like any addict, he wanted plenty of the drug for himself; like any addict he wanted all others to be spared the terror of the addiction, for finally the addict loses control to the drug. *Phaedrus* is an attempt to prevent our addiction, to keep us healthy.

Phaedrus is more than that, though, for the pharmakon of writing (always true to its nature as the combined opposite of itself) is both the possibility and the impossibility of Platonic thought. Plato attempts to use *Phaedrus* to explain the human condition. Right from the beginning, however, he admits he cannot do it, because he must begin by describing the essence of human life, the soul: "To describe it as it is," his Socrates admits, "would require a long exposition of which only a god is capable; but it is within the power of man to say in shorter compass what it resembles" (sec. 246a). Plato wants to give us "truth," but he can't. He has to replace it with what it is not, writing. I think *Phaedrus* is a record of his frustration as well as one of his most powerful attempts to use writing as the replacement of itself, thereby making it "truth." Plato wanted desperately to demonstrate how truth validates thinking and thinking validates writing, but every time he picked up his pen, his very own process of writing—which enabled his thinking and then enabled the replacement of what a god could say as the "truth"— defeated him. He wanted to use writing to reveal the "truth," but at every scratch on the page he had to fight against the haunting possibility that "truth" is writing. Inscription always seems to turn around, and Plato wanted it to go straight.

III. Inscription

> Writing is in no way an instrument for communication, it is not an open route through which there passes only the intention to speak.
>
> Barthes, *Writing Degree Zero*

The drug of Plato's addiction, the source of his sickness, is for us now and for those always to come, the source of his life. Anyone who gives up the drug and becomes healthy, anyone who agrees not to play with this forever open replacement, trades Plato's (permanent) life of sickness for what?

1. WHATEVER GOES AROUND COMES AROUND.   Plato's reversal of arguments in *Phaedrus* is brilliant. No one would deny that. His method of displaying what seems like common sense— love as an insane disease best avoided—and then turning it around to show how it is in fact the opposite of what it seems— love as the only way of knowing the good—is both pleasing and convincing. And Plato uses this method of reversing apparently obvious ideas again and again in *Phaedrus*. Ammon reverses Theuth's praise of writing, Socrates reverses Phaedrus's ideas about rhetoric and writing, even toadies and prostitutes have

their good sides (sec. 240b). *Phaedrus's* effect on the reader resembles that of the "Allegory of the Cave," in which the person
in chains must turn 180 degrees to discover the source of light
and the "real" world outside the cave. The question that this
sort of reversal wishes to deny, however, is, Once one starts
turning, how does one stop or know where to stop? Plato's
answer, of course, is, I'll tell you. He first explains that we are
facing the wrong way, seeing nothing but the shadows of reality.
He also explains just how far we are to turn so that we face
reality itself. That is why no one after him should need writing.
After all, he has used it to reveal how one discovers and communicates "truth." Why should anyone else need it? More importantly, since he has played with the medium so long and
knows it so well, he knows how dangerous it can be. As a writer
he must have realized how his works were never finished, how
no dialogue ever quite said everything that needed saying or
captured what needed saying to the absolute exclusion of everything else that could be said. He decided to use writing to
turn us 180 degrees and then destroy it so that future turns could
not be made. Fortunately, it didn't work.

I'll give two examples. The first, I think, would have made
Plato cringe; in fact, he would have predicted it if *everyone* continued to write *everything* that could be written. It is Ronna Burger's 1980 book, *Plato's* Phaedrus: *A Defense of a Philosophic Art of
Writing*. The book is quite fine, in my opinion. In effect, Burger's
project is the same as mine—to save writing from Plato. The
difference is that she defends Plato and argues that he did not
mean his attack on writing the way it seems on first reading.
Phaedrus, she argues, rather than being an attack on writing, is
really a cautionary defense. Because writing has the potential of
foreclosing thought, it is dangerous. Thus, one must always read
in a dialectical fashion, always questioning the text, never accepting what it says at face value. Moreover, in an indirect way,
Phaedrus defends writing as an activity, because all the attacks
on writing made by Ammon, who is a god and thus has no need
for writing, and Socrates, who placed himself above writing,
show that humans *do* need writing. Humans are not gods like
Ammon, and Socrates' refusal to write was an act of hubris in
which he tried to behave like Ammon. This hubris, of course,
led to his death, as it had to (pp. 1–7, 79–109).

In my opinion, Burger's book is a well-done example of New

Criticism, showing how *Phaedrus* sets down the law and then conforms to its own law. The canon remains the source of authority, the reader (critic) plays the role of subservient priest-interpreter of what is finally greater than she. I, of course, read *Phaedrus* differently. I think Plato meant what he wrote (or had Socrates "say") about writing. And I think the well-known attack on writing in "The Seventh Letter" supports me because it says almost the same thing as *Phaedrus*, except even more forcefully.

Ultimately, however, it doesn't matter whether Burger is right or I am right or some other position is right. What matters is that Burger discovered her opinions through the act of writing them down, just as I have done and just as Plato did. What can be said in writing is always open. Whichever turn the text takes, it can always turn onward or turn backward. Writing reveals the possibility of saying the truth, but it is always only a possibility, for writing is never finished. Given Plato's desire for knowledge, I don't think he could bear the thought of the truth as an unclosable, infinitely operating, external system. I don't think he would like Burger's book any better than mine because both purport to tell Plato what he meant. He did not want to hear my voice or Burger's or anybody else's. He wanted us to hear his. If I were only a reader and a talker, I might very well be reduced to that, which might satisfy Plato, but it wouldn't satisfy me. And I don't want to be a New Critic either. I'm not the least bit interested in demonstrating the superiority of Plato's understanding of the "truth." If he is a better writer than I am, so be it. But let's not forget that he was just one more writer among many, except that he came to hate the thing he could not do without.[10]

The second example is James Golden's 1984 essay "Plato Revisited: A Theory of Discourse for All Seasons." This too is a truly fine interpretation of Plato whose purpose is to explain that Plato does in fact offer a comprehensive, sound, currently relevant theory of communication. The last section of the essay shows how Plato's theory of dialectical communication works. Plato's theory begins with clear definition, moves through division and collection, and operates rhetorically in a carefully sequential pattern consisting of (1) raising a question, (2) developing an answer, (3) refuting the answer, and (4) modifying the original answer (pp. 30–34). Golden argues that Plato's dialectical communication theory "draws upon science for its definition and structure, upon philosophy for its subject matter, and upon rhetoric for its strategies" (p. 32).

I do not disagree with Golden. His essay is an erudite, informative, and highly readable piece of scholarship. I do, however, think he has fallen for Plato's trick and given up his own voice. He has read the entire Platonic canon and developed a clear, accurate explanation of what Plato *says* about communication theory. Plato, however, does not do what he says, not anywhere and especially not in *Phaedrus*. It is easy to forget that Plato is a writer, writing alone, with a motive. What seems like a dialectical movement toward truth in his dialogues is really a written text whose end is known at the beginning and whose every aspect is managed through the revisionary, recursive process of writing. There is absolutely and utterly no way to recapture what Plato has done outside of writing.

In *Phaedrus*, for example, all the procedures articulated by Golden seem to work. Plato's Socrates defines his terms, explains and uses the processes of division and collection, offers a hypothesis with examples for support, refutes the hypothesis, and finally offers a new, modified position—a position that reveals the nature of divine love. Well and good, except that nothing about *Phaedrus* worked that way. It emerged in writing; thus, the final position of the dialogue was available all along to its writer-reviser. Now that is not good-faith dialectic at all. In good-faith dialectic, two lovers work together toward truth. In Plato, however, a preconceived position is arrived at in writing, then the whole text is (re)constructed around the final position toward which the text will be made to appear as a progress. I think Plato knew that and it horrified him. He wanted to believe in truth as something one could move toward. He did not want to think of truth as a system that, if operated well enough, could discover any position, work backwards from that position, and then seem to work forward to it.

I'll put it this way: Do *you* want to be like Phaedrus? No, I thought not. Well, if you sit at Plato's feet and do what he says, that's who you'll be because he will tell you how to think and talk and at the same time tell you that what you are doing *is* thinking and talking. Actually, you'll just be repeating him, and you'll never see what writing has allowed him (to seem not) to do.

I think Plato would like Golden's essay just fine, for Golden has taken him at face value.[11]

2. THE MOVING AND THE FIXED. "Self-motion," according to Socrates' second speech, "is of the very nature of soul"; dialectic, Socrates explains, is a continuous movement toward truth; and the erotic relationship between two philosophical lovers is a quest for godly understanding. Writing, on the other hand, just sits there. It doesn't go anywhere, it never changes, it has no existence outside the physical, it depends on the whim and talent of a reader. In short, it is as opposed to Platonic philosophy as anything could be. Yet it is the origin and possibility of that philosophy. Not only was it impossible for Plato to leave his philosophy for posterity in speaking, he could never have thought of it in the first place in speaking. *Phaedrus*'s very existence is the unsaying of its argument. It could come to be only through the fixed medium of writing.

Every time Plato's Socrates gets close to revealing "truth," he backs away, saying that it can only be apprehended through what it is like or that it finally depends on mystic intuition. Thus, readers who take *Phaedrus* seriously find themselves in the system of Platonic philosophy, a system that always *promises* final revelation of truth. This same system, however, denies access to writing, the mode that would reveal the truth of the system's own operation. The reader constantly must ask, Have I got it now? And the text constantly replies, No, not yet. Only writing (or its image, formal speaking) can have the rhetorical and psychological effect of being complete; only the writer (or rhetor) can know fully how many gaps and inadequacies had to be hidden for such a feeling of closure to come about. Plato uses writing's capacity to have the opposite effect of its process better than anyone else ever has. He uses it to generate a longing for understanding and closure, while at the same time hiding the knowledge that the thing that allowed him to generate the longing is the thing that precludes it. The deficiency of humans who do not know "truth" is not the inadequacy of their souls or the weakness of their intellect; the deficiency is inherent in the system that created the longing in the first place. Plato's text can be complete only if we agree to forego writing, thus making ourselves permanently inadequate, for completion exists only outside the writing process.

The Platonic idea of soul found itself in writing. Soul, says Plato's Socrates, is originless, indestructible, uncreated self-motion that is always true to itself. "That which owes its motion to something else," on the other hand, "even though it is itself the cause of motion in another thing, may cease to be in motion and therefore cease to live" (sec. 245c). Of course such a thing would be created, destructible, dependent on an origin, and capable of falsehood both to others and to itself. Above all, it would depend on something outside itself for motion. Left alone, it would be doomed always to stillness. Note the following oppositions:

Soul	Writing
self-moving	dependent on outside operator (reader) to live
originless	dependent on an outside operator (writer) to occur
uncreated	dependent on preexisting, precreated system of inscription to exist
indestructible	easily destroyed
true to self	capable of falsehood even against itself

Plato's Socrates describes soul as the opposite of writing. And how does he describe it? In writing. I think the idea of soul in *Phaedrus* finds itself in its opposite, writing, which promises the possibility of originality, permanence, and truth, among other things, but never delivers except through the rhetorical effect of closure, which the writer made up in the despair of knowing the writing of truth would never be finished. Yes, of course, most of the ideas in *Phaedrus* come from Socrates, the Pythagoreans, the Orphics, and other pre-Socratics, but only with Plato do they take a form we can know today, and that form is writing. Indeed, only writing lets us conceive of a form that cannot be described while at the same time allowing us to describe such a form. And writing does more, it then makes the description of the undescribable available in history.

Phaedrus, more than anything else, is the record of what happened when Plato employed a medium of possibility, writing, to develop a system of conclusion (the one impossibility of writing). The operation of *Phaedrus* is an operation of repression as *Phaedrus* tries to emerge from itself as writing by denying itself. When Plato's Socrates says a created soulless thing can be "the cause of motion in another thing," we know that created, soulless writing brought to the West the idea of soul as Plato wrote it down. Plato's thought could not take possession of itself as the origin of Western thought until it was created in inscription. It could not begin to move Western thought until it got fixed.

3. MY WRITING? OR, WRITING ME? The truth of everything and all people after Plato is writing: you are, one might say, either what *you* write down or what somebody else writes down about you. Religions, philosophies, governments, laws, mores, possibilities for personhood, modes of being human all emerge from writing. Those who must be what somebody else writes down will suffer all their lives from the separation of body and soul, will feel themselves somehow inadequate to and unworthy of their true selves, will be victims of someone else's inscription. Those, on the other hand, who become writers themselves, will understand how the idea of soul came about, for they themselves can operate the medium that forever promises yet never delivers itself. More importantly, they will know what to think of those who claim to know the truth and want them to spend their whole lives following them to that ever-delayed moment of incommunicable revelation. Those who begin to write (really write the way Plato did), may at first think they have lost a fundamental possibility—the movement toward truth. Actually, they haven't lost anything at all except the dream of such a movement, a dream that was discovered in writing in the beginning. Such a loss is a case for celebration, not a time for mourning.

Writing could have been introduced to the West as a celebration of endless possibility. It could have opened the ultimate mode of democracy because it allows everyone the time and the place to discover the rhetoricity of whatever text presents itself as the closure of truth. The first thing the writer learns is the impossibility of writing to close itself down in truth. The *only* real possibility for a philosopher-king to rule is in an oral society where there are no writers to reveal the king's essentially rhetorical nature, where there are no writers to reveal that the king, who presents himself as possessing the knowledge of philosophy, was made up in writing and could have been made up in an infinite number of other ways. What sort of person would deny to others the source of the power of the king?

The ultimate problem of *Phaedrus,* therefore, is its destructive distortion of the human condition, for it sets up a field in which discovery of self precedes its expression, in which a first, unique voice opens the way to such a discovery, and in which speaking originates knowledge. *Phaedrus* itself, however, does not work this way. Look, for example, at how expression works throughout the text.

The truth, Plato's Socrates would have us believe, is inherent in our souls, which have fallen from association with the gods whose image they bear. We learn truth through memory: if two lovers, Socrates says,

> have not previously embarked on this pursuit, they now apply themselves to the discovery of truth from every available source of knowledge and from their own personal researches; they find in themselves traces by which they can detect the nature of the god to whom they belong, and their task is facilitated by the necessity which constrains them to keep their eyes fixed upon him; by the aid of memory they lay hold on him and are possessed by him, so that they take from him their character and their way of life. (sec. 252d–253a)

In contrast to the process of "memory" through which the philosopher "knows" what is already recorded in the traces of the soul's past, writing, Ammon tells us, "is a receipt [drug, charm, specific] for recollection, not for memory." It shows great folly, Plato's Socrates continues the attack, to think "that written words can do more than remind the reader of what he already knows" (sec. 275), for the *re*memory enabled by reading external marks is clearly inferior to the "true" memory inscribed internally in the soul.

Actually, it's the other way around. Writing is the process that allows one to externalize one's self, to generate the possibility of an "I" and a "me." Only through writing can one operate systematically, recursively, and sporadically enough to seize control of one's "other" voice. While it is true that the idea of the soul as a prisoner in the body goes back at least as far as the Orphics and had been kicking around Greece for more than a century before Plato wrote, the literature on soul and immortality originates with Plato. The only possible way one could work out a systematic, *fixed* idea about the soul was in writing. What makes Plato important is not that he invented the idea of soul, or even the idea of a split between soul and body. What makes Plato important is that he opened the idea in history as writing so that it could remain open for all time. Imagine what would have happened to Plato's idea of soul if it had continued to be kept orally for the last twenty-three centuries! If the soul has traces of truth inscribed in itself, the only way to "read" that inscription is to externalize it, get it out in the light of day—in writing.

At the end of *Phaedo*, Plato's Crito asks Plato's Socrates, "In what way shall we bury you?" Socrates replies, "In any way that you like," but you must get hold of me, and take care that I do not run away from you" (Jowett, sec. 499). Then Socrates explains once again that he is not his body: "I cannot persuade Crito, my friends, that the Socrates who is now conversing and arranging the details of his argument is really I: he thinks I am the one whom he will presently see as a corpse, and he asks how to bury me."[12] After drinking the poison, Socrates concludes, "I shall no longer be with you, but shall go away to the joys of the blessed."

This passage is truly remarkable. Crito may not have known how to "get hold of Socrates," but Plato surely did: he *wrote him down*. Moreover, when Socrates says it is *his* soul that is "conversing and arranging the details of his argument," one cannot help realizing that what is really arranging Socrates' argument is Plato's writing, not the fictional Socrates' soul. Or perhaps a better way to put it is to say that Plato's writing *is* Socrates' soul and that the fiction of writing is the origin of the Western idea of soul in the first place. Plato may have fooled a great many other people about how what he "says" emerged, but he could not fool himself and he hated writing as a result. He wanted to originate, not write. But to originate, he had to write, which made him always already copied down.

To mask the origin of his thought as writing, Plato always speaks with a prior voice. There is never any voice speaking here and now in Plato. In *Positions*, Henri Ronse draws Derrida out about the idea of "différance," which combines differ and defer (pp. 3–14).[13] That surely is what is at work in *Phaedrus* (and in the above passage from *Phaedo*) as Plato constantly defers his own voice through prior (dead) voices of authority and differs from what he himself would say by never saying anything. You cannot write with a never-before-heard voice, because writing depends on all the other written texts before it. You cannot speak with a never-before-heard voice because the voice of any speaker depends on the voices of all the speakers before it. You can, however, speak with the never-before-heard voice of a now-dead speaker who never wrote. All you have to do is write down what (you say) he in his now-dead position of authority said. Thus what you "say" differs from what *you* say because what *you* say is merely what he said, and of course now that he is dead (martyred!) what he said defers any possible interrogation by its already gone presence. But you can only do that in writing, and you can only catch someone else doing it by trying to write in his or her space.

One more thing needs saying before I finish. I have argued that Plato knew Platonism was available only through writing, yet he tried to deny to writing both validity and any opportunity to continue in history. No, I don't know why, but yes I am absolutely sure he knew what he was doing. He knew that the "speech" he left for us to "see" was preceded and enabled by writing. The work of Eric Havelock and Julian Jaynes makes me sure.

Havelock's *Preface to Plato* argues that Plato is pivotal in Western thought because he provided the means for an oral culture to "wake up." Havelock writes primarily about the *Republic* with the purpose of explaining Plato's attack on poetry. The attack is so devastating, Havelock believes, because epic poetry was the organizing principle of oral culture. In effect, the listener to the oral poet entered a sort of hypnotic trance and thus became a vicarious participant in the action itself. Plato's *writings*, however, offer the "discovery of intellection," "a mechanism of reasoned calculation," "a 'subject,' a 'me,' whose separate identity" makes possible disinterested, analytical speculation (p. 201). What Plato *writes* is revolutionary because he represents the invention of literate culture in the middle of oral culture. After Plato "the personality which thinks and knows" distinguishes itself from the "body of knowledge which is thought about and known." Of course, a body of knowledge separate from any particular thinker can exist only in writing. What happens after Plato is the revolutionary process of "'me thinking about Achilles' rather than 'me identifying with Achilles.'" Two remarks by Havelock are particularly striking. The first locates the "discovery of the soul" chronologically with Plato: "The *psyche* which slowly asserts itself in independence of the poetic performance and the poetised tradition had to be the reflective, thoughtful, critical psyche, or it could be nothing. Along with the discovery of the soul, Greece in Plato's day and just before Plato had to discover something else—the activity of sheer thinking" (p. 200). The second remark shows how the technology of writing made Platonism possible in the first place. How, Havelock asks, "did the Greeks ever wake up?" And where did dialectic come from? They woke up through learning to write, and dialectic came from writing:

> The fundamental answer must lie in the changing technology of communication. Refreshment of memory through written signs enabled a reader to dispense with most of that emotional identification by which alone the acoustic record was sure of recall. This could release psychic energy, for a review and re-arrangement of what had now been written down, and of what could be seen as an object and not just heard and felt. You could as it were take a second look at it. And this separation of yourself from the remembered word may in turn lie behind the growing use in the fifth century of a device often accepted as peculiar to Socrates but which may well have been a general device for challenging the habit of poetic identification and getting people to break with it. This was the method of dialectic. . . ." (p. 208)

Jaynes makes a similar kind of case. Early humans, he argues, were ruled by a bicameral brain, a brain which gradually broke down during the first and second millennia B.C., leaving the left brain in charge. As a result of this breakdown, Jaynes argues, an "analog self that can 'do' or 'be' something quite different from what the person actually does or is" originates (pp. 219–20). The person develops an "analog" through which an infinite number of alternate actions can be taken in the abstract while never taken in fact. Through this analog a person can imagine himself or herself doing and being quite different from any actual action or existence. "The importance of writing in the breakdown of the bicameral voices," Jaynes continues, "is tremendously important. What had to be spoken is now silent and carved upon a stone to be taken in visually" (p. 302). "What," Jaynes asks, "is writing?" His answer is profoundly problematic for the innocent reader of *Phaedrus:*

> Writing proceeds from *pictures of visual events* to *symbols of phonetic events.* And that is an amazing transformation! Writing of the later type, as on the present page, is meant to tell a reader something he does not know. But the closer writing is to the former, the more it is primarily a mnemonic device to release information which the reader already has. The protoliterate pictograms of Uruk, the iconography in the early depictions of gods, the glyphics of the Maya, the picture codices of the Aztecs, and, indeed, our own heraldry are all of this sort. The informations they are meant to release in those who look upon them may be forever lost and the writing therefore forever untranslatable. (p. 176)

Yes, I do think that writing is the origin of the soul and of dialectic, and I think it functions to tell not only readers but also writers something they did not know. And I think Plato knew that too. He could never accept the fact that instead of his writing writing, writing wrote him. It is, however, high time we dismiss his *Phaedrus* as a serious document about writing, for the text is deceitful and false. It attempts to say the opposite of what its author knew to be true and hated with all his heart.

4.
PHARMAKON AND PHARMAKOS

Drugs, Scapegoats, and Writing

In spite of all, Plato's stature in Western civilization tempts one to seek some sort of rehabilitation of *Phaedrus*. Such a rehabilitation is possible. Derrida shows the way. "Only a blind or grossly insensitive reading," he argues at the beginning of "Plato's Pharmacy," "could indeed have spread the rumor that Plato was *simply* condemning the writer's activity. Nothing here is of a single piece and *Phaedrus* also, in its own writing, plays at saving writing—which also means causing it to be lost—as the best, the noblest game" (*Dissemination*, p. 67).[1] Yes, Plato can be seen as saving writing, but I'm fairly certain that none of us in composition studies will be much relieved by what has been "saved" once writing has undergone Plato's cure.

I. The Drugging of Writing

This pharmaceutical nonsubstance cannot be handled with complete security, neither in its being, since it has none, nor in its effects, the sense of which is always capable of changing. In this way, writing, touted by Theuth as a remedy, a beneficial drug, is later overturned and denounced by the king and then, in the king's place, by Socrates, as a harmful substance, a philter of forgetfulness.

Derrida, *Dissemination*

No single word in English captures the play of signification of the ancient Greek word *pharmakon* (with its associated words *pharmacia, pharmakeus,* and even *pharmakos*). *Drug* comes closer than any other English word. Derrida traces the links in the chain of "pharmaceutical" words that make "an act of presence" in Plato's dialogues: *medicine, philter, remedy, poison, charm, spell, recipe, substance* (which leads to occult virtues, cryptic depths, even alchemy), *antisubstance* (which leads to nonidentity, nonessence, nonsubstance), *pharmacia* (which means administration of both poison and remedy), and *pharmakeus* (which means wizard, magician, poisoner). And yet more, for *pharmakon* means *artificial* color and paint, which, among other things, disguises and perfumes the corpse: In Plato's texts, "the magic of writing and painting," Derrida explains, "performs like a cosmetic concealing the dead under the appearance of the living. The *pharmakon* introduces and harbors death. It makes the corpse presentable, masks it, makes it up, perfumes it with its essence" (p. 142). In sum, *pharmakon,* the word used to describe writing throughout *Phaedrus,* is overdetermined, signifying in so many ways that the very notion of signification gets overloaded. Except, that is, in one case, for *pharmakon,* as well as all the things it can *represent,* signifies anything not divine.

In the *Republic* Socrates tells Adeimantus that God is perfect, unchangeable by any external influence (sec. 381). In other words, God can have no relationship with the pharmakon, the drug (poison, remedy, charm) from the outside that penetrates and changes the thing it penetrates by inscribing itself on the inside. Whereas immortality and perfection are allergy free and consist in having no relation with an outside, whereas health and virtue proceed from the inside, the pharmakon enters from the outside and in remedying, poisons. Before writing, that most human of things, can open the way to divinity, Plato must save and then purify it.

In the theoretical matrix Plato leaves for us, the only way to save writing is to condemn it. Such a condemnation saves both writing and Platonism by creating the opening in which truth becomes possible. The catch is that the Platonic frame of reference can open a text to the possibility of truth only by making truth a *possibility;* for truth to remain itself, it must remain forever a possibility, never an actuality. Thus, truth as a possibility depends on the impossibility of truth's appearing in writing.

As a way of keeping this "saved" writing pure, Plato gave the West his own version of sophistry (which, for reasons that I hope will be obvious, I spell with the same silent *p* that appears in the Greek and English word *pneuma*). This Platonic psophistry is not the sophistry of Protagoras or Gorgias (which I will refer to with the usual spelling), or even that of Lysias or Isocrates. Psophistry, like the Platonic Socrates, is a fiction. Yes, of course, psophistry must bear some resemblance to the sophistry of Lysias, Gorgias, Protagoras, and Isocrates, just as the Platonic Socrates must bear some resemblance to the historical person. But by writing a psophistry that differs from that of the sophists, by writing a psophistry that defers the need for theirs by replacing it, Plato creates the field where true knowledge can occur without ever really being there.

Even though, as I have tried to show, Plato had to use some of the tricks of the rhetoricians as well as some of the sophists' strategies for case making in order to create what we now call *Phaedrus* (or to create anything else in the Platonic canon for that matter), Plato would have us believe that much more than rhetoric and psophistry emerges from *Phaedrus*; he would have us believe that genuine knowledge in the Platonic sense emerges from *Phaedrus*. Plato manages this seeming impossibility by bringing psophistry on stage in his own text and letting it have its say. At the same time, he brings the system that allows this psophistry—a system based on writing and false rhetoric—on stage too, thereby focusing the reader's attention both on the saying of psophistry (early in *Phaedrus*) and on the system that allows psophistry to be said (at the end). He calls attention to writing as a pharmakon, a double agent always operating in more than one way.

Used by the psophists (those fictional villains whom Plato needs to vilify in order to exempt himself), writing is the pharmakon that poisons truth, for psophistry operates as nothing more than the strategy of position taking. Indeed, psophistry can be made to hold any position; the adept psophist can present any position as the closure of truth. But the psophist can do this only by excluding truth as a possibility. The psophist substitutes the ability to convince others for the inability to know what others should be convinced of (in Plato's jargon, one would say the psophist substitutes *doxa* [belief] for *sophia* [wisdom]).

Used by Plato, however, the same pharmakon becomes an

antidote. Because of psophistry's capability of closing itself down in apparent truth, Plato reveals psophistry as the absence of truth by revealing truth as the one thing beyond closure. Truth occurs only in dialectic, the constant detour through the voice of the other and therefore the impossibility of closure. Dialectic always awaits the response of the other, a response that then requires a new speaking and then generates a new response and so on. Whereas the writing of psophistry maneuvers the reader into believing whatever the psophist has set out to prove, Plato's writing cancels itself out by bringing psophistry and its impossibility face to face. What remains is an opening, one might almost say an absent space, in which and through which a dialectical process can operate.

In short, Plato (and Derrida) would have us believe that Plato, though he uses psophistry, is not a psophist himself. "The argumentation against writing in the *Phaedrus* is able to borrow all its resources from Isocrates or Alcidamus," Derrida explains, "at the moment it turns their own weapons, 'transposing' them, against the sophists. Plato imitates the imitators in order to restore the truth of what they imitate: namely, truth itself" (p. 112). For Plato, therefore, writing is the replacement of dialectic with its "other"; writing is, in fact, dialectic with the self. Thus it must be written on the soul. At the moment of its inscription, it disappears because it is inscribed on the absent place. More importantly, as long as writing remains writing (before it becomes persuasion or psophistry), it remains open; it remains dialectic.

By "taking" *Phaedrus* as the source of the *possibility* of truth, not the closure of truth; by "taking" writing as the remedy for a diseased desire for the closure of truth; by "taking" writing as nothing more than a replacement for speech and dialectic; the writer can open the possibility of dialectic within the writer's own self. Rather than a place or a destination, rather than the shelter of some closed and complete revelation, truth becomes an *opening*. Any writers who agree to enter Platonic writing will find themselves in just such an opening; thus, most struggle with all their might never to go there. If pressed, they substitute the opposite of Platonic writing by turning to psophistry, which is the only alternative the Platonic frame of reference permits. This psophistry allows writers to avoid the infinite opening of dialectic, the infinite detour that always (and only) *approaches* truth.

Most composition teachers carefully hold their students in the Platonic frame of reference while at the same time precluding dialectical writing. Such teachers want a complete essay intended to generate a certain state of mind or a "particular change in the reader's image" (Young, Becker, and Pike, p. 217). That, however, is the one thing they will never get if their students use Platonic writing, for Platonic writing, regardless of its point of departure or "topic," will finally carry the students into a dialectical search for truth.

In effect, composition teachers ask their students to write in a Platonic frame of reference where writing operates as the ever-reversible pharmakon. In the beginning, students enjoy a state of pre-Platonic internal certainty in which they think they know what they believe about such topics as abortion, capital punishment, football, Russia, and zoology. The moment they begin to write, however, the pharmakon of writing poisons the internal security of whatever they choose to write about. Writing constantly shows them that they are not sure of, have insufficient basis for their belief in, do not know enough about, and cannot quite finish with whatever they are writing on. At this point, writing is operating Platonically—which is to say it is operating dialectically, internally, on the soul—as the students dispute with themselves in the opening of trying to know what they know. The "disease" of internal certainty (which is merely another name for the "disease" arising from the desire for ideological closure where dialectic is forever precluded) is being "cured." Though the students, as they struggle with writing, may think their internal certainty, indeed their entire state of mental well-being, has been poisoned, in fact, the poison is Plato's remedy for the disease they do not know they have. Their teacher, however, who also operates in the Platonic frame of reference, has demanded that they use what seems like a poison (the writing that kills their internal certainty) and is really a remedy (for the disease of internal certainty) as a poison (the medium that allows them to present a closed, persuasive essay that could lead a reader into internal certainty).

Writing, being the ever-reversible pharmakon, will, of course, do this, but anyone inexperienced in the Platonic frame of reference has difficulty reversing the internal, dialectic nature of writing, removing it from the soul where it can be "true" and inscribing it in ink where it must be both false and deceitful about its own process. By this point, things have gotten out of hand for many students; thus, they give up entirely and replace Platonic writing not with its opposite, psophistry, but with its negation, what I call antiwriting, which usually looks something like this:

> Three Reasons for Stopping X
>
> X is one of the most important problems in today's modern society. There are three main reasons why X should be stopped. This essay will explain those reasons.
> First, a lot of people X because it is the popular thing to do. They do not realize how harmful it can be in their later lives. All young people should realize that the best thing to do is have fun later when it will last. Doing the popular thing now because it is fun is a big mistake, because this sort of fun doesn't last.
> Second, a lot of people don't realize that taking the easy way now is a bad idea. The way to have a bright future that will last is to work hard now and wait until later to X. For example, Horatio Alger did not X a lot when he was young. Instead, he worked hard for a bright future, and he ended up with a wonderful family, a good job, a lot of money, and a beautiful home.
> Third, the Bible says young people should not X. The Bible has been around a lot longer than those who X. If young people will be patient like Job was and if they work hard like he did, they will end up with children and all the good things life has to offer.
> In conclusion, I feel that people should not X. We should elect leaders and hire teachers who do not X. Because X is popular, and the easy way, and against the Bible, you can see X should be stopped.[2]

The teacher's Platonic frame of reference has pushed students into this sort of antiwriting, which is so common in writing courses at all levels. Students' intuitive knowledge that psophistry is the *best* they can hope to produce—a dialectical writing on the soul having been precluded from the beginning—magnifies the power of the temptation to retreat into this sort of antiwriting. Without knowing jargon words like sophistry and deconstruction, the students know all along during the process of their attempts to turn dialectical writing into psophistical writing that the teacher will be able to deconstruct their essays. Thus they must be willing to turn dialectical (soul) writing against itself in order to develop incomplete psophistical positions knowing all along that these positions will immediately be treated the way Plato's Socrates treats his Lysias. This explains the attraction of essays like the above "Three Reasons for Stopping X." By inscribing antiwriting, the student avoids poisoning his or her internal security. Better yet, since the student has inscribed neither Platonic writing nor psophistry, nothing at all exists for the teacher to deconstruct. The student has submitted something like this:

> I am not writing. I hold no position. I have nothing at all to do with discovery, communication, or persuasion. I care nothing about the truth. What I *am* is an essay. I announce my beginning, my parts, my ending, and the links between them. I announce myself as sentences correctly punctuated and words correctly spelled.

Plato (and Derrida) would have us believe that the way out of this seemingly endless circle, where the remedy (soul writing) for disease gets perverted into a poison (psophistry) or, worse yet, gets perverted into nothing at all (antiwriting), is wizardry. The Greek word for *wizard*, Derrida points out, is *pharmakeus*. A psophist is a pharmakeus who uses the powers of wizardry to destroy truth by changing truth (*sophia*) into opinion (*doxa*). This pharmakeus uses the pharmakon of writing to trick the reader by presenting the reader's opinion as the truth. The antidote to this pharmakon is the pharmakon administered by another pharmakeus, another wizard. Paradoxically, the pharmakon administered by this second pharmakeus (in Plato's case, Socrates) is the same pharmakon as that administered by the first pharmakeus (the psophists) except that this time the pharmakon has been turned around into its opposite.

The good pharmakeus destroys the power of the evil pharmakeus by exposing his method. "The fear of death," Derrida explains, "is what gives all witchcraft, all occult medicine, a hold. The *pharmakeus* is banking on that fear. Hence the Socratic pharmacy, in working to free us from it, corresponds to an operation of *exorcism*, in a form that would be envisaged and conducted from the side and viewpoint of god" (p. 120). Psophistry's powerful hold over the modern writer comes from the fear that writing cannot close itself down in the presentation of truth. Accepting that fear or addiction not as a poison but as a remedy makes it its own remedy. As psophistry and dialectic struggle against each other, "*pharmakeus* against *pharmakeus*, *pharmakon* against *pharmakon*" (p. 124), psophistry offers ideological certainty through the rhetorical (doxological) closure of truth; dialectic counters this degraded psophistry by showing that truth must be excluded for that closure to occur. Dialectic, in other words, poisons the poison of closed truth and ideological certainty. Plato would have composition teachers ask themselves What kind of pharmakeus am I? A good one like Plato's Socrates or a bad one like Plato's Lysias?

II. Plato's Cure

Imagine for a moment a student writer faced with the task of writing a paper on any issue about which there is the possibility of disagreement. Almost as a reflex, a move learned in the Platonic frame of reference, the student attempts to rediscover the voice of the lost or hidden god-father who can "pronounce" the truth of the issue. But the moment the student agrees to write, this pronouncement gets deferred because the student differs from the one who could make such a pronouncement. The moment such students pick up their pens, they have deferred their positions permanently because their writing consists of the process of choosing what among the many things that could be inscribed will actually appear in their papers. Their efforts lead ineluctably to psophistry: they will do the best they can to anticipate the arguments against their position, to adapt their own arguments to the audience at hand, and to present as closed and complete a position as possible. Like Plato, however, they can pursue the links only so far. Never will writing bring them to the point of completion.

Like Plato, the student seeks knowledge with no sign or supplement—knowledge that is itself in itself by itself. For writing to reveal such knowledge, it would have to erase itself, becoming the "no thing" in which the "true thing" could reside, the non-outside of the perfect, impenetrable inside. Any writing that does not erase itself, any writing that remains available indefinitely and indiscriminately can never be more than the stopping point of a failed dialectic. Any finished text has become the opposite of its true self, for if it were true writing, if it were the writing that occurs on the soul as a dialectical search for truth, it would not yet have finished. When it was arbitrarily stopped, it changed into its opposite.

This reveals the difference between a dialectical position and a psophistical one. A dialectical position always holds itself in question; only a psophistical one claims to be complete, hence the seemingly endless process of deferrals that constitute *Phaedrus*:

1. Socrates defers his business in order to hear Lysias's speech (Plato having already deferred his own business in order to create the writing where Socrates can have any business at all).
2. After Lysias's speech, Socrates defers his true opinions about love in order to give a speech that defeats Lysias by making Lysias's case better than Lysias could make it himself.
3. After Socrates' first speech, he defers his decision to leave the plane tree and return to Athens because of the need to correct the error he has committed against love.
4. Socrates' second speech is less a speech than the constant series of maneuvers through which he defers what he would really say if he could speak with the voice of a god.
   a. He defers the beginning of his speech with a series of comic etymologies, thus setting a tone that makes the reader extremely wary of concluding what the speech finally "says."
   b. Then he defers the beginning of his speech again with a definition of soul; this definition is itself the deferral of the true definition that only a god could give.
   c. The speech itself explains how the philosopher's mode of operation constantly defers the perception of truth.

Rather than simply apprehending truth directly, which the fallen soul cannot do, the philosopher must reapproach such an apprehension through dialectic (the constant deferral of one voice to another and the perpetual deferral of closure). And to enable themselves to begin the journey at all, philosophers must replace direct love of truth with the inspiring but insufficient love of the beloved. The face of their god, which is the thing they desire most to see, is what must be gone. Its absence prevents their being wise and limits them to being "lovers of wisdom."

5. After Socrates' second speech, when one would expect the dialogue to end in order to maintain its "organic structure," Socrates and Phaedrus decide to defer their departure from the plane tree a second time in order to discuss rhetoric and writing. (Note that Socrates' famous call for organic structure would not appear in *Phaedrus* at all if the dialogue had ended with his second speech. Plato must defer the ending of his own dialogue in order to have a place to explain where endings in general should occur.)

6. The first principle of rhetoric turns out to be the never-ending deferral of itself, for it presupposes "knowledge of the truth" (secs. 259e–260e).

7. Writing appears in the first place only through the deferral of dialectic, only as "a shadow" of the knowledge of dialectic (secs. 276a–e).

8. And then this final deferral (all italics mine):

To *believe* . . . that a written composition on any subject must be to a large extent the creation of *fancy*; that nothing worth *serious attention* has ever been written in prose or verse—or spoken for that matter, if by speaking one means the kind of recitation that aims merely at creating *belief*, without any attempt at *instruction* by question and answer; that even the best of such compositions can do no more than help the *memory* of those who already *know*; whereas *lucidity* and *finality* and *serious importance* are to be found only in words spoken by way of instruction or, to use a *truer* phrase, written on the *soul* of the hearer to enable him to learn about the *right*, the *beautiful* and the *good*; finally, to realize that such spoken truths are to be reckoned *a man's legitimate sons*, primarily if they *originate* within himself, but to a secondary degree if what we may call their *children* and *kindred* come to *birth*, as they should, in the *minds* of others—to *believe* this, I say, and to let all else go is to be the *sort of man*, Phaedrus, that you and I might well *pray* that we may both become. (secs. 277e–288a)

Stirring and inspirational though this is, loaded with the characteristics of closure as it is, it does not end *Phaedrus*; rather, it defers that end permanently. The whole paragraph presents itself as an emptiness waiting to be filled through the process of dialectic. One can choose almost any noun, verb, or modifier in the passage (note the words I have italicized) only to discover that this "word" in fact conceals a catachresis (the name that is no name) hiding an unending series of questions, uncertainties, replacements, deferrals, differences, and supplements. Defining any of those italicized words would open an unclosable dialectic. With this sentence, Plato has taken *Phaedrus* away, leaving an emptiness that did not exist before the act of "reading." Only a dialectical, perpetual *approach* to the beautiful and the good can fill this emptiness. After Plato, writing becomes the opportunity for beginning the dialectical procession toward truth; writing itself will always empty itself out at the moment of inscription. Platonic writing calls continuously to dialectic, which always waits to be filled by the question What do you mean?

Now this recalls those students trying to write essays on issues about which there can be disagreement (which, of course, excludes almost nothing). If such students consent to attempt Platonic writing, the first thing they will lose is what they thought they would use writing to say. Their conception of writing as the vehicle one uses to transport an idea fails at the beginning because it demonstrates that no such thing as an idea exists in isolation. Any idea depends first on the idea of an idea, which is problematic enough in itself; then within that problem, it depends on the other ideas from which it can differ, on one hand, as a way of knowing itself and like which it can seem, on the other hand, as a way of supporting itself.

Students realize that their studies of the controversial issues they have chosen inaugurate the danger of an endless search

(Plato would call it an education). Of course, the teacher's demand for essays on a certain day precludes any such search. The students' response is predictable. They have seen enough of Platonic writing to know they are not ready to close down their inquiries and inscribe them. As a way of giving in to the demand for essays, they turn to psophistry, which is the only alternative available in the Platonic frame of reference chosen by the teacher. Psophistry allows the students to construct texts that the reader will find sufficiently difficult to deconstruct; it also allows them to substitute the opinion of their reader for the knowledge they still lack. They attempt to escape from writing by convincing the teacher that they have thought enough, know enough, and have written convincingly enough for their arguments to be acceptable. In effect, they conspire with the teacher in the use of psophistry by replacing the absence of their own knowledge with their ability to generate a desired opinion in someone else. That's what Plato feared above all else; it's what *Phaedrus* struggles against. And it's what drives most writing teachers into literary studies.

Having undergone Plato's cure, writing teachers operate in a world where truth "exists." Of course, it "exists" only as a possibility, but this forever absent "existence" makes it all the more attractive and powerful. In this world, the only writing of value is dialectical writing as the writer opens and holds open an eternal internal dialectical journey toward truth. Anything less than this is psophistry, nothing more than a concatenation of rhetorical tricks designed to manipulate readers so as to make them believe their opinion is the truth. For the writing teacher operating in a Platonic frame of reference, however, writing courses unavoidably become psophistry because such courses can never be more than courses in rhetoric. They begin and end with invention, arrangement, and style. Neither the students in the courses nor the institutions that house the courses are willing to permit disinterested, protracted journeys toward truth; the idea of lovers seeking truth together and wishing to travel in the sphere of the same god is laughable, if not illegal, in the writing classroom. Two options result.

Most beginning writing teachers internalize the Platonic dichotomy, learn to view writing contemptuously because, even at its best, it is mere psophistry, and quickly turn their attention toward literature. There they can begin what seems like a journey toward truth as they surround themselves with canonized texts and with fellow travelers who claim to be on the same journey. Their classes become dialectical searches for truth as these teachers dispute with themselves and with the best of their students the meanings of the texts under scrutiny. The teachers become Plato's Socrates, their students become *Phaedrus,* and the journey toward truth opens endlessly before them. The literary canon reinforces the idea of truth as "possibility" because of its constancy and power. Best of all, it allows truth to take on an even more objective appearance because the dialectician, rather than being limited to the truth recorded invisibly in only two souls, can work with the truth as it has been metaphorically externalized by a whole series of "great souls." Some of the teachers in this category continue to teach writing, of course, but they do so only quite casually in a sort of dues-paying way until they can get away from the task. Should fate trap them into teaching writing frequently, they simply see it as an impediment on their true journey toward truth, not unlike Plato's Socrates' problems with the likes of Lysias, or Plato's own problems with Isocrates.

Numerous other beginning writing teachers, though, internalize the Platonic dichotomy as above, but, for reasons known only to them (perhaps they believe their souls are small and incapable), they remain for years (sometimes throughout an entire lifetime) in the composition classroom. Because they see what they do as psophistry, they regard their endeavor as skill-building—more like carpentry than like philosophy. Thus they expect to be both treated poorly and underpaid (after all, they have nothing to do with truth), and they struggle mightily to keep their pedagogy as rigidly structured as possible in order to keep it manageable in a forty-hour work week. They guard against any sort of dialectical endeavor with a vigilance bordering on the frantic, preferring to limit instruction in writing to the rules of grammar, spelling, and organization.

Yes, Plato saves writing by making it the medium for an internal, dialectical journey toward truth. And he presents his (soul) writing as the pharmakon, the drug that can cure those souls who believe themselves to know a closed and permanent truth. But this cure comes at a great price for writing, because it makes writing just one more metaphor for the romantic notion of the well-examined life, and it requires that everything written down in a writing class present itself as nothing more than a failed, dead, and incomplete dialectical search for truth.

Two examples drawn from my own experience will show the effect of Platonic writing on students. When I was teaching freshman composition at NYU in the spring of 1978, the best writer in my class stopped me one day to complain about a grade. She had gotten what she considered a bad grade on a paper she thought deserved better; she agreed the paper wasn't very good, but she thought it was some distance better than the grade I had assigned. After I refused to change the grade, she said she felt as if she were in the Hotel California, the Eagles' haunting metaphor for the "good life" where, once there, "you can check out any time you like, but you can *never* leave."

Since that day, I have thought many times about the way she came to write that paper. I had assigned the task of writing a persuasive essay on a controversial issue. My frame of reference was clearly, though unconsciously, Platonic; above all, I valorized the endless, dialectical search for truth. The student had chosen to writing about abortion, which she strongly opposed and thought should be outlawed in the Constitution. She had requested a conference because she was having great difficulty getting started. When I asked what she was going to write about, she hesitated a few moments and then said abortion. She was clearly uncomfortable, probably because she assumed I supported legalized abortion. As a way of drawing her out, helping her start, I asked what she might say. She responded quickly and succinctly, "It's wrong." When I asked why it was wrong, she shrugged and replied, "It just is," as if the possibility that it might be right were inconceivable. When I asked how she might go about writing that it was wrong, I immediately saw her utter despair. She was exceedingly reluctant to carry her beliefs into the sort of writing she knew I would demand. She knew from the beginning that she could not submit a paper like this:

> In the Ten Commandments, God said we should not commit murder. A lot of babies aborted in today's modern, scientific world are capable of living and get flushed down the toilet. There ought to be a law against that because it's murder.

I think this situation typifies that of most inexperienced writers whose teachers force them into a self-conscious Platonic frame of reference. Anything more than a simple statement like the above exceeds what the student wants to write. Yet the above statement of dogma does not exist in the sort of writing we require in Plato's academy. As this student knew all too well, having sat for years in English classrooms, if she "seriously" pursued the issue of abortion by bringing it into Platonic writing, her idea, which could have been written down so simply as above, would suddenly slip away from itself, finally becoming endless supplementation, endless deferral of any incontrovertible pronouncement against abortion. Because the text was to be on abortion, it would enter an arena populated for many years by all the other texts on the same subject which would preempt, humiliate, and expose it as incomplete.

Before she began to write, this student knew how she felt: abortion is wrong and oughtn't to be allowed. For her, writing was the poison that enters from the outside, penetrating the interior of her conclusion and propelling that conclusion outside into the arena of discourse where it will immediately be inadequate. In Platonic terms, of course, the dis-easy state she entered by trying to write about abortion should "cure" her belief in truth as closure and remedy her desire for ideological certainty. Once she began Platonic writing, she should open truth as a possibility and begin to write on her own soul. Though this "true writing" would never conclude itself with a written text, she should save writing by losing it; that is, she should keep it pure by forever beginning to write but never actually reaching the point of editing the final draft.

This particular student, however, escaped through antiwriting. She replaced writing with its negation, which said only, I am writing, and thus was nothing at all. She merely replaced X with *abortion* in the above "Three Reasons for Stopping X" sample of antiwriting, dressed it up and lengthened it, and dared me to fail her. She won the dare.

In the fall of 1975, I taught an honors composition class at Baylor University. The texts for the semester were *Job* (New English Bible) and Archibald MacLeish's *J.B.* The brightest student in the class was a young man planning to become a minister. The course was agony for him, and finally for me too. Before the class began, he had never read *Job*, though he had heard numerous sermons preached on it over the years. As he read the text for the first time, he found himself unable to deal with it. He simply could not find a way to make it say what he needed to hear.

We probably had a dozen conferences, some quite long and heated, not to mention numerous other conversations as we walked to and from class or when he would accost me walking across campus. Each of his essays after the first undid the previous essay, and the fifth and final essay undid itself as well. I put no grade on the last paper because I did not know what else to do with it. It did not fit into any sort of idea I had at the time of essayness, yet I knew its author was exceptionally bright and had worked very hard indeed. Because he had made clear A's on the other four, I simply gave him "credit" for number five and an A in the course.

I can now imagine him in his dorm room trying to find a place where his writing can start. Plato's remedy has poisoned his internal certainty. The ideological closure he brought to Baylor from a small Texas town and a fundamentalist church is diseased and dying. To write the essay that will be the antidote to Plato's remedy—the bad poison to drive the good poison out, one might say—he needs to use terms like *God, faith, justice,* and *reward.* He needs those terms to operate as pure signs; not signifiers temporarily and arbitrarily linked to significations, but pure, crystalline, fixed signs. His desperation borders on panic as he tries to write, but too many voices, too many questions assail him. Through Derrida's description at the end of "Plato's Pharmacy," I can see my student attempting to inscribe Platonic writing. He cocks his ear, trying to distinguish between two repetitions:

> He would like to isolate the good from the bad, the true from the false.
>
> He leans over further: they repeat each other. . . .
>
> The walled-in voice strikes against the rafters, the words come apart, bits and pieces of sentences are separated, disarticulated parts begin to circulate through the corridors, become fixed for a round or two, translate each other, become rejoined, bounce off each other, contradict each other, make trouble, tell on each other, come back

like answers, organize their exchanges, protect each other, institute an internal commerce, take themselves for a dialogue. Full of meaning. A whole story. An entire history. . . . (pp. 169–70)

And so the replacement of dialectic that is writing on the soul, the opening of truth, goes. It is, says Derrida, the eternal inauguration of itself: "If writing is *inaugural* it is not so because it creates, but because of a certain absolute freedom of speech, because of the freedom to bring forth the already-there as a sign of the freedom to augur. A freedom of response which acknowledges as its only horizon the word as history and the speech which can only say: Being has always already begun" (*Writing,* p. 12).

I now think I understand the dynamics of both of those cases. In the first case, I felt I had opened a student's narrow-minded social fanaticism by showing her that her point could not be made in any sort of definitive way. Because I forced her into a Platonic frame of reference where she had to choose between the romantic process of a well-examined life and psophistry, she chose nothing at all. I did not expect her to write an essay, merely to struggle endlessly with the impossibility of writing an essay and to record for me the evidence of that struggle. But she had a life to live and my Platonism would have prevented it. In the second case, I wanted to dismantle a world view from which I myself had "escaped." Again I did not expect an essay, and in fact every time my student gave me one, I gave him an A and then took the essay apart, showing him in detail why it was not "true," until finally he went me one better by writing something that did not pretend to truth. He slipped out of the Platonic frame of reference, where he had been forced to choose between Platonic writing, on one hand, and psophistry on the other.

What I did not realize at the time was that my goal was to make both students permanently inadequate. Under my tutelage, they would learn how to remain in a state that would forever foreground what they did not know. The goal was not to know or to act, but to contemplate. In each case (a Roman Catholic girl from New York and a Southern Baptist boy from Texas), the purpose was to change from the simplistic, fundamentalist "delusion" of adequacy to the self-dialectical, contemplative, (p)sophisticated "reality" of *in*adequacy. What I did not realize at the time was the price of such (p)sophistication. One must take a final look at Plato, again through Derrida, to see that price.

III. Scapegoats

In tracing out the complicated linkages and multiple significations of the pharmaceutical terms in what he calls the "text of Plato," Derrida discovers that one term, *pharmakos*, is excluded. Though *pharmakon* and *pharmacia* appear frequently, though Socrates is actually called a *pharmakeus* in *Meno* (sec. 801b), and though *pharmakos* "can, on one of its faces, be considered the synonym, almost the homonym, of a word [*pharmakeus*] Plato 'actually' used" (p. 130); *pharmakos*, like Plato himself, appears nowhere in the dialogues. In one way, *pharmakos* means the same thing as *pharmakeus*, except that *pharmakos* has the overlay of being a scapegoat, an evil force, an outsider. The pharmakos functioned sociologically, Derrida explains, to save society by being excluded from it as a scapegoat or killed by it as a sacrifice:

> The city's body *proper* thus reconstitutes its unity, closes around the security of its inner courts, gives back to itself the word that links it with itself within the confines of the agora, by violently excluding from its territory the representative of an external threat or aggression. That representative represents the otherness of the evil that comes to affect or infect the inside by unpredictably breaking into it. Yet the representative of the outside is nonetheless *constituted*, regularly granted its place by the community, chosen, kept, fed, etc., in the very heart of the inside. These parasites were as a matter of course domesticated by the living organism that housed them at its expense. "The Athenians [Derrida quotes Frazer as saying] regularly maintained a number of degraded and useless beings at the public expense; and when any calamity, such as plague, drought, or famine, befell the city, they sacrificed two of these outcasts as scapegoats." (p. 133)

Derrida argues that the word *pharmakos* is as visible in Plato's canon through its absence as it would be through its presence.

This is so because all the other words in its family appear there in prominent positions. More importantly, I would add, it is so because Socrates, the central figure in Plato's writing strategy, became Athens's most famous pharmakos, the scapegoat, the force of evil, the corrupter of youth whom the city killed (permanently expelled) in order to keep itself intact. One can indeed become a pharmakos, a truth seeker whose greatness of soul exceeds normal human circumstances, but society will exact its revenge. Suffering that revenge is a high price to ask students to pay before they become writers. It is, however, the price Platonic writing requires.

Undeniably, Platonic writing has a powerful attraction. Those who embark on it can believe themselves to have superior souls, souls that wish to escape the limitations of the human condition. Merely embarking on the never-to-be-completed journey toward truth sets these people apart as philosopher-kings who can revel in the satisfaction of knowing their love of wisdom should place them in roles of social authority. Those who choose Platonic writing, or, more generally, the Platonic frame of reference, should, however, keep in mind the three options it allows for the teaching of writing.

In the first, truth opens endlessly as a possibility as writers write on their souls. In the second, writers who refuse soul writing must turn to psophistry, where writing becomes an utterly value-free technology. In this second option, writing, like aviation engineering, plumbing, or the wheel, is merely one more technological tool whose skillful use has nothing to do with truth or morality. Writing well and knowing what one ought to write remain utterly separated. In the third option, psophistry gets debased even further as writing becomes nothing more than the corporal housing for thought. In this option, writing becomes antiwriting, a sort of physical regimen focused on spelling, grammar, punctuation, and patterns of organization. Here, one teaches writing as a way of disciplining thought's house, making it neat and correct.

Anyone who wishes to reconstruct *Phaedrus* can do so by accepting the Platonic, dualistic frame of reference in which truth remains possible through its permanent absence in the dialectical quest. In this frame, any written text must be inadequate and all the operations of (mere) rhetoric must be eschewed. Also, the composition teacher self-deconstructs, or, more likely, becomes a philosophy teacher. And that's not as odd as it sounds. The Platonic frame of reference has determined English departments since their inception. In the first essay by an English professor in the first issue of *PMLA* (which in 1884 was called *TMLA* for Transactions of the Modern Language Association), James Morgan Hart sets out the point of view that has dominated the MLA ever since. Three things, according to Hart, do not belong in English departments: logic, rhetoric, and philology. Of logic and rhetoric, Hart says:

> Fortunately the Logic question is fast settling itself. The growth of this study has been so rapid of late, its drift toward mathematics and the experimental sciences so unmistakeable, that no disciplined mind of the present day can look upon logic and literature as having anything in common. As to Rhetoric the course is not so clear. There are still too many persons of influence and culture who persist in looking upon the instructor of English literature as necessarily the instructor of rhetoric. I am unable to share this opinion. To me rhetoric is purely formal drill. . . . The proper object of literary study in one word is to *read*, to grasp an author's personality in all its bearings. And the less rhetoric here, the better—in my judgment. Rhetorical exercises are, of course, useful. So are the parallel bars and dumb-bells of a gymnasium. Need I push the comparison further? (pp. 84–85)

Apparently the answer to Hart's rhetorical question was yes, for in a footnote he goes on to say, "I do not wish to be understood as arguing in general against the utility of training in Rhetoric and Composition. In fact, such training seems to me an indispensable part of the school-curriculum. The above strictures are aimed solely at Rhetoric and Composition, as they are often taught in College. . . . It seems to me that Rhetoric, if taught at all in college, should be taught by the professor of Philosophy."[3]

There is, however, another caution for those about to be inveigled by the Platonic frame of reference, a caution even more powerful than the danger that the teaching of writing will become the teaching of philosophy. Even if psophistry were sophistry, how dangerous could it be? The answer to this question lies at the heart of Platonism. The dialectical journey undertaken by superior souls allows the philosopher to escape from the cave, to see the light, and to return to the cave with a superior knowledge of both the "real" and the "ideal." Sophistry endangers such a journey because Plato's liberated soul, upon returning to the cave, must compete with all those sophists who do not know the truth and who may, in fact, through rhetoric defeat the Platonic soul. Thus, the true danger posed by sophistry and rhetoric is that they threaten the Platonic soul's control over the masses. And where is such a threat an important problem? Only in societies whose members are unable to undertake the journey toward truth and unable to recognize the trickery of sophistical rhetoric.

But what would happen if *everyone* had a sophistical education? What would happen if everyone knew how metaphysical, political, and ethical decisions were made? Then wouldn't everyone know how to recognize sophistry and thus be aware of how a given position developed and how it worked its force on its audience? And wouldn't that be democracy, where there aren't any philosopher-kings and there aren't any "great souls" and all people stand on equal footing in attempting to sort out the various rhetorical strategies they encounter each day. If everyone had a sophistical education, if everyone could recognize sophistry and understand the rhetoricity of all metaphysics, wouldn't that prevent anyone from claiming superiority by claiming to be on a journey toward truth? Wouldn't the teaching of writing enable a democratic society by showing how to construct a position, how to deconstruct one, and how not to be fooled by those who claim to know the truth, even if they make the claim by explaining that the truth of the truth is that no one knows it?

Those who work in composition studies ought to be very careful about any attempt to rehabilitate *Phaedrus*. But composition studies can't survive in Plato's academy without some theoretical matrix. That matrix, I believe, is the sophistry that psophistry effectively killed off. I'd like to advance it as an alternative theoretical matrix for a rhetoric liberated entirely from philosophy. But before I can do that, I must inhabit fully the philosophical situation that enabled these first four chapters, and that takes me to Derrida, he who would like to rewrite Plato by writing him down and showing his already-writtenness.

△

5.
"THE MOST IMPROBABLE SIGNATURE"

The Derridean Theory of Writing

> If I seen him bearing down on me now under whitespread
> wings like he'd come from Arkangels, I sink I'd die down over
> his feet, humbly dumbly, only to washup.
>
> Joyce, *Finnegans Wake*

Whether Jacques Derrida's work proves to be enduringly important to the study of literature in the United States remains to be seen. Obviously, his texts have stirred up sufficient controversy to spill over into society at large.[1] There is, oddly enough, no question about his importance to writing theory (see Winterowd, *Composition*, pp. 84, 197, 307), even though American writing theorists have not discussed his work nearly so much as have literary theorists. Because the key move in each of his texts (especially those published between 1965 and 1973) is to "deconstruct" the West's concept of "communication" by showing how that concept begins with and depends upon the suppression of writing, writing theorists in the United States must understand his ideas and take them into account in some way, even if only to reject them. As anyone who reads his books cannot help but see, Derrida is, more than anything else, a writing theorist.

Two difficulties, alas, plague anyone trying to study Derrida's impact on writing theory. First, his analytical methods make everything harder, not easier. American writing theorists have such a long tradition of seeking the easier, quicker way that hardly anyone in the field welcomes a theoretical position making everything harder and slower. Second, of course, his texts are hard to read.

I have nothing to say about the first difficulty except that the study of writing remains an immature discipline just so long as it believes in and seeks the magic system or the special program that will teach students to write quickly and efficiently. And I don't have much to say about the second difficulty either except to agree that it exists. Unquestionably, with a little more time and care, Derrida could have written his texts much better than he did. He does explain why his texts are so hard to read. He attempts, he says, to write in "the space in which is posed the question of speech and meaning." Such writing "attempts to keep itself at the point of exhaustion of meaning," which risks meaning nothing: "To be entangled in hundreds of pages of a writing simultaneously insistent and elliptical, imprinting . . . even its erasures, carrying off each concept into an interminable chain of differences, surrounding or confusing itself with so many precautions, references, notes, citations, collages, supplements—this 'meaning-to-say-nothing' is not . . . the most assured of exercises" (*Positions*, p. 14).[2] Perhaps because I remain an undeconstructed logocentrist* (words marked with an asterisk are "defined" in chapter 6 below), I remain skeptical both about this explanation and about the needlessly poor writing that characterizes most of Derrida's pre-1974 canon. My "faith" tells me that any obscure, difficult text could have been written clearly had the writer genuinely wished for clarity and been willing to put in the work it requires.

CAVEAT EMPTOR

Before "beginning" my essay, I must address a third problem. (Of course it says something about the ontology of "an essay" for me to imply in a fourth paragraph that my own essay has not yet "begun" and in fact will not "begin" for seventeen more paragraphs. I am, however, fully confident that Derrida's deconstruction of prefaces in the "Outwork" of *Dissemination* and his deconstruction of the "interior" of an essay in "Living On · Border Lines" justify my eighteen-paragraph caveat. Since, as "Outwork" would have it, my essay cannot be said to "begin" anywhere, I am free to pretend it "begins" wherever I like. And since, as "Living On · Border Lines" demonstrates, my essay "proper" will speak its own "other voice" however much I struggle to keep that voice silent, the longer I wait to "begin," the longer I can keep the floor all to myself.) Even though in 1982 Derrida explained at length that the "apocalypse" his analyses lead to is a gala rather than a catastrophe (*D'un ton*, pp. 9–17),[3] the texts he published before 1975 speak in a more ominous tone than his more recent texts admit. In fact, something about the way Derrida wrote in the decade between 1965 and 1975 is scary. The reader has the clear feel of being at the end of a Yeatsian gyre, waiting for a terrible change. The third problem, then, is the apocalyptic threat of deconstruction. This caveat, which I do not consider part of "this" text, addresses that threat of apocalypse.

When I think of the apocalypse, I do so in what Derrida would call logocentric terms. Because I was raised a Southern Baptist in the Mississippi Delta at a time when everybody I knew accepted a New Testament millenarianism as "God's way," apocalypse, for me, has always meant Christ's militant return to reestablish his kingdom forever. This whole scenario is logocentric because in it Christ constitutes a beginning, an ending, an absolute authority, and an origin of meaning. When Christ speaks, at least in the Southern Baptist theology of my childhood, he speaks absolute meaning. In effect, what he says *goes*—no equivocation, no ambiguity, no margin for error. In that scenario, the trumpet on the last day needs no interpretation. Somehow it sounds at one with its meaning. If you hear it, in other words, you'll know what it means even if you've never heard of the Revelation of St. John. After the trumpet sounds, when God binds Satan, casts sinners in hell, and admits the saved to heaven, again that voice will speak its own absolute meaning. No arguments, no uncertainty, no interpretation: simply the absolute union of signifier and signified as the voice of God says what is and what will be.

Derrida describes a different sort of apocalypse. When he speaks "with a newly adopted apocalyptic tone," he is playing with the idea of apocalypse, reversing it entirely. Rather than an event that ends the play of meaning and finally reestablishes the origin of meaning in the mouth of God, rather than some terrible holocaust during which all "the lost" get sent off to perdition, Derrida's apocalypse exists all around us all the time. It reverses the New Testament idea of apocalypse by denying the absolute origin on which a New Testament type apocalypse would depend. Even so, Derrida's apocalyptic tone troubles me, and I suspect it troubles other American humanists, both those who have made a serious effort to read his books and those who have not. Having "outgrown" belief in one apocalypse and affiliated ourselves with the tradition of humanistic learning, we American humanists have difficulty taking seriously new prophets of a new apocalypse, especially those who claim to be deconstructing the tradition we have spent so many years learning. Derrida, however, operates firmly within the same humanistic tradition as we do. Though he often ends his analyses by saying that no words, no concepts, no "way of thinking" currently exist to say and think what needs saying and thinking, he operates consistently through the major philosophical and literary texts of the West and readily admits that he could not operate at all without those texts.

To begin with, Derrida's "apocalyptic" analysis reveals that there won't be an apocalypse, at least not one where meaning simply asserts itself with no need for some "other mode" of expression. "What we know," Derrida argues "is that there has never been, never will be, a unique word, a master-name."[4] Instead, there has always been and will always be the play of signification, as signifier refers to signifier in an endless chain that never leads back to an origin. Rather than accepting this new, nonapocalyptic apocalypse with nostalgia; rather than longing for the time when signification could be regarded as secondary to, inferior to, and subservient of meaning, "we must *affirm* this, in the sense in which Nietzsche puts affirmation into play, in a certain laughter and a certain step of the dance." Vincent B. Leitch calls this "other" apocalyptic vision Derrida's "intractable gaiety" (p. 17); David Kaufer and Gary Waller think it begins a celebration by opening the possibility of infinite free play (p. 69).[5]

What causes so much concern among philosophers and critics is that Derrida argues again and again—especially in the essays written in the sixties and early seventies—that a period of metaphysical thought has "come to a close." As a result, no form of expression or indication[6]—whether speech, writing, gesture, or solitary mental life—can any longer be thought to reveal "an absolutely objective core of meaning." In other words, no possibility exists for having meaning simply available. This does not mean that Derrida has set himself in opposition to the now-closed tradition of metaphysical thought; nor does it mean that he thinks of himself as outside it. Indeed, he repeatedly argues that his work can be done only within that tradition, if for no other reason than no alternative tradition exists; thus, the tools and strategies for deconstructing that tradition must come from the tradition itself.[7] Derrida's essays themselves, however, never get beyond cryptic hints about what might come after such a deconstruction. (I assume that *Glas* and the "Envois" to *La carte postale* do not represent the models for a "new" kind of writing that can now appear in the wake of Derrida's deconstructive apocalypse. For an argument that they *do* represent such a new writing, see Ulmer.)

Frankly, I do not know—nor, in my opinion, is there any way to predict—what forms of reading, writing, and thinking Derrida's deconstruction of Western thought might lead to.[8] But since the bulk of this chapter (once it "starts") articulates a Derridean "philosophy of composition,"[9] it seems only fair to admit the uncertainty that still surrounds Derrida's analyses. The rest of this caveat—though admittedly through a glass *very* darkly and with surgical brevity—summarizes Derrida's own cryptic hints about whatever beast of a new age currently slouches toward Bethlehem. Four effects of Derridean analysis seem obvious: self-contained, complete meaning is impossible; expectations of reading change; conceptions of writing change; and, as a result of these first three, a new sort of apocalypse is at hand, though what sort of appearance it may make remains impossible to predict.

MEANING.   At the end of *Speech and Phenomena*, Derrida states bluntly that the possibility of absolute knowledge simply present to itself, independent of any mode of expression, and free from any taint of language is the closure of history. And he believes "that such a closure has taken place" (p. 102). Thoughts unthought of as yet, thoughts that must be "sought for across the memory of old signs," will be required to "know" what begins beyond this closure. On one hand, we must continue to question the old system of metaphysics from within, but on the other, we must escape to

> the openness of an unheard-of question that opens neither upon knowledge nor upon some nonknowledge which is a knowledge to come. In the openness of this question *we no longer know*. This does not mean that we know nothing but that we are beyond absolute knowledge (and its ethical, aesthetic, or religious system), approaching that on the basis of which its closure is announced and decided. Such a question will legitimately be understood as *meaning* nothing, as no longer belonging to the system of meaning.

To begin speaking in this new age, "we will have to have other names than those of sign or representation." These new names will allow us to generate discourse in a metaphysical system where "the indefinite drift of signs," the continual "errance and change of scene" generate the desire for absolute knowledge while forbidding absolutely its presence. (p. 103)

READING.   At the end of "Form and Meaning: A Note on the Phenomenology of Language," Derrida argues that reading must ask "an entirely other question" from what it has asked before: No longer, "What is the line of thought?" Rather, what is the circularity that makes two lines of thought, each wishing to exclude the other, "pass into one another indefinitely"? (*Margins*, pp. 172-73). In trying to decide between matter and form, the reader oscillates endlessly until there is "neither matter nor form, nothing that could be recast by some philosopheme, that is, by some dialectics, in whatever sense dialectics may be determined. An ellipsis both of meaning and of form: neither full speech nor a perfect circle. More and less, neither more nor less" (*Margins*, p. 173).[10]

WRITING.   In *Grammatology* (pp. 85-87), Derrida speculates on the end of what he calls "linear writing," which is some four thousand years old and which, through its triumph over nonlinear writing, originated the West. This triumph, however, was not complete: "A war was declared, and a suppression of all that resisted linearization was installed." Linear writing "creates" the ideal of history: "the unfolding of presence[*], where the line relates the final presence to the originary presence according to the straight line or the circle." Nonlinear writing, in contrast, "spells its symbols pluridimensionally; there the meaning is not subjected to successivity, to the order of a logical time, or to the irreversible temporality of sound." Nonlinear writing, which Derrida also calls "mythographic" writing, allows a kind of technical, artistic, religious, and economic unity that linear writing disrupts. To regain access to this unity, "we must" (here Derrida quotes Andre Leroi-Gourhan) "desediment 'four thousand years of linear writing.'"[11] But the process of linear writing has been so ingrained in Western thought that Western thinkers can no longer "see" it. Rather than *a form* of thought, it has *been* thought; thus, "meditation upon writing and the deconstruction of the history of philosophy become inseparable." Derrida says, however, that the night of linearity has recently begun "to lighten a little at the moment when linearity . . . relaxes its oppression because it begins to sterilize the technical and scientific economy that it has long favored." Though "the end of linear writing is indeed the end of the book," nonlinear writing may still allow itself to be encased inside the form of a book:

> It is less a question of confiding new writings to the envelope of a book than of finally reading what wrote itself between the lines in the volumes. That is why, beginning to write without the line, one begins also to reread past writing according to a different organization of space. If today the problem of reading occupies the forefront of science, it is because of this suspense between two ages of writing. Because we are beginning to write, to write differently, we must reread differently.

Derrida justifies the claim that a new writing has dawned by referring to the sort of writing in fiction, drama, poetry, film, and philosophy that has occurred in the twentieth century. Twentieth-century writing, he argues, is "gradually destroying" the linear or "epic" model because modern thought cannot be written in the linear pattern, a pattern that assumes the existence of meaning before and outside of language. Not that modern thought is new to the world; quite the contrary, recent studies of writing have shown how the limits of Western metaphysical discourse have always been in place. The current access to pluridimensionality "makes all the rationality subjected to the linear appear as another form and another age of mythography. The meta-rationality or the meta-scientificity which are thus announced within the meditation upon writing can therefore be no more shut up within a science of man than conform to the traditional idea of science. In one and the same gesture, they leave *man, science,* and the *line* behind."

Two principles follow from Derrida's apocalyptic analysis of linear writing: the first about the process of writing, the second about the process of reading. Hartman, writing about *Glas,* makes the point about writing. *Glas* itself, he says, questions the ability of linear writing to move toward certain knowledge. Derrida "saves" the fact of the written character, but he does so by insisting, like so many contemporary artists, "that the materializing imprint of words is more than the deformation of some ideal thought"; saving writing amounts to the most radical critique of "naïve, phonocentric materialism" (*Saving,* p. 35). J. Hillis Miller, writing about canny and uncanny critics, makes the point about reading. The uncanny, or deconstructive, reader follows the text's linear attempt at logic until logic itself fails in impasse or aporia. But the moment logic fails, the moment the discourse the text wishes to privilege is exposed as harboring another discourse it cannot silence or comprehend, the reader has penetrated to the heart of language itself ("Stevens' Rock," pp. 335–38).[12]

THE UNNAMABLE, MONSTROUS, TERRIFYING, ABNORMAL APOCALYPSE.   In all three of his 1967 books, the books with which he burst upon the international scene, Derrida says his analysis finally moves toward an unnamable monstrosity. In *Speech and Phenomena,* he argues that "the very essence of consciousness and its history," the essence of the West, is that speaking transcends writing. "One cannot attempt to deconstruct this transcendence without descending, across the inherited concepts, toward the unnamable" (p. 77).

In *Writing and Difference,* Derrida argues that play disrupts presence. While play "is always play of presence and absence[*]," it is also the prior medium in which presence and absence can be differentiated. Play is the already absent present in which absence can constantly undermine the confidence presence attempts to claim. One can respond to "the lost or impossible presence of the absent origin" in one of two ways: in a saddened, negative, nostalgic, guilty way as Rousseau does, or with the laughter of Nietzschean affirmation, which "is the joyous affirmation of the play of the world and of the innocence of becoming, the affirmation of a world of signs without fault, without truth, and without origin which is offered to an active interpretation. *This affirmation then determines the noncenter otherwise than as loss of the center.* And it plays without security." These two possible responses lead to two possible "interpretations of interpretation." In the first, the reader "seeks to decipher, dreams of deciphering a truth or an origin which escapes play and the order of the sign." In the second, the reader "affirms play and tries to pass beyond man and humanism, the name of man being the name of that being who . . . throughout his entire history—has dreamed of full presence, the reassuring foundation[*], the origin and the end of play." Derrida sees these two possible interpretations of interpretation as "absolutely irreconcilable," and he sets for himself the task of studying "the *différance*[*] of this irreducible difference." As he watches the birth of what his study reveals, he too averts his eyes "when faced by the as yet unnamable which is proclaiming itself and which can do so, as is necessary whenever a birth is in the offing, only under the species of the nonspecies, in the formless, mute, infant, and terrifying form of monstrosity" (pp. 292–93).

In the "Exergue" to *Of Grammatology* as he prepares the space where he will carry out his analysis of writing, Derrida opines that the science of writing he attempts, a science that "shows signs of liberation all over the world, as a result of decisive efforts," runs the risk of "never being able to define the unity of its project or its object. Of not being able either to write its discourse on method or to describe the limits of its field." His hope is that the discourse of the West has reached "the point of being now able to produce its own dislocation and itself proclaim its limits." The method requires "patient meditation and painstaking investigation on and around what is still provisionally called writing." The future, however, "can only be anticipated in the form of an absolute danger. It is that which breaks absolutely with constituted normality and can only be proclaimed, *presented*, as a sort of monstrosity" (pp. 4–5).

DECONSTRUCTION.   Entering a world where meaning is lost, where reading and writing are radically changed, and where an abnormal, unnamable, absolutely dangerous monstrosity is undergoing parturition would give anyone pause. To the faint-hearted, however, I can give all assurances that what's actually there is not so shockingly, radically revolutionary and nihilistic as is sometimes claimed. No doubt, most Derrideans will accuse me of trying to bring Derrida's ideas into the realm of and under the sway of logocentric discourse, the very discourse he tries to call into question. Perhaps I am indeed guilty of that. In my defense, however, let me say two things: (1) This book is the record of a struggle, not the presentation of a conclusion. (2) This book is frankly and overtly parasitic on Derrida's canon. Parasites by definition extract only part of their hosts.[13] In an effort to draw Derridean theory into composition studies, I have decided to dismember (and, yes, probably mangle) Derrida's texts. But as he surely knows all too well, their very existence *as* texts makes such dismembering inevitable.

Chapter six below, which was written before this chapter as a way to make this chapter possible, "defines" what I consider to be the key terms in the Derridean lexicon. Except for the extensive quotations in this caveat, which, as I explained, is not part of this text, I have included very few quotations from Derrida. Since I am writing so flagrantly and preemptively in his space, it seems only appropriate to relegate most of his text to my endnotes and to use brief parenthetical documentation to point to the many places in his texts that have been repeated in my text. For Derrida's actual "words," one must see my notes.

With assurances given and defenses erected, I can "begin" my essay, which I do at the "beginning" by explaining Derrida's notions about writing.

I. Classical Writing

The apocalyptists usually set forth their messages under the name of some ancient worthy, e.g., Adam, Enoch, Noah, Abraham, or some other figure of note.

New Oxford Annotated Bible

In almost every essay he writes, Derrida attempts to reveal how Western metaphysical discourse constitutes itself. Though Derrida tends to write about texts and to use a jargon unfamiliar to American writing theorists, and though he would no doubt be horrified to wear the label I am about to give him, in effect, his essays explore the process by which written texts emerge. Though he describes an entirely abstract process—as opposed, for example, to the empirical processes described by such composition specialists as Janet Emig, James Britton et al., and Glenn J. Broadhead and Richard C. Freed—all of his analyses attempt to explain how a given text came into existence and how it continues to operate. What these analyses reveal startles everyone at first, causing most readers, as Derrida himself admits (*Positions*, p. 68), to reject them out of hand. Again and again, Derrida attempts to show that writing precedes speaking and that from the beginning of the West, "the history of truth, of the truth of truth, has always been . . . the debasement of writing, and its repression outside 'full' speech" (*Grammatology*, pp. 3–4). Admittedly, such statements seem preposterous. The way to show how Derrida arrives at them is to show how he defines writing, beginning with how he defines what he calls "classical writing."

In the classical notion, writing is tertiary. First there is thinking, then speaking serves as an instrument to represent thinking, and finally writing serves as an instrument to represent speaking. This means not only that writing remains exterior to and dependent on speaking and that speaking remains exterior to and dependent on thinking, but also that all systems of signification remain exterior to and dependent on whatever they signify. Language, in other words, must come after, remain outside of, and depend absolutely on meaning. Each exterior thing, by carefully proclaiming its exteriority to whatever it represents, both affirms the presence of and denies the need for the actual appearance of whatever it represents (*Grammatology*, pp. 75–83). This elaborate series of hedges allows thinking simply "to be," to exist without ever needing to reveal itself.

Since Plato, however, everything that has been taken seriously as "thinking" has appeared in and depended on writing. Preliterate cultures simply cannot "think" in the post-Platonic sense of the word. But for thinking itself to remain pure, writing can never be more than a set of imperfect utensils. The relationship of writing to thought parallels that of body to soul, with writing as the fallen, decaying "home" where meaning and thinking temporarily reside (*Grammatology,* pp. 34–35). In the classical notion, the progress of human civilization moves inexorably as humans first learn how to think, then how to convey those thoughts through sound, and finally how to represent the sounds in writing. But writing itself never affects in any way the meaning it carries (*Margins,* p. 312).

In the chain of replacements between thinking and writing, speaking, which stands closer to thinking and precedes writing, always enjoys privileged status. The reasons for this privileged status are easy to see. One's own speech appears to link signifier and signified in a necessary and absolute way. One's ideas are clear and full, belonging to the presence of one's own self-identity (Culler, pp. 107-9). Speakers seem not to borrow anything from outside themselves; rather, speech generates a diaphanous chain of signifiers that disappear leaving their meaning intact. Through speech, in fact, meaning seems to emerge from nowhere. Thus thinking and understanding, Derrida explains, seem to be acts in absolute proximity to themselves, acts that have no need of language (*Speech,* pp. 77–80). Such an experience "lives and proclaims itself as the exclusion of writing." Such an experience precludes "an 'exterior,' 'sensible,' 'spatial' signifier interrupting self-presence" (*Grammatology,* p. 98).

Privileging speech has enormous ramifications in almost every area of human life. For example, it allows the concept of the "ideal" to emerge. Ideal objects remain forever independent of any here-and-now; ideal objects, though infinitely repeatable, remain forever unchanged. But any ideal, since it exists outside the world, depends on a medium where it can be constituted and expressed without somehow being changed (*Speech,* pp. 75–76). Such a medium would efface itself completely, leaving the idea whole and uncontaminated. The spoken voice, vanishing even as it occurs, names this medium.

But since Western thought and culture depend absolutely on writing, since they could never have emerged and surely could not operate even one day without it, writing becomes, in Richard Rorty's phrase, "an unfortunate necessity." The Western writer wants to capture the reader by using only a few entirely transparent words to demonstrate knowledge in some absolute way. In effect, such writing attempts to end writing by using it to obviate itself in the presence of pure knowledge ("Philosophy," p. 145). Derrida's analyses reveal two problems with this desire: first, writing always leads to more writing; second, writing in fact precedes and enables speaking.[14] Most who have tried seriously to write can accept the former. The latter, on the other hand, needs a good bit of explaining.

II. Writing and Speaking

> In the beginning was the Word, and the Word was with God, and the Word was God. He was in the beginning with God; all things were made through him. . . .
>
> John 1:1–3

Without question, arguing that writing precedes speaking invites scorn, if not contemptuous ridicule.[15] It takes time just to get up enough patience to listen to the possibility. Once one does, however, the argument and the analyses it generates are undeniably intriguing. As the key move in making his case, Derrida distinguishes between what he calls "writing in the narrow sense" and "writing-in-general," which he also sometimes calls arche-writing (*Grammatology*, pp. 109–12). Writing *in the narrow sense* means inscribing speech, thus making visual a preexisting system of oral communication. In this view, thinking comes first, followed by communication. Writing appears as a species of communication, a species that operates only in the absence of what it represents. Thus, from the moment it appears, writing exists quite some distance from what it substitutes for, always occupying the role of insufficient servant. Writing appears in history only because of speech's inability to remain present in time.

Through an enormous and painstaking set of readings, however, Derrida has tried to show that all the characteristics of writing in the narrow sense—all the deficiencies that make it tertiary, repetitive, metaphoric, and metonymic—also exist in speaking, also exist in thinking, exist even in Being. In other words, what Derrida calls writing-in-general—the operation of supplement*, différance, repetition*, replacement, absence of presence, absence of closure, absence of the transcendental signified*—already constitutes everything that would present itself as prior to and purer than writing. If one assumes that writing operates at the tertiary level, then one also assumes that something secondary and something primary precede writing. Derrida's analyses overturn these assumptions by showing that when one tries to work back to the level that precedes, founds, and enables writing, one finds nothing more than the exact same operation of writing—supplement, repetition, différance, absence. More importantly, the only way to attempt such a working back, indeed, the only way "to think" of it in the first place is in writing.[16]

Derrida presents his hypothesis by defining "sign" as replacement. Any sign exists only to stand for whatever no longer appears or cannot fully function in its own right. A fully sufficient signified (or meaning) needs no sign to take its place. Thus, the original insufficiency from which writing suffers—that it is not the "thing itself" but merely a replacement for and repetition of such a "thing"—describes every sign. No sign is "the thing itself," for no sign can appear until the "thing itself" has already disappeared or become inadequate (*Margins*, pp. 314–20).[17]

In both *Margins* (pp. 316–21) and *Grammatology* (pp. 42–44, 62–63, 237–39, 302) Derrida explains the essential qualities that constitute writing and then shows how speaking has those same qualities. Writing has three particular qualities:

1. Since writing remains in effect far beyond the life of the author, it can continue to "speak" more or less infinitely. And since authors cannot control what readers may find in their texts, the ways future readers may interpret those texts remain inexhaustible.
2. Written signs break with their contexts, escaping into contexts and taking on meanings that the writer not only did not intend, but also was incapable of intending. No context can enclose writing, which constantly grafts itself to other chains of writing and signification. Everyone who has read much interpretation, and especially the worst excesses of New Criticism, has seen interpretations go far beyond anything the author could have conceived. In effect, Derrida merely says what we all know: if a written document manages to survive long enough, readers will make it say things the author could neither have thought nor understood.

3. Spacing makes writing vulnerable to such breaks with context. Written documents exist in space (*Grammatology,* pp. 68–70). They remain available by breaking with everything around them, by becoming discrete form and transportable mass. Readers can differentiate texts from what they are not because texts proclaim their beginnings, endings, boundaries, and even their containers (e.g., book and magazine covers, essay folders, and so on). Even the insides of texts depend on such spacing devices as chapters, sections, pages, paragraphs, sentences, clauses, phrases, words, letters, and diacritical marks, all of which depend on the spaces that separate them, allowing each entity to achieve an identity by both association with and separation from all that surrounds it.

This same spacing allows for extraction and grafting. An entire text or any part of a text remains forever liable to extraction from its current context, an event that immediately rearranges its entire process of signification. By the same token, texts and parts of texts find themselves grafted onto other texts and find that other texts graft onto them. Just as a text must space itself from all the other texts around it in order to become a discrete text, the very need for spacing shows the need for the other texts, which play in and around this text all the time. And no text can avoid either of these operations. For a text to be read, the reader must extract it from the author's protection. Any author who has experienced the agony of watching a reader (no matter how friendly) read knows the violence of this process of extraction. The author, sitting and watching helplessly, feels the text slip away, take on unintended even unimaginable meanings; feels, in fact, betrayed. And just as the text gets "extracted" by the reader—at first usually by a friendly, well-known reader, but in future by nearly anyone—the text also finds itself grafted onto other texts: the texts whose form or method it borrows; the texts with which it differs; the whole milieu of written texts upon which it depends to be recognizable as itself. Moreover, other texts come along immediately and graft onto this one, changing it with every new grafting.

This description of writing rarely generates much opposition. The next step, however, does, for Derrida argues that the same characteristics that describe writing appear in speaking. In a

literate culture, speaking *seems* free from the deficiency of out-
living or escaping the speaker's control. My spoken words appear to be mine; they cannot escape me because they disappear
as soon as I utter them, leaving no possibility of their being
misrepresented. But in fact, spoken words can behave the same
way as written words do. Indeed, spoken words may be even
more liable to betray one in one's absence or after one's death
than written words. Who knows, for example, what Christ really
said, or Socrates, or the early Homer and Beowulf poets, or even
Vygotsky and Saussure?[18]

Even those of us who live in highly literate cultures see our
speech escape us, get carried away from us by others, and then
repeated beyond our control. All of us have been undone by our
speeches that have left us and entered the mouths of others.
And in oral cultures, where speech remains the repository of
culture, history, and theology, the process of repetition, restate-
ment, reformulation and *change* goes on infinitely. By no means
does our speech stay within our control. Once uttered, it becomes
available for interpretation, repetition, and reformulation even
by those who did not hear it, even after we are dead.

Furthermore, because speech, like writing, cannot be confined
to our presence and our control, it too breaks with its context.
It too is subject to extraction and grafting. For speech to function
at all, it must be recognizable and repeatable across a broad range
of accents, tones, and voices. This makes the spoken word behave exactly like the written word. Iterability[19]—the possibility
of being repeated not only apart from the meaning intended by
any given speaker at any given time, but also apart from any
intention to mean at all—allows speech to be speech. But at the
same time it requires that each spoken signifier remain forever
severed from any specific meaning. Thus, each spoken signifier
functions exactly as any written signifier, as a floating mark that
never was and never can be pinned (or penned) down to a single
production or a single meaning.[20] Like writing, speech can be
extracted from one context and inserted in another. Indeed, the
continuity of speaking communities depends on constant extraction from speaker to speaker and constant repetition and
change of what any given speaker says. Moreover, conversation
grafts itself onto other conversation and in turn has new conversation grafted onto it. In other words, the spacing that allows
discrete speech to appear also requires that an infinite host of

other speeches attend each seemingly discrete speech in order to give it a body of other speech to be discrete from. The spacing that allows speech operates exactly the same way as the spacing that allows writing.

In short, if endless repetition, constant reinterpretation, continual extraction from context to context, and infinite grafting of text to text describe writing, then writing describes speaking. In *Speech and Phenomena* Derrida gives the example of the signifier "I," which, in speech, presents itself as pure unsymbolized self-intuition. But because the signifier "I" exists apart from any given speaker, rather than presenting such a pure presence, it merely serves a symbolic function. As a result, whatever speaker is designating her- or himself must use this symbolizing function— even if the speaker is unknown, or dead, or fictional. The spoken "I" seems to stand for a fully self-aware, wholly integrated and available "self." But as we know all too well in a post-Freudian world, such an integrated, complete "self" can never be more than illusion. The signifier "I" that replaces and stands for such a whole self, in fact *creates* the possibility of that self by standing in for what would never have existed in the first place had a symbol that distorts it not taken its place.[21] The "I" that operates symbolically by pointing toward the absent, whole, self-aware "self" in effect symbolizes what never was and creates the possibility of a "never was" by replacing it and revealing its absence. And the complications continue. For the written "I" creates the spoken "I" by standing for it and thus giving it something to differ from. In other words, there can be no such concept as a spoken "I" without a written "I" to replace it and call attention to it by revealing its absence (pp. 92–97).[22]

Having shown that a description of writing is also a description of speaking, Derrida next shows why writing cannot in fact derive from speech. If speech had ever been joined with meaning so that it erased itself leaving pure meaning present, writing would have been not only unnecessary, but also anathema: a form of speech that existed prior to writing would have been joined with meaning; thus, writing, which would merely have represented speaking and immediately would have failed to capture it perfectly, would have been the most important thing to avoid. In fact, however, speaking always operated as writing. It presented itself in the absence of the meaning that would have appeared if it could have without allowing a set of signifiers to intervene. In other words, speaking *is* writing in every manner of its operation.

Even more oddly, speaking did not become "speaking" until writing replaced it and, by both differing from it and deferring it, called attention to its absence. Truth and meaning, therefore, are not simply present anywhere: not in solitary mental life, not in speaking, not in any combination of the two. Truth and meaning are absences that become objects of desire, one might almost call them fetishes, because writing and speaking reveal them as always existing absences (*Grammatology*, pp. 56–57). Speaking, in short, like writing, remains forever incomplete because what it would present if it could actually present what it *re*presents becomes "gone" only when speaking or writing appear on the scene to stand for the "thing" that can be recognized as "gone" now that a symbol appears to stand in its absent place.[23]

III. Writing-in-General

The *Word* (Greek 'logos') of God is more than speech; it is God in action, creating, revealing, redeeming. Jesus is this *Word*. He was eternal; personal; divine. *Was*, not became. He was sole agent of creation. Apart from him both physical and spiritual life would recede into nothingness.
New Oxford Annotated Bible, (note to John 1:1–3)

"Writing-in-general," therefore, names a process of movement. Derrida often calls this process the trace* (*Speech*, pp. 85–86; *Grammatology*, pp. 72–73). Writing represents something that has already gone, that in fact must be gone for writing to appear at all. Though writing, as the paradigmatic signifying system, constantly points to what it replaces (both speaking and meaning), the "thing itself" that writing points to (whether speaking or meaning) can never appear in writing. The hard thing (for me at least) to think, however, is that writing actually creates both speaking *and* meaning: (a) by differing from them and thus calling attention to them by that difference, and (b) by deferring them and thus generating the desire for what now can be recognized as absent. (Derrida calls this compound process of differing and deferring "différance.")

As a way of beginning itself, Western discourse attempts to

escape the play of différance and the movement of the trace. It does this by debasing writing while at the same time using it as a necessary evil in transcribing speech and transporting meaning. By showing that speech operates exactly like writing, Derrida locates any sort of final meaning (which he would call a transcendental signified) as a sort of permanent absence. This absence puts play in play—that is, it starts the process of signification, which endlessly points toward the meaning that would destroy it were such meaning to appear. Derrida accuses Western discourse of using play to end play, by which he means using systems of signification to present meaning, the thing that had to be absent for signification, play, and the *possibility* of meaning to occur in the first place (*Grammatology*, pp. 17, 31).[24] Any human enterprise that purports to escape play by effacing itself in the presence of meaning can be shown to be writing, to be inscribed, to be a mark that repeats and replaces without being able to limit the field of play.

In effect, Derrida's deconstructions of Husserl, Rousseau, Lévi-Strauss, Saussure, Plato, Freud, and others, work through the same analytical process. He shows how Western metaphysics sets up a hierarchy of oppositions, beginning with speech against writing, in order to create "thinking," while not requiring "thinking" to explain itself, its origin, or its foundation. The key move in doing this is to use writing at every stage and in every act while at the same time claiming that writing is secondary to speech, which is nearest "thinking" and the "self" that generates it. Again and again Derrida shows how any description of writing also describes the thing for which writing stands. Though writing is admittedly replacement, secondarity, and play, whatever is supposed to precede and inform writing, whatever is supposed to escape play or be primary or be present in its own right always turns out to operate just like writing.[25] Writing, in other words, created the West, not the other way around. And thus, whatever Western thought generates or achieves is never more than writing, never more than secondary, repetitive, playful, longing for what must be absent for play to begin.[26]

Because the West emerged through writing, and because everything Western that would count as thinking appears in writing, the devaluation of writing plays a crucial role. First, it allows the formation and integrity of the individual as an absolute origin of meaning; second, it keeps meaning intact by constantly calling attention to itself as an inadequate servant of the greater truth it attempts to bear.[27]

In writing, the writer remains confused, unsatisfied, unfinished. By conceiving writing as the replacement for speech, by treating it as an inadequate medium for capturing the meaning that simply emerges in speech, the illusion of pure meaning lives on (*Grammatology*, p. 22). Of course, deconstructing this conception of thinking, speaking, and writing does not make writing innocent (*Dissemination*, pp. 181–82, n. 8). Rather, it merely shows that "writing does not *befall* an innocent language." Because every writer knows the forever-playing, unfinished process of writing, writing must serve some other medium. If it does not, then such things as self, meaning, and truth—things that writing *symbolizes* and by symbolizing points toward the absence of— become the effects of writing rather than the origins that enable and inform writing. Deconstructing the West's devaluation of writing does not set writing up over speech, thus reversing the old hierarchy. Rather, it shows both how metaphysical systems operate by privileging one concept over another and how meaning emerges from différance and from the repression of the opposite of meaning.

In a deconstructed notion of writing, the writer knows both that the text cannot be reduced to its meaning and that no way exists to get back before the writing to the speaking or thinking that would found and validate the writing (*Positions*, p. 64).[28] Writing always leads to more writing: to displacement, substitution, gradual forgetting, and gradual distancing from the origin (*Grammatology*, p. 200). The writer must operate a system while never expecting the system to deliver what it promises; for writing infinitely defers what it promises in order to keep the *promise* in motion. Writing will never do what the written text appears to do: fix and communicate closed meaning.

IV. Absence and Presence

. . . as it is written, "They shall see who have never been told of him, and they shall understand who have never heard of him."

Romans 16:21

What writing *will* do is play around, limitlessly and end-lessly. Derrida compares this play to a mirror, which, like a written text, represents yet never actually "contains" anything. One cannot "have" what a mirror contains; one can only see the mirror endlessly repeat what it appears to contain (*Dissemination*, p. 323). Perhaps more to the point, only by looking at the mirror from an unchanging position can one see this appearance. Turning away from the mirror reveals something much different from what the mirror shows, and changing positions before the mirror changes what the mirror itself shows.

The angle of vision from which Derrida usually opens an analysis strikes almost everyone as odd, if not downright perverse. Consistently and persistently he looks not for what the text under analysis "says," but rather for how the writing itself works. Reading to discover what a text "says" already devalues writing by assuming that the reader can extract what the writing carries. Derrida's reading strategy focuses on a variety of odd, apparently idiosyncratic, phenomena about writing. Those who allow Derrida to demonstrate his strategy, however, usually have their conception not only of writing but also of communication in general changed in fundamental ways.

To begin with, instead of seeing writing as the presentation of knowledge, one sees two absences. The writer must be absent before the reader can begin to read. And the meaning the text purports to represent must be absent for any sort of representation to occur in the first place. Writing cannot construct a text that then vanishes leaving "the signified content which it transports and in general teaches" (*Grammatology*, p. 160; see also pp. 41, 267, 300). Because the presentation of pure meaning would equal the transcendental, blinding, silencing, all-sufficient presence of God, meaning remains forever a possibility but never an actuality.[29] For 273 pages in the "Envois" to *La carte postale* Derrida plays with the absences that constitute writing. The "Envois"—a hodgepodge of allusions, personal anecdotes, and hilarious play—breaks apart.[30] Almost every paragraph has part of two lines missing. And the text both begins and ends with the demand that the reader (whoever he or she is) burn all the postcards. The text demonstrates the theory that writing exists at least as much by what it excludes, suppresses, and leaves blank as by what it includes, represents, and fills in. Moreover, the text depends on writing's structural possibility of miscarrying and never reaching its destination.

A more important, though less obvious, "absence" is what Derrida calls the "attending discourse," the discourse that brings writing into existence and tends its continued life (*Dissemination*, pp. 324–30). In a discourse, two voices appear to speak: on one hand, the "I" of the discourse; on the other, the semiotic system into which the text must fit so as to be recognizable *as* a text. The "I" resembles what Wayne Booth calls the implied author (pp. 71–73), a sort of provisional presence that invokes the reader's attention and then serves as the moral, ethical, perspective-orienting channel through which the discourse can emerge. The semiotic system, in contrast, enables writing in the first place. Such a system allows texts to be recognizable as texts by providing rules for how texts operate, defining such roles as writer and reader,[31] and setting boundaries within which the concept "text" becomes thinkable.

These two discourses struggle continuously. The "I" attempts to make a unique statement, to reveal whatever "knowledge" the text has been shaped to carry. The system, on the other hand, constantly reveals how this particular discourse is woven into the web of similar discourses. By providing any given discourse with the context of all the other discourses that precede and surround it, the system reveals what this discourse borrows, what it lacks, and how it speaks only by using words and patterns that come already loaded with uncontrollable connections.

The attending discourse operates as a third discourse that unites the discourses of the "I" and the system. The attending discourse itself has no specific location, and never in fact speaks audibly (or visibly). It serves as a "pure passageway for operations of substitution," as a sort of channel through which the "I" can communicate with the system and the system with the "I." It lets a writer say "I" as if "I" were a self-sufficient, univocal origin. But "I," however much it may appear to do so, does not originate itself; rather, both "I" and the possibility of writing "I" exist in the system. Since the writer must have that "I," and since the writer does not wish merely to repeat the system, the writer must find some passageway into and out of the system through which the "I" of the system can be expropriated. By like token, the system continues to live only so long as someone repeats it. Thus, the system needs a passageway through which to enter the writer's text in order to expropriate it by making it repeat the operation of the system.

This oscillation between the "I" struggling to speak outside the system and the tyranny of the system's "I" is a process of différance. Each specific text defers the originality with which it would speak if it could speak outside the constraints of a system. At the same time, it differs in two ways: first, from the system it modifies at the moment of entry into the system; second, from what it would be if it could merely efface itself in the presence of pure meaning rather than keeping alive a system from which it would like to escape. Most important of all, the attending discourse allows the writer to play the role of "I" as if it were not a role, as if, in fact, it were a pure presence, a fully integrated, self-sufficient origin for and generator of meaning (*Dissemination*, pp. 324–326).[32]

The operation of the attending discourse raises several questions vexing to anyone who wishes to conceive writing as inscription of speech and transfer of meaning. All these questions revolve around the identity of the writer, a concept Derrida deals with under the heading "presence" (which I try to explain in detail in chapter 6 below). If the attending discourse allows a systematic "I" to expropriate the voice of the writer and vice versa, then "I" exists as much outside and before any given writer as it does from within. Thus, at least in part, the "I" foments against "the writer" by splitting the notion of "I" in two and showing that "I" always functions like a written word. While the "I" of the system remains inert until some writer enters the system and triggers its operation, without the system the writer has no "I" and thus no way even to begin a discourse. Any writer's attempt to unify his or her presence into a single unified "I" always reveals the graphic, divided origin of the "I."

The writer who attempts self-discovery and self-presentation in writing discovers, perhaps with horror, that what appears in the space called "self" is continuous play. The concept "self" is a signifier, a free-floating possibility of meaning; it is not a signified, a fixed, secure point of reference. As long as one merely speaks one's ideas, the concept "self" can appear as a closed signified, as a "me" generating pure meaning in a medium that erases itself leaving that meaning behind. If one attempts to write, however, both the meaning and its origin begin to play, begin, in fact, to seem more like unfulfilled possibilities than present realities. The frightening thing about viewing writing from a Derridean perspective is that the recursive, unfinished, unclear, unsatisfactory, frustrating process of writing describes everything that would like to present itself as prior to and manipulative of writing—everything including "us." We are all written.

I realize, of course, how odd this sounds. And I also realize that it begs the question about its relationship to the teaching of writing. While that relationship is, admittedly, highly abstract, I think it exists. A deep and abiding part of American myth depends on belief in the virtue of the strong silent type, the person of action rather than words. Such a person knows what is right and how to do it. Most of our students subscribe to the idea of such a person. But such a person can only be written—in a novel, for example, or in a movie or a political speech. Many of our students want to continue believing that such people exist outside writing—out there in the "reality" that writing supposedly describes. The possibility that the indefinite, uncertain, never-finished play of writing creates the strong silent type rather than merely describing him or her calls too much into question. This is, I think, fairly easy to see.

To show it, however, I must argue that the "I" is an absence of yet another sort than that described above under the rubric "attending discourse." Once the "I" emerges through the passageway of the attending discourse into the system, it divides once again. In fact, the location "I" can occur only through a division. "I" cannot recognize myself as "I" until "I" am able to play both the role of subject and the role of object. Thus, strictly speaking, the place where "I" recognizes itself is a sort of floating set of oppositions. Whatever could constitute an "I" as itself, whatever could signify either to itself or to others that "I am," already operates as a signifier, and any signifier can only operate in the absence of what it stands for (*Positions*, p. 29). Before any "I" can recognize itself, it must divide and be willing to be *rep*resented. As Miller states, "The self in this process is not a source but a function, and an empty one at that. It is a negative element in a system" ("Two Rhetorics," pp. 11–12).

This division shows itself most clearly in writing, where there must be an "I" to generate the discourse and a "you," or "alternate I," to validate it. For example, when I write a sentence, I rarely think it says what I want it to say. But the "I" who writes and the "I" who evaluates operate at some distance from each other, frequently even grow angry at each other: the writer finds the evaluator picky while the evaluator finds the writer lazy or incompetent. The act of writing sets up a continuous internal struggle between the "I" attempting to emerge and consolidate itself in inscription and the "you" who validates the discourse, determining whether it is acceptable.[33] The writing "self" remains forever divided. The last thing apt to happen in writing is "self-discovery." Instead, what happens in writing is a forever becoming-present (*Dissemination*, p. 310). "I" and "you" become a dance of oppositions, each operating in the absence of the other, each depending on the absence of the other to appear at all, each negating and affirming the other.

Entry into writing calls the most fundamental of assumptions into question, beginning with the assumption that "I" am "myself." "I," rather than standing alone as a discrete, knowable entity, becomes the spacing, the place of differentiation where the effect of "I" can operate as a signifier. A signifier, however, merely stands in for a signified. The signified itself, the pure, univocal "I," must always and forever be gone so that the operation of the effect can continue indefinitely. This leaves the "who-'I'-would-be-if-'I'-could-be-present-as-a-signified-with-no-need-of-signification" permanently hanging in the balance. "Within this hanging-in-the balance," Derrida explains

> with its numerous intersecting planes, he who says *I* in the present tense, in the so-called positive event constituted by his discourse, would be capable of only an illusion of mastery. At the very moment he thinks he is directing the operations, his place—the opening toward the present assumed by whoever believes himself capable of saying *I*, I think, I am, I see, I feel, I say (you, for example, here and now)—is constantly and in spite of him being decided by a throw of dice whose law will subsequently be developed inexorably by chance. (*Dissemination*, pp. 297–98)

As the writer moves through the passageway of the attending

discourse into the "I" of the system, both the certainty of "plain" meaning and the foundation of "who I am" slip away. Writing, rather than merely recording the meaning generated by the student's "extralinguistic self," reveals the supposed "extralinguistic self" as an apparatus through which the *possibility* of meaning passes. And this apparatus does not precede and inform writing; rather, it exists only *in* writing: "Not that the apparatus can be considered my self or my property, but it stands in my place and *I* is only the differentiated structure of this organization, which is absolutely natural and purely artificial, differentiated enough to count within its structure the moment or the place of the autarchic illusion of the sovereign subject" (*Dissemination*, p. 299).

As composition is currently taught almost everywhere, including in my own freshman class this semester, it is, to quote Hartman, based on "the wish to put ourselves in an unmediated relation to whatever 'really' is, to know something absolutely." My students and I "desire to be defined totally: marked or named once and for all, fixed in or by a word, and so—paradoxically— made indifferent," free from the différance that constitutes not only language but also self. But learning to write exposes the impossibility of achieving this desire, and the impossibility of this desire is what makes writing so frightening to teachers and students alike. "The desire for self-definition, fullness of grace, presence; simply to expose the desire to own one's own name, to inhabit it numinously in the form of 'proper' nouns, words, or the signatory act" leads us to writing. Once there, however, writing escapes us, infecting not only speech but also thought and even self, revealing the trace, the constant play of différance where desire to be defined can originate in the first place. The "genuine logos," it turns out, "is always a dia-logos" (*Saving*, pp. 97, 109–10). Every discourse carries another discourse. The "I" can never separate itself from the "you" that the "I" needs to differentiate itself from in the first place in order to allow discourse to begin; nor can it free itself from the discourse of the "you," which never finishes interrogating the text and showing its flaws; nor can it free itself from the discourses of the system in which it operates. The silence of the unthought, the repressed, the forgotten, and the implied all attend the discourse of the "I" (see *Margins*, p. xxviii).

The student, of course, conceives of both meaning and understanding as immediately self-present. They simply *are*. As a result, neither needs a system of communication to exist. But when the student tries to write meaning down so that a reader can understand it, something terrible happens. On one hand, the written words replace the meaning that should need no system of replacements; on the other, understanding never quite gets behind those written words to the meaning they should reveal. The more the student struggles to make writing behave itself and communicate exactly what the student "means," the more meaning itself becomes questionable. The student, who wants to maintain the assured, silent presence of novels, movies, and politics, discovers how to make up such a person in writing, but knows that the person is just that—made up in writing. Many students cannot deal with the possibility that writing is not a magical kingdom where the obscure becomes clear and understanding perceives knowledge. Their whole constellation of beliefs trembles. "I" appears more and more as a signifier, as an effect of language, rather than as a defined soul, or an absolute entity independent of expression.[34]

The great power of writing is that it allows the writer to evaluate life. Carrying out such an evaluation, however, has a double price. First, it requires giving up participation in ongoing life for the isolation of the writing process. But by paying this first price, one gains the ability to raise oneself above one's life in order to enjoy and "own" that life. Unfortunately, at least from the student's perspective, the deconstructive nature of the writing process leads to the second price: writing *itself* constitutes the life one "owns" when one uses writing to seize control of life. Inside the inside that writing is supposed to be the outside of, there is nothing but more writing (*Grammatology*, p. 142). From the student's perspective, this is a high price indeed, much higher than the beginning writer operating in a naïve, positivistic, frequently fundamentalist world can manage to pay without considerable support and time.

As Derrida speculates on Freud's analysis of the *fort/da* game, he carefully and frequently hedges his analysis by repeating, "je ne dis pas que Freud dit" ("I am not saying that Freud says") (*La carte*, pp. 330–32; my translation). But in fact, he *is* saying that Freud says. And he says Freud's description of his grandson's game of tossing "himself" away and then retrieving "himself" describes the act of writing, an act of self-separation as the writer separates himself from himself, generating a rift that cannot be closed up. The process of writing reveals that a unified, prewriting "self" never existed. Understanding the nature of this permanent rift clarifies two constant problems in the composition classroom: the poor writer who begs constantly to know what the teacher wants and the insecurity of almost all students about their writing.

The poorest students have greatest difficulty realizing that writing is a play of absences. They bring to their texts a radically oversimplified belief that writing should convey the knowledge that exists outside of and prior to writing. Because they can never find that knowledge, their texts never really begin; thus, what occurs in their texts is a lost voice crying to know itself. Such writers never get to the point of trying to write. They never get past the theological assumption that *what to write* will take care of the writing itself once they know *what to write*. Everyone who has any significant experience teaching writing at all knows those students who never quite begin. What we don't know in trying to understand what's going wrong is that their theological preconceptions prohibit the beginning of the play of meaning. The texts they complete seem hopeless because they are not yet texts. The students are trying desperately to construct texts that will serve meaning. Of course the play that constitutes meaning can't even begin until the closure of knowledge the student seeks has already disappeared as a possibility. Such students are caught in a double bind: they seek the knowledge that would enable and control writing *before* they start to write, but starting to write forecloses the dream of such knowledge.

The insecurity of most students comes from the problem of authority. In all classes, the act of writing puts authority in question as the act of writing inscribes itself everywhere, both exceeding what the student could hope to control and revealing what the student does not yet know. Thus most student writers feel less than author of their texts whatever shape those texts finally take. In composition classes, the authority of the author is put even more radically in question because both authors and readers (even if a reader is a peer evaluator) oppose the texts from the beginning. Authors oppose their texts at every moment during the composing process as they argue with their texts about what the texts ought to say. And readers (especially in a collaborative learning class) read specifically to seek those places where texts are not yet complete, not yet satisfactory. Given the effect of writing on the "self-in-general," the heightened sense of this effect in composition classes makes for a justified, understandable, radical insecurity.

V. Grafts = Dissemination

> But there are also many other things which Jesus did; were every one of them to be written, I suppose that the world itself could not contain the books that would be written.
>
> John 21:25

Not only are *we* written, *what we write* is also written. Those of us still saddled with romantic notions of genius and originality find this even harder to accept than we do the divided "I." Even so, no matter how much a text struggles to keep itself pure and different from other texts, it originates as a weaving of prior texts. It must graft itself onto something else in order to become itself. Shakespeare's unabashed process of borrowing and copying may more accurately describe the composing process for all texts than any of us—especially those like me who have spent years trying to teach research and documentation—have any reasonable willingness to consider. The range of signifying systems upon which the writer depends includes everything from a vocabulary, whose defined differences open the play of meaning, and a syntax, whose rules rigidly limit the shape of statements, to a history of written texts whose tradition of document design tells the text under composition what it is.

Logocentric discourse, as Hartman points out, operates on the assumption "that saying and meaning coincide, that the exact or just word can be found." But writing shows how words have multiple meanings, meanings that always exceed what the writer intends. Writing also shows the uncertainty of texts by showing how they interlace with parts of other texts. "Using words that have been used already," Hartman continues, "we trace or cite or echo them in ways that change and perhaps distort" (*Saving*, p. 8). The writer faces the possibility that "no knowledge except in the form of a text" exists, and that textual knowledge "is devious and dissolving, very unabsolute, as it leads always to other texts and further writing" (*Saving*, p. 24).

Both Derrida's own texts and his descriptions of the way he writes depend on the idea of graft, that process of inserting something alien into a preexisting host. Referring to his own writing as a sort of inserted, grafted reading, Derrida says, "It is necessary to read and reread those in whose wake I write, the 'books' in whose margins and between whose lines I mark out and read a text simultaneously almost identical and entirely other" (*Positions*, p. 4). Derrida's texts operate in the rupture created when he inserts his text into another text, a text that would rather keep Derrida out. "Therefore, extraction, graft, extension," Derrida explains, "this is what I call, according to the process I have just described, *writing*" (*Positions*, p. 71). The examples of this theoretical position in Derrida's astonishingly large canon are numerous, *Glas* being the most extended. The most accessible and self-conscious example, however, may be "Dissemination" (*Dissemination*, pp. 287–366), where Derrida claims to write in the angles and corners of Philippe Sollers's novel *Numbers*.[35] Without Sollers (or Husserl, or Freud, or Rousseau, or Nietzsche, or Shelley, or whichever text he has chosen to write *in*) Derrida *has* no text. Like Derrida's texts, however, whichever host text he invades also exists in the spacing of the texts it invades, as do those texts too, and the ones before them, and so on. "The gap that separates the text from itself and thus allows for scission or for the disarticulation of silent spacings" (*Dissemination*, p. 356) both allows the transplants *and* makes writing without transplanting impossible.[36]

Because writing depends on graft, on attaching itself to other texts, writing always disseminates itself, going places, carrying meanings and revealing connections the writer not only does not intend but cannot, in advance, even imagine (*Dissemination*, pp. 39–41, n. 39). Everyone who has ever "finished" a text and given it to someone else knows this feeling of dissemination. Because the process of writing was never complete, the text will almost surely do things the author did not expect and would not choose. Hartman calls this loss of "parental" control "the wandering of the written word" (*Saving*, pp. 48–49). Derrida, who calls writing "the miserable son," says that writing, when asked about its father, "does not answer this question—it writes (itself): (that) the father *is not*, that is to say, is not present" (*Dissemination*, pp. 145–46).[37]

Because writing depends on graft, the writer never occupies a position from which to control its process. As writers write, they produce something different from what they expected, which leads to the frightening question What if this is a graft with no body proper? In other words, what if rather than grafting a finite idea onto some other finite idea I have in fact nothing with which to work but a series of graftings so complex that the recognition of a body proper remains forever impossible? What if my text is a "*skew* without a straight line," a "*bias* without a front," "a *snag* in writing that can no longer be mended, a spot where neither meaning, however plural, nor *any form of presence* can pin/pen down [*agrapher*] the trace" (*Dissemination*, pp. 21, 26)? Conceiving of writing as the act of recording what one thinks may well be the most frustrating possible approach to writing because it presumes that some way of "thinking" outside and prior to writing exists. Derrida argues convincingly that "there is no extratext," because "the graphic—graphicity in general—has always already begun, is always implanted in 'prior' writing. . . . There is nothing before the text; there is no pretext that is not already a text" (*Dissemination*, p. 328; *Grammatology*, pp. 165–66).

VI. A Pretext for Writing

To him who conquers I will give some of the hidden manna, and I will give him a white stone, with a new name written on the stone which no one knows except him who receives it.
Revelation 2:17

Most students, of course, go to school to learn the "pretext," the knowledge that writing serves to represent and keep around. For those who seek the pretext, "writing is the evil of representative repetition." It is the "double that opens desire," allowing the writer to contemplate closure but forever binding the writer inside the writing process (*Grammatology*, p. 312). I think this explains why so many American students have so much difficulty with writing and find psophistry (e.g., replacing their inability to know with their ability to persuade) and anti-writing (e.g., writing whose only purpose is to demonstrate mastery of the rules of writing) so attractive. They have a theological belief in the disembodied existence of knowledge. Their ideas of history, culture, morality, and decency all depend on knowledge freed from the need for or corruption of expression. As long as they never attempt writing, as long as they never allow themselves to get caught in the endlessly recursive, never-completed process of writing, their knowledge can remain untainted. For such students, failing to write or retreating into psophistry or antiwriting is an act of self-defense. They believe in themselves and their souls; they believe in absolute knowledge. Such beliefs depend on freedom from writing. Students will go to great lengths to defend those beliefs.[38]

For them, writing is a dangerous transgression.[39] What had been whole, what had been "present" to the student's self as long as it remained outside inscription disintegrates the moment the student tries to inscribe it. Foundation, origin, the transcendental signified, peace, belief, and everything else that gives life certainty recedes in writing faster than the pen (or even word processor) can move after it. The student who expects to solidify and control thought in writing finds just the opposite happening. This explains why most students, even the best writers, denigrate their writing so frequently. They know what an uncertain mess it grew from. They also know the degree to which the process of writing has compromised whatever they wished to present. The students struggle endlessly with any given text, attempting to employ "resolutely overdetermined words that slip the leash of meaning without escaping meaning" (Hartman, *Saving*, p. xxiii). They see intuitively that their texts will depend on repression to emerge, that once written their texts will disseminate themselves in ways the students cannot even guess at, that in writing the perception upon which they have built their understanding of the world gets called in question, and that knowledge itself refuses to *appear* anywhere. It is no wonder that they fear writing so and go to such great lengths to avoid it.

Their texts depend on repression because they must repress everything they know that contradicts what they finally write. Few writers indeed, and almost no student writers, can construct a text without realizing places where something they know contradicts what their text says. For a while, such contradictions can be answered, but if the essay is to end, the writer must simply decide that enough contradictions have been accounted for and let the others remain unanswered. By like token, writers know they cannot follow out all the connections implied in their texts; rather, they must "draw a line around the material to be treated, . . . give it an edge or border which appears as a natural stopping place in all directions beyond which there is nothing relevant to the subject, and . . . treat what is left inside the charmed circle totally and with total continuity" (Miller, "Figure," pp. 112–13). Writers must learn to ignore or conceal breaks in the circle that separates the text from its outside, and they must learn to ignore or conceal those strands within the circle that have not been followed to their conclusion. Perhaps most difficult of all, they must repress the ongoing phenomena of the world around them. In order to participate in writing at all, they must cease participating in life's continuing "events."

And this last act of repression disrupts in a much more profound way than simply withdrawing from a conversation or skipping an evening out with friends, for writing replaces perception with an endless, breaching deferral.[40] Writing-in-general, Derrida argues, precedes not only speech and thinking, but also perception. Writing reveals that no pure perception exists. Indeed anything that "becomes" perceived, anything that appears before consciousness has been "written down," has become a signifier that operates just as any written signifier must. As students attempt to "write down" the reality that they have always believed in, suddenly they become readers of the phenomena swirling around them, thus making those phenomena into a text. Even more frighteningly, as they turn inwards to attempt to describe the perceiver of those phenomena, they become readers of themselves, thus changing themselves from a finite, knowable "self" into yet another text. "We are written," Derrida argues, only as we write, by the agency within us which always already keeps watch over perception, be it internal or external. The "subject" of writing does not exist if we mean by that some sovereign solitude of the author. The subject of writing is a *system* of relations between strata: the Mystic Pad, the psyche, society, the world. Within that scene, on that stage the punctual simplicity of the classical subject is not to be found. In order to describe the structure, it is not enough to recall that one always writes for someone; and the oppositions sender-receiver, code-message, etc., remain extremely coarse instruments. (*Writing*, pp. 226–27)

More astonishing yet, for the student writer, the finished text disseminates itself continuously without coming to rest on a final meaning. Even the student who wrote the text cannot overcome "the impossibility of reducing a text as such to its effects of meaning, content, thesis, or theme" (*Dissemination*, p. 7).[41] If texts operate this way, and if the writing process makes both "external" phenomena *and* the "internal" perceiver into texts, then the writing process sets in motion an endless, radical movement of deconstruction.

In other words, novices who enter writing give up knowledge of themselves. In return for this sacrifice, they get writing. To be sure, writing *promises* truth, but all the while writing defers truth in order to keep the promise, and not its fulfillment, in operation. Students learn quickly that the process of writing wreaks havoc with what they are trying to use writing to represent. And they learn just as quickly that they can protect both themselves and their closed belief systems by keeping them free of writing. The moment something that "belongs" to them gets into the world of writing it's lost. As Kaufer and Waller have explained, students come to college trained to believe that reading means uncovering the theme or thesis and that writing means describing the summary. Both operations presume writing is exterior to whatever it vehiculates. "We are," they explain, "trying to change an ideology—but students think we are trying only to undo whatever small successes their secondary teachers were able to claim" (p. 77). In effect, many of our writing assignments, rather than dealing with problems, *are* problems.[42] The problem for students is finding a way to avoid writing while generating texts near enough to writing to pass for it.

Of course, students don't object to inscription that signifies itself as nothing more than inscription: clear organization, good transition, mature sentence patterns, correct punctuation, and correct spelling. What they object to is using writing to explore and communicate "thinking." Once they begin writing, their thinking is breached, and nothing will ever come to heal that breach, close up the gap, bring back fullness and belief.

VII. In the Boa-Deconstructor's Coils

Draw near to me, you who are untaught, and lodge in my school.

Sirach 51:23

The degree to which entry into writing threatens the novice, however, is even more perilous than I have yet described. In fact, most composition teachers have always read their students' work with the eye of a deconstructor.[43] Derrida's readings of such writers as Rousseau, Husserl, and Plato differ only in insignificant ways from our readings of our students' papers. When Derrida explains in *La carte postale* that his reading of the role of Freud's daughter Sophie in *Beyond the Pleasure Principle* asks questions of Freud's text that neither Freud nor the text intended to answer (p. 349), he describes what the writing teacher customarily and without apology does to the writing student's text. Anyone who reads much of Derrida becomes annoyed with his methods, feeling strongly that Derrida has done something to the text that the text never intended, something that the text, in fact, attempts to prevent. The tension between what the text wants and what Derrida wants to do to the text is palpable, to many maddening and even dishonest.[44]

This tension offers a lesson for us in composition. It resembles the tension between a student writer's text and what the writing teacher does to it. Our resistance to Derrida's readings lets us know how the student writer feels about the way we treat student texts. No text and no writer likes to have an analyst seek the inadequacies the text was designed to conceal, even if the analyst is the friendliest, most benevolent person in the writer's life. Though most writing teachers try to show *both* strengths *and* weaknesses in their students' texts (usually with emphasis on *strengths*), writing teachers read in ways the students cannot imagine, never intended, and would not choose.[45] Students' texts, in effect, undo themselves before the teacher-analyst's gaze; everything the students couldn't hide appears to defeat them. Indeed, the writing teacher's purpose has nothing at all to do with understanding what the students have tried to write; quite the contrary, the teacher—who writes in the margins of, between the lines of, between (and even inside) the words of, and in the spaces all around the students' texts—sets out from the beginning to show those moments in the texts where the texts do not accomplish their own goals, even though such analyses may be embedded in considerable praise for what the students have accomplished. Miller's description of reading deconstructively describes what most of us do when we respond to a student's paper: "The focus of my readings is on the 'how' of meaning rather than on its 'what,' not 'what is the meaning?' but 'how does meaning arise from the reader's encounter with just these words on the page?' " (*Fiction,* p. 3).

Like Derrida's, the writing teacher's readings are acts of writing that decompose texts. The teacher need not, and usually does not, set out to overturn the texts or embarrass their authors. In fact, the readings provided by good composition teachers are quite friendly, even heartening and encouraging. But then Derrida does not always set out to overturn or destroy the texts he reads. His readings of Plato, Foucault, Freud, Sollers, Jabes, and others show that at length.[46] Showing a text where it fails merely makes reading part of the process of writing. But such a process does not end in the production of a "complete" text; it ends because the limits of the writer's ability or patience or time have been reached.[47] Seeking out the undecideables, the false verbal properties, the oppositions that resist and disorganize a text does not mean the text must be removed from useful reading or the text has no value. Such a reading strategy merely describes what the best writing teachers have always done with their students' work. They seek constantly for a way to intervene in their students' texts, to reveal the oppositions and the failures of those texts. And they practice Derrida's "double writing" (*Positions*, p. 41; *Dissemination*, pp. 173–287) as they themselves write in and around their students' texts in order to keep the process of writing in motion.

Students, facing such a deconstructor and knowing how their texts will be read, write with a double gesture, too. One gesture inscribes a text on some apparent subject—drugs, or space exploration, or perhaps a poem by Donne. The other gesture, however, inscribes the plea for a good grade, attempts to sew a seamless garment too formidable for the coming deconstructor. But the "finished" text never really expects to be treated as finished; quite the contrary, the text fully expects to be told how and why it has failed to be what it set out to be. Yet such a demonstration need not be harsh or intimidating. The students know their texts can and will be dealt with that way. They expect the teacher's reading to be what Derrida calls "a necessary infidelity" (*Grammatology*, p. 39).

Just as Derrida's reading of Rousseau "is ordered around its own blind spot" (*Grammatology*, p. 164), the composition teacher becomes "blind" to the student and the student's text in the process of reading that text. Rarely, if ever, does a teacher fail to see what the student has attempted. The teacher's reading has nothing to do with whether the student's attempt can be discerned. Rather, the teacher responds to the text *as if it were a text* by looking to see how it works and where it fails. Just as deconstruction is "an incision" that allows the discourse to be dismantled (*Positions*, p. 82), the composition teacher's reading of a student's paper begins with an incision allowing the student's paper to be dismantled. The teacher's incisions, like Derrida's, depend on clipping out examples of the writing, dismembering the text in order to expose its operations (see *Dissemination*, p. 305).[48]

The text the teacher generates in the margins and the blank spaces of the student's work resembles more than anything else the sort of text Derrida creates in *Glas*. The teacher's marginal, idiosyncratic, deconstructive text would infuriate anyone who expects writing to be well-constructed, unified, and focused on a clear thesis. Just as *Glas* confuses and estranges readers, causing them to resee everything that gets pulled into one of its columns, the teacher's text, existing in and around the student's text, estranges the student from the student's own work.[49]

Oddly enough, I do not fear making the claim that composition teachers read like deconstructors. While I expect such a claim to raise a few eyebrows, I do not expect the howls of protest that literary critics and philosophers have raised against Derridean analysis. Because those of us who have taken composition studies seriously during the last twenty years have never thought it possible to shut a text down in a closed meaning, we do not fear that articulating such a possibility will somehow undo our discipline the way it might undo professional literary interpretation or philosophical speculation. Since we have never done anything *but* writing, we have nothing to fear from the revelation that our discipline is *merely* writing. Professional interpreters, on the other hand, and especially those who purport to tell what texts mean, have a great deal to fear. Because we have known about the recursive, never-finished, frustrating process of writing all along, theories of reading and writing suggesting an indeterminate text merely make explicit our own long-standing, tacit assumptions.

Because Derrida does not see any text as closed, he never attempts to explain what it "says." Rather, he treats the text much as any good writing teacher would. In what seem like marginal comments, he shows deficiencies, agrees or disagrees with the writing, makes jokes, plays with words, reveals derivations, and makes connections; and he always summarizes the text's strengths and weaknesses. At no point does he attempt to double what the text "says," to "leap over the text toward its presumed content, in the direction of the pure signified" (*Grammatology*, pp. 158–59). Instead, he reviews the operation of the text, revealing what it attempts to hide and exposing the assumptions that set it in motion. He admits all along to a strategy of transgression, of doing what the text would least like to have done to it. The working hypothesis with which he begins to read any text presumes that the text is not complete.

Those who attempt to keep deconstruction out of the writing class usually retreat into some form of Platonism where they oscillate between the two forms Platonism usually takes: psophistry and antiwriting. Psophistry teaches students nothing more than how to persuade an audience. The success or failure of writing depends on the effect the writing has on the intended audience. Then there is antiwriting. Because of writing's effect on thought and belief, some teachers fear writing and maneuver constantly to avoid it, preferring the safety of antiwriting. In the world of antiwriting, everything exists as uninterrogated binary oppositions, with the integrity of the first term in each pair dependent on the depreciation of the second: correctness/incorrectness, coherence/incoherence, development/insufficiency, transition/rupture, fullness/ellipsis, standard usage/deviant usage. In such a composition frame (up?), there are lists of rules, criteria for correctness, features of necessity, and required patterns of presentation. All these "standards," however, merely erect barriers between student and teacher on one hand and writing on the other hand. They substitute themselves for writing, removing teacher, students, and all from any need to write, leaving them in the world of innocent presence, allowing them to escape deconstruction by never venturing to write in the first place. In such a world, writing *does* signify: it signifies itself as correct spelling, good transition, good sentence variety, clear organization, tight coherence, and correct punctuation. But it does this by separating writing from meaning—and from thinking and even from Being.

The alternative to teaching psophistry or antiwriting is to teach writing as process. But that alternative too often implies either a neutral or a "good" pedagogy. Those of us who have adopted it must recognize just how thoroughly that pedagogy commits us to a Derridean philosophical position. And more importantly, we must recognize the degree to which writing as process threatens much of what our students hold dear. In a process class, students cannot even become *beginning* writers until they agree to insert their texts into the numberless host of prior texts in whose wakes, margins, edges, angles, borders, and silent spaces their own texts must be inserted. And they must agree to enter an intertextual situation where their texts stand in the middle of and depend absolutely on other people's discourse, discourse even less under their control than their own.[50]

Most of all, we must recognize that with process writing comes the end of a writer's ability to believe his or her discourse is founded on meaning outside the play of différance. Underestimating the overwhelming power of the system into which we attempt to introduce students simply leads to massive problems of oversimplification for them and for us. Once students begin writing, all that they "knew" before entering writing loses its finiteness, and the system with which they are left questions both their identity and the possibility of self-definition, leaving them nothing but writing as a weapon to fight against the infinity writing itself has opened.

△

6.
A
T(R)OPOLOGICAL
GROUP

Nine Terms in the Derridean Lexicon

Throughout his early writing, and especially in *Writing and Difference*, Derrida explains that there are no neutral terms. When a writer applies one term to a second term as a way of elucidating, controlling, or defining the second term, the first term cannot be neutral. Like the term to which it is applied, it has both a history and a sediment of prior meanings. Because I am a writer, *I* have no neutral terms. I cannot arraign the following Derridean words in some neutral court. Nor, in fact, do I wish to. I have read Derrida with the eye of an American composition teacher who teaches writing and teaches others how to teach writing every working day of his life. Though I often find what I learn from Derrida unsettling, sometimes even annoying, what I learn is, I think, worth knowing.

The Derridean lexicon is admittedly off-putting at first, especially to those unfamiliar either with French structuralism and poststructuralism or with the tradition of philosophers from Hegel through Husserl and Nietzsche to Heidegger. And Derrida's texts are filled with "in jokes" that usually annoy American humanists rather than make them chortle the way a member of the cognoscenti at the École Normale might. Nevertheless, the lexicon is not so impenetrable as it seems on first glance. And in Derrida's defense, one must remember that he did not write for laborers in the American composition industry.

Derrida says, in effect, that the terms in the group to be discussed cannot be defined: "The movement of these marks per-
vades the whole of the space of writing in which they occur,
hence they can never be enclosed within any finite taxonomy,
not to speak of any lexicon as such" (*Dissemination*, p. 25). In a
note to this passage, Barbara Johnson also warns against trying
to define Derrida's terms:

> Because Derrida's discourse operates in a displacement
> of traditional binary logic, it tends to amass and fore-
> ground a series of terms like those listed here which con-
> tain within themselves skewed contradictions and which
> render undecideable any proposition in which they occur.
> It is therefore tempting for translators and other prefacers
> to try to facilitate the reader's entrance into Derrida's writ-
> ing by constructing a "lexicon" of such terms. Derrida is
> here both inviting and warning against such a procedure,
> which, while it points up Derrida's neologistic innova-
> tions, reinscribes the effects of those innovations within
> a finite, pointillistic topology. (p. 25, n. 24)

Even John Searle, though to be sure quite sarcastically, says
that those wishing for definitions manifest the logocentrism that
Derrida deconstructs ("Word," p. 74). Thus the risk I take in
writing what follows is obvious.

Though I do not expect anyone to read this chapter from start
to finish, I have tried to write it sequentially (linear, logocentric
writing raises its ugly head yet again!) so that one definition
leads to another. I must, however, admit that beginning resembles jumping on a moving merry-go-round: one must jump on
somewhere, and wherever one jumps on is where one starts in
moving around the merry-go-round itself. Though I hope each
definition can be read alone, I have arranged the terms in such
a way as to work through Derrida's theory of writing so that the
basic operation of that theory gradually appears. Nevertheless,
this chapter reads like a one-note samba, the same term defined
the same way nine times. I comfort myself with the beliefs that
readers have nine different points of entry and that no one needs
to read all nine definitions to learn the tune—by heart (ad nau-
seum!).

Because I am exploring the relationship between Derridean

thought and the teaching of writing in the United States, I have tried to show what each term "indicates" about the process of writing, especially student writing.

Presence

> I done me best when I was let. Thinking always if I go all goes.
>
> Joyce, *Finnegans Wake*

Though Derrida argues that the strategy goes back to Plato, Descartes more clearly than anyone else introduces the procedure whereby Western thinkers assure their self-presence:

> I thought that I should . . . reject as absolutely false anything of which I could have the least doubt, in order to see whether anything would be left after this procedure which could be called wholly certain. . . . I decided to suppose that nothing that had ever entered my mind was more real than the illusions of my dreams. But I soon noticed that while I thus wished to think everything false, it was necessarily true that I who thought so was something. Since this truth, *I think, therefore I am,* was so firm and assured that all the most extravagant suppositions of the skeptics were unable to shake it, I judged that I could safely accept it as the first principle of the philosophy I was seeking. (p. 103)

Since Descartes, the most elaborate attempt at a reduction to the origin of thought appears in the works of Edmund Husserl. Husserl names the place where the self is present to itself "solitary mental life." Here, meaning, rather than depending on a system of replacements, simply "is" as pure, unmediated self-presence. Husserl divides communicative systems into those that indicate and those that express: any form of externalizable language through which sounds or visible images *represent* "solitary mental life" would be indication; expression, on the other hand, would be the pure self-knowability of solitary mental life. Throughout *Speech and Phenomena* Derrida shows that at no point can expression rid itself of its need for indication. For expression to be separated from indication, meaning would have to be "present to the self in the life of a present that has not yet gone forth from itself into the world, space or nature." The place of pure expression would be an unmediated pure interior, simultaneously and univocally known to itself: in "solitary mental life the pure unity of expression as such should at last be restored" (*Speech*, pp. 40–41). "While in real communication," Derrida continues, "existing signs *indicate* other existences which are only probable and mediately evoked," in solitary mental life expression is supposed to be "full." Any sort of sign, of course, must be "foreign to the self-presence of the living present." In order for presence to be itself, nonsignification would become its principle of principles. Presence, in effect, would have to be "the experience of the absence and uselessness of signs" (*Speech*, pp. 58–60).

Demonstrating the fundamental maneuver of deconstruction, Derrida reverses the hierarchy Husserl (or, in *Grammatology*, Rousseau) attempts to set up. He shows that solitary mental life does not precede and inform systems of indication; instead, systems of indication create the possibility of solitary mental life by replacing it, representing it, and showing that it is gone. Further, pure self-presence, rather than the originary medium in which solitary mental life exists, itself depends on a prior medium. That prior medium, according to Derrida, is writing: "The repression of writing as the repression of that which threatens presence and the mastering of absence" allows the writer "to exclude or to lower (to put outside or below) . . . the body of the written trace as a didactic and technical metaphor, as servile matter or excrement" (*Writing*, p. 197).

Whereas "presence *ought to be* self-sufficient," it in fact depends on some sort of supplement, some sort of addition that will allow it to know itself. But, of course, any sort of addition to pure presence makes an excess, makes presence more than itself and thus no longer itself. Pure presence cannot be "*supplemented*, that is to say it does not have to be supplemented, it suffices and is self-sufficient; but that also means that it is irreplaceable; what one would substitute for it would not equal it, would be only a mediocre makeshift." The essence of presence, Derrida explains, "if it must always be repeated within another presence, opens originarily, within presence itself, the structure of representation. And if essence *is* presence, there is no essence of presence nor presence of essence. There is a play of representations and eliding. . . . Thence the letter. Writing is the evil of representative repetition, the double that opens desire and contemplates and binds . . . enjoyment" (*Grammatology,* pp. 311–12).

Students' notions about writing come bundled with their desire for constant self-presence. They think, for example, that their writing must have a thesis and that everything in the paper must pertain to this thesis so that the paper will have coherence. And, of course, they think their writing should display what Hartman calls "total intelligibility." Hartman goes on to explain, however, that the "desire for totality" must finally lead to a theological conception of writing and reading wherein "truth is revealed rather than read." Hartman shows just how radical the attempt to know oneself and know what one thinks must be. "What," he asks, "can it mean to place mind on its own axis and free it from books—to make mind its own text . . . ? Can we transcend telling toward, more simply, showing? Would that bring about . . . a return to things themselves? Yet does not the very existence of words indicate a breach with the phenomenality of things, or with an ideal of showing, of evidentiality, taken from that sphere?" (*Saving,* pp. xix, xvi). Students, of course, think themselves deficient because they fail at saying what they mean. The belief in a "what-they-mean," however, presumes from the beginning a presence existing outside language. And, as Jonathan Culler has shown, beliefs in self-referentiality and self-presence are inextricably tied to the idea of coherence. Students interpret coherence to mean that a thesis can know itself completely with no need in the beginning for a system of indication to allow the thesis to *become* itself (*On Deconstruction,* pp. 200–1).

Anyone who has taught composition has heard students say, "I know what I want to say. I just don't know how to say it." In effect, this is a declaration of faith in the existence of presence. In a way, it is true. Nonwriters *do* in fact "know" what they think before they become writers. More than anything else, the act of writing teaches them not what they know, but what they don't know. As long as they can keep their ideas out of writing, those ideas seem to be present instead of *re*presented. For students struggling to preserve the sanctity of their thoughts and beliefs, "the possibility of the representer befalls represented presence as evil befalls good, or history befalls origin. The signifier-representer is the catastrophe." Of course, student writers want "to reach the point where the source is held within itself, where it returns or reascends toward itself in the inalienable immediacy of self-possession." Unfortunately, as the student sees it, any sort of representation of ideas corrupts them because "the representative is not the represented but only the representer of the represented; it is not the same as itself" (*Grammatology*, pp. 296–98; see also Derrida's study of the Egyptian god Theuth in *Dissemination*, pp. 84–94). The moment the student attempts to extract thought from presence, not only thought but also its matrix—presence itself—gets called into question. Writing designates not so much a field of discovery or self-discovery as "the place of unease, of the regulated incoherence within conceptuality" (*Grammatology*, pp. 237–40). If what the thinker thinks could be present in its own right, the mediation of signs would be unnecessary.

While this recondite theory seems quite far from any composition class, it calls into question much of what we assume about the initiation into writing. Rather than allowing the student a mode of self-discovery, we invite students into an arena where self-discovery (or full self-presence) is forever promised yet infinitely delayed. Presence, Derrida shows again and again, could only fulfill itself outside language, outside any possible system of signs. Thus, the mode for knowing what you want to say can truly exist only outside language where any sort of "what-you-want-to-say" doesn't exist in the first place. Once students find themselves *inside* language, and especially inside writing, they have already entered the arena where presence is only and always promised but never fulfilled (*Speech*, p. 99). "God," Derrida explains in *Grammatology* "is the name and the element of that which makes possible an absolutely pure and absolutely self-present self-knowledge. From Descartes to Hegel and in spite of all the differences that separate the different places and moments in the structure of that epoch, God's infinite understanding is the other name for the logos as self-presence" (p. 98).

Transcendental Signified

. . . I was sweet when I came down out of me mother. My great blue bedroom, the air so quiet, scarce a cloud. In peace

and silence. I could have stayed up there for always only. It's
something fails us. First we feel. Then we fail.

Joyce, *Finnegans Wake*

The phrase "transcendental signified" stands for a meaning without a signifier, a meaning that would neither need nor
allow something to stand for it. "The sign," Derrida argues,

> is usually said to be put in the place of the thing itself,
> the present thing, "thing" here standing equally for mean-
> ing or referent. . . . When we cannot grasp or show the
> thing, state the present, the being-present, when the pres-
> ent cannot be presented, we signify, we go through the
> detour of the sign. . . . The sign, in this sense, is deferred
> presence. Whether we are concerned with the verbal or
> the written sign, with the monetary sign, or with electoral
> delegation and political representation, the circulation of
> signs defers the moment in which we can encounter the
> thing itself, make it ours, consume or expend it, touch it,
> see it, intuit its presence. . . . And this structure presup-
> poses that the sign, which defers presence, is conceivable
> only on the *basis* of the presence that it defers and *moving
> toward* the deferred presence that it aims to reappropriate.
> According to this classical semiology, the substitution of
> the sign for the thing itself is both *secondary* and *provisional*:
> secondary due to an original and lost presence from which
> the sign thus derives; provisional as concerns this final
> and missing presence toward which the sign in this sense
> is movement of mediation. (*Margins*, p. 9)

As a result of the "absent presence" the sign stands for, it must
draw its meaning from its similarities with and differences from
the other signs in its system. If there were such a thing as presence, such a thing as solitary mental life, the transcendental
signified would appear there as pure meaning and escape the
need to refer to other signs. Rather than being a sign among
other signs, rather than drawing its value from its relationships
with the other signs in its system, the transcendental signified
would be the absolute existence of unsignified meaning and
would "place a reassuring end to the reference from sign to sign."
No way exists, however, to reduce "the sign or the representer

so that the thing signified may be allowed to glow finally in the
luminosity of its presence. The so-called 'thing itself' is always
already a *representamen* shielded from the simplicity of intuitive
evidence. . . . The self-identity of the signified conceals itself
unceasingly and is always on the move" (*Grammatology*, pp. 48–
50).

Throughout *Speech and Phenomena* Derrida tries to show that
logic, rather than being a maneuver founded in presence and
acquainted with the transcendental signified, is a trope, an effect
of rhetoric. Because rhetoric, as Paul de Man shows in both
Blindness and Insight and *Allegories of Reading*, permeates language
at every point, no possibility of discovering a core meaning and
then prettying it up with "mere rhetoric" exists. In other words,
an essay with flawed logic does not have a flaw in the thinking
that preceded and enabled the core; instead, the flawed logic
results from a failure in managing the rhetorical trope that generates logic. Nothing closed and secure stands outside the discourse to shelter it. Moreover, such terms as unity and coherence,
which appear so frequently in composition texts and composition
lectures, are, like logic, tropes. They are rhetorical effects. Because language moves "by marginal differentiation through a
signifying series that can never quite circumscribe, or comprise
a body" (Hartman, *Saving*, p. 104), the writer must use the tropes
of logic, coherence, and unity to achieve the effect of discrete,
persuasive, complete discourse.

Ironically enough, most American composition teachers ask
their students to construct essays that do not surprise the reader,
essays that have such clear introductions and good coherence
that nothing confuses the reader on the way to the end of the
essay. In fact, however, those students who "write" at all are
constantly surprised by their own texts. And their teachers are
disingenuous in pretending to be surprised by texts that fail to
master the tropes of logic, coherence, or unity. If students' texts
really surprise their readers, Miller smiles disbelievingly, then
the readers must admit that until they read these texts they are
innocent about language. In fact, hardly anything in a student
text surprises an experienced writing teacher. Quite the contrary,
the teacher has demanded that the students disseminate their
"meaning" over several hundred words, all the while pretending
that this meaning can know itself and present itself in exactly
that amount of space and be present at every moment in that

space. Such rhetorical effects take years to learn, and no one ever fully masters them. Discovering a flaw in the tropes of logic, coherence, or unity hardly surprises a teacher.

Even more ironically, luring students into writing both compromises their ability to believe in the ordinary and makes them into permanent self-deconstructors. Most composition programs purport to teach expository prose. More than anything else, expository prose is the discourse of presence and the vehicle for the transcendental signified. The code for such prose is straightforward, referential language. Such language exists to bear and show the knowledge that informs it. Its most salient characteristic is ordinariness. English departments carefully distinguish expository writing courses from creative writing courses, for in creative writing the writing *may* take precedence over the knowledge it bears. Indeed, in creative writing, the writing may in fact *be* the knowledge the writing bears.

Expository writing, in contrast, is much safer. The writing there shelters itself under the protection of the greater, prior knowledge. But both Miller and Stanley Fish demonstrate at length that no such thing as "ordinary" language exists, and Miller calls straightforward, referential language a "mirage" (Fish, "How Ordinary" and "Normal Circumstances"; Miller, "Composition," p. 40). Both Fish and Miller work from a Derridean base in which "everyday language" can never be innocent or neutral but must be fraught with the language of Western metaphysics and with "a considerable number of presuppositions of all types" (*Positions,* p. 19). The very idea of ordinary language exists only through its difference from whatever nonordinary language would be; thus, the idea of ordinary language depends on, plays off, and is inextricably intertwined with whatever it must differ from to be itself (*Margins,* p. 325). Mastering the operation of "ordinary language" would depend absolutely on an intimate knowledge of *extra*ordinary language. "Ordinary language," like logic, coherence, and unity, turns out to be a trope, a rhetorical effect. Anyone who masters use of "ordinary language" *must* know how to generate the rhetorical effect of ordinariness, an effect requiring *extra*ordinary skill and willingness to take risks.

In view of all this, we must recognize that when we try to teach composition as ordinary writing (instead of whatever creative, or extraordinary, writing would be), we put students in an impossible, nonexistent situation, by asking them to master a system permeated at every point with the play of rhetoric, the language of the extraordinary. It is only a slight exaggeration to say that many "expository" writing courses are not writing courses at all, for writing is the one thing they preclude from the beginning. Because writing would call the presence of both teacher and students in question, because it would put the transcendental signified forever out of reach, these courses deteriorate into antiwriting, where students demonstrate mastery of syntax, patterns of organization such as cause-effect and comparison-contrast, and categories of writing such as exposition, narration, description, and persuasion. Such writing courses generate infinite numbers of texts that proclaim themselves as correct syntax, patterns of arrangement, and categories such as exposition. They hardly ever generate any writing.

In a writing course, students would begin by inquiring about the operation of language and about its relation to whatever lies outside it and depends on it for *re*presentation. Thus, any student who agrees seriously to attempt writing, who agrees to put presence and the transcendental signified in question, becomes a deconstructor willy-nilly. "Relentless lucid inquiries into the constituting powers of *language*," Leitch explains, "reveal its 'creative' and 'monumentalizing' functions, teaching active suspicion of all language formations. All writing, one's own especially, would become subject to depropriation—deconstruction. Lucidity, if pushed far enough, engenders vigilance about language— its productions, slippages, congealings" ("Deconstruction and Pedagogy," p. 23). The reason most students flee writing whenever they can is that they wish to subject language to being, signs to truth, speech to thought, and writing to speech (see Derrida, *Speech*, p. 23). Such students expect writing to reveal truth, to bring the "thoughts" of solitary mental life into the world. As every experienced writer knows all too well, however, writing never does this. In fact, in an almost palpable way, writing generates the absence of closed truth and self-presence, and with that absence the longing for its filling (see *Speech*, p. 88).

Student writers believe in the transcendental signified. In desperation, they use thesauruses, ask friends for help, and frequently use words whose customary place in the semiotic system they do not know. Because they believe in the existence of a transcendental signified, they seek the word that, as Derrida puts it, "would refer to no signifier, would exceed the chain of signs, and would no longer itself function as a signifier" (*Positions*, pp. 19–20).

If Derrida is right, no such transcendental signified exists or could exist outside the presence of God. Thus, when we tell our students to pick a thesis or to discover a central idea and treat it fully, we merely exacerbate their fears of writing. They believe fully in self-presence and the transcendental signified. Though perhaps not consciously, they also know all too well that the more they write the less their own presence is self-assured and the further the transcendental signified that would pin (or pen) down their meaning in absolute clarity slips away.

The Trace

> To put it all the more plumbsily. The speechform is a mere
> sorrogate. Whilst the quality and tality (I shall explex what
> you ought to mean by this with its proper when and where
> and why and how in the subsequent sentence) are
> alternativomentally harrogate and arrogate, as the gates may
> be.
>
> Joyce, *Finnegans Wake*

What (dis)appears in place of the transcendental signified is the trace, which creates the transcendental signified both by never appearing, so as not to become the transcendental signified itself, and by replacing the transcendental signified by its own constant movement. When I first began to try to read Derrida in 1978, I felt I was the mark in a find-the-pea con game. Every time I guessed where the pea was, it wasn't there. To a degree, I was right. Discourse operates infinitely because what the discourse represents never appears. The trace names this process of infinite deferral and movement. The trace has at least the following four aspects.

First, the trace is Derrida's name for what is never there. No element in any signifying system "can function as a sign without referring to another element which itself is not simply present." Each element, in fact, is constituted by the trace within it of the elements from which it differs. "Nothing, neither among the elements nor within the system, is anywhere ever simply present or absent. There are only, everywhere, differences and traces of traces" (*Positions*, p. 26). Writing is merely "one of the representatives of the trace in general, it is not the trace itself. *The trace itself does not exist*" (*Grammatology*, p. 167). Any process of signification begins only because something is absent. Were pure understanding available, it would be the silent, self-awareness of divinity. Were pure communication available, it would be a transcendental intuiting from one divine understanding to another. Signifying systems, in contrast, begin when such pure understanding and such pure communication no longer exist. As any signifying system operates, the traces of the now-gone pure knowledge and communication play in and around the system all the time. But the system depends both on those purities' being absent and on the play of the traces of those purities whose promised arrival keeps signification in operation—infinitely.

Second, operating a signifying system causes one to erase as much as to inscribe. Inscription itself (which in the Derridean world can be either spoken or written) seems to make sound and meaning visual. In fact, however, as the words appear on the page, they erase the pure meaning that would obliterate them if such pure meaning could appear in its own right. Indeed, words on a page depend on the erasure of such pure meaning because written words can never be pure meaning. They can only represent it once it has gone. The trace "can only trace itself out in the erasure of its own 'presence,' so that tracing is not simply the mere other or outside of erasing" (*Dissemination*, p. 364). The trace "is never as it is in the presentation of itself. It erases itself in presenting itself, muffles itself in resonating, like the *a* writing itself, inscribing its pyramid in *différance*" (*Dissemination*, p. 23). (Note that Derrida's neologism *différance* and the usual French word différence are distinguishable only in writing.) This explains the forever recursive process of writing. Writing *never* fixes meaning. Something always remains incomplete or unclear. Writing itself erases the possibility of the end of writing. Strange as it seems, only the absence of writing could fill the absence created by the process of writing, which forever traces the absent figures that must remain absent for writing (whether oral or written) to operate.

Third, if a writer could enter the self-presence of his or her own being, know what was there, and then record that for others to see or hear, writing would be free from all traces of omission, distortion, ignorance, and incompleteness. If writing could free itself from all the traces of past use, all the connotations and denotations sedimented around every word and phrase, it could simply vanish in the presence of its meaning. But such writing never occurs. The desire to work writing backwards to its origin in meaning merely returns one to the metaphysics of presence: "What the thought of the trace has already taught us is that it could not be simply submitted to the ontophenomenological question of essence. The trace *is nothing*, it is not an entity, it exceeds the question *What is?* and contingently makes it possible" (*Grammatology*, pp. 74–75). The trace "is in fact the absolute origin of sense in general. Which amounts to saying once again that there is no absolute origin of sense in general. The trace is the différance which opens appearance and signification" (*Grammatology*, p. 65).

In "White Mythology," Derrida demonstrates the futility of trying to expunge the trace and reveal the origin behind it. In principle, of course, concepts ought to be separable from the metaphors that express them. In fact, however, not only is such an attempt difficult, the terms and procedures to separate the two are themselves metaphorical. There is no way for metaphysical discourse, or any discourse for that matter, to free itself from rhetoric. "White Mythology" reveals even "concept," "foundation," and "theory" as metaphors (*Margins*, pp. 207–71). And "the only weapon against a metaphor," Miller explains, "is another metaphor, along with an awareness of our linguistic predicament in not being able . . . to declare what a thing is, except by saying it is something else" ("Two Rhetorics," pp. 106–7).

Fourth, as with most other Derridean concepts, the trace calls identity into question. Not only is the trace erasure of absolute thought and the transcendental signified, it is also

> erasure of the present and thus of the subject, of that which is proper to the subject and of his proper name. . . . The trace is the erasure of selfhood, of one's own presence, and is constituted by the threat or anguish of its irremediable disappearance, of the disappearance of its dis-

appearance. An unerasable trace is not a trace, it is a full presence, an immobile and uncorruptible substance, a son of God, a sign of parousia and not a seed, that is, a mortal germ. (*Writing*, pp. 229–30)

Accepting writing as the forever-disappearing traces both of the system itself and of what the system represents clarifies two problems student writers have with the writing process. First, because the trace operates in the absence of an origin, its movement never really "begins" anywhere. Wherever the writer attempts to begin, the trace has already begun there and left the marks of its now absent presence. Student writers frequently say they don't know how to begin. And even experienced writers know the hardest part of writing anything is beginning. The only difference between the novice and the professional is that the professional has given up on finding a place to "begin." The writing process never really starts anywhere. Or said differently, wherever in the process one makes the first stroke, whether with pen or keyboard, writing has already begun and the writer can only play among the traces of what writing excludes in order to be itself. The novice, who seeks a mode of inscription free of the trace, waits interminably for that mode to appear, carrying with it its unsignified, pure meaning. The professional, knowing that writing plays infinitely, agrees to play. Student writers, believing in presence and searching for the transcendental signified where their meaning could come to rest in the full presentation of itself, constantly feel something amiss about their writing. Experienced writers have become so accustomed to the feeling of incompleteness during the writing process that they can tolerate it.

Second, before writing, the novice expects writing to capture and present the meaning that writing should serve. To the novice's absolute frustration, the marks on the page have the effect of erasing rather than presenting that prior-to-writing meaning. Inscribing one's thoughts seems to operate simultaneously with the disappearance of those thoughts as they would appear if they did not need to be *re*presented. Beginners are apt to think something is wrong with them because they can't get writing to behave. The more they write, the more they need to write. Experienced writers have merely accepted writing as the "prize" they get for agreeing to write. They know from the beginning that whatever they write will graft onto other texts, have other texts graft onto it, and lead always and infinitely to more writing, never to the closure of meaning that the student expects writing to reveal.

Absence

> I wish I had better glances to peer to you through this
> baylight's growing. But you're changing, acoolsha, you're
> changing from me, I can feel. Or is it me is? I'm getting mixed.
> Joyce, *Finnegans Wake*

Absence in the Derridean lexicon does not play the role of master term replacing presence and standing for a sort of transcendental signified in reverse. It does not indicate a nihilistic nothingness nor does it imply that meaning doesn't exist. Absence does, however, reveal the constant play of meaning in language. It does show that what language would be reduced to if it could be reduced to its meaning, its transcendental signified, was always already absent, or the play of language would never have begun. Rather than the absence of full presence, absence is the prior medium in which the desire for presence can become aware of itself. Because the absence of self-present meaning is the precondition of speaking or writing, absence, instead of opposing or negating presence, precedes and enables it. "One cannot help wishing to master absence," Derrida admits, "and yet we must always let go" (*Grammatology*, p. 142).

Not surprisingly, the beginning writer trembles at the thought of operating such a system. Words, rather than operations that unveil meaning, turn out to be empty places. They exist as what Culler calls rifts or gaps waiting to be filled but never quite filled up (p. 142). The process of writing, as Derrida shows, reveals the "out-of-placeness" of language where what is supposed to stand behind language, inform it, and control it, remains forever out-of-place, just beyond reach (*Dissemination*, p. 182, n. 8). The "truth" of whatever matter the student takes up always turns out to be missing when the student tries to explain the matter. The words that would close the text, allowing it to implode into the blinding presence of truth never present themselves. Instead, the student can conceive of "the truth of the matter" only as an opening (*Writing*, p. 160), as the possibility where words finally adhere to their reality and cease playing. Commencing any sort of prewriting risks falling into a hole with no bottom, what Derrida calls "*'the chance for a book'* into which one can only plunge, and that one must maintain while destroying it. The dwelling is inhospitable because it seduces us, as does the book, into a labyrinth. The labyrinth, here is an abyss: we plunge into the horizontality of a pure surface, which itself represents itself from detour to detour" (*Writing*, p. 298).

The beginning writer's words seem to cancel themselves almost as if they were in fact under erasure (Spivak, p. xvii; Derrida, *Dissemination*, p. 354). Experienced writers, of course, know that readers must "construct ghost chapters whenever there is a gap in the text" (Comley, p. 131). Inexperienced writers do not know this. They expect meaning to present itself in their writing. To their horror, words cross themselves out, present meaning always remains just out of reach, and what should be present is always absent. Worse yet, the student writer's text can only become itself once the writer is absent:

> To write is to produce a mark that will constitute a kind of machine that is in turn productive, that my future disappearance in principle will not prevent from functioning and from yielding, and yielding itself to, reading and rewriting. . . . For the written to be the written, it must continue to "act" and to be legible even if what is called the author of the writing no longer answers for what he has written, for what he seems to have signed, whether he is provisionally absent, or if he is dead, or if in general he does not support, with his absolutely current and present intention or attention, the plenitude of his meaning, of that very thing which seems to be written "in his name." (*Margins*, p. 316)

Student writers, whether in composition classes or some other, know all along that their texts will be read in their absence. And they know that those texts will not implode into pure meaning.

Absence names the thing not "there" in writing, the thing never quite "there" at all. Writing reveals that the thing not "there" in writing is not anywhere else either. The "there" that the Western thinker so desperately seeks is always gone, had to be gone in order for someone to recognize its absence and seek it in the first place. But the medium in which the now recognizably absent presence can be recognized is also the location where this absent presence must always be absent. The medium constitutes itself and organizes its search for presence only in the absence of such presence.

Différance

> Talis is a word often abused by many passims (I am working out a quantum theory about it for it is really most tantumising state of affairs). A pessim may frequent you to say: Have you been seeing much of Talis and Talis those times?
>
> Joyce, *Finnegans Wake*

The neologism *différance* first appeared in English in David Allison's translation of *Speech and Phenomena*. Derrida himself has written an extended explanation, published simply as "Différance" and printed both at the beginning of *Margins of Philosophy* and at the end of *Speech and Phenomena*. Trying "to explain" *différance*, trying to tell what differs, what gets deferred, and what *différance* "is" (Derrida marks through the linking verb thus: ƚꞩ) runs the risk of falling

> back into what we have just disengaged ourselves from. In effect, if we accepted the form of the question, in its meaning and its syntax ("what is?" "who is?" "who is it that?"), we would have to conclude that *différance* has been derived, has happened, is to be mastered and governed on the basis of the point of a present being, which itself could be some thing, a form, a state, a power in the world to which all kinds of names might be given, a *what*, or a present being as a *subject*, a *who*. (*Margins*, p. 14)

The word *différance* itself comes from the French verb *différer*, which, as Allison first explained, combines the meaning of two English verbs, to differ and to defer (*Speech*, p. 82, n. 8). Simply put, différance "combines and confuses 'differing' and 'deferring' in both their active and passive senses" (*Positions*, p. 98,

n. 3). "It is read, or it is written, but it cannot be heard. It cannot be apprehended in speech, and . . . it also bypasses the order of apprehension in general" (*Margins*, p. 3).

In part, of course, différance appears as early as Saussure's description of how language operates. "In language," Saussure argues, "there are only differences. Even more important: a difference generally implies positive terms between which the difference is set up; but in language there are only differences *without positive terms*" (p. 120). Derrida's *différance* undeniably resembles Saussure's *differences*. At the end of *Positions*, for example, Derrida designates "as *différance* the movement according to which language, or any other code, any system of reference in general, is constituted 'historically' as a tissue of differences" (p. 104, n. 31). But Derrida attempts to go further. Whereas Saussure sees the differences in a semiotic system as the set of everchanging relationships the speaker manipulates in order to generate meaning, Derrida describes différance as the infinite disappearance of either an origin of or a final resting place for meaning. Insofar as Derrida describes différance, he consistently does so by explaining what it is *not*.

Différance, he says, "is literally neither a word nor a concept." He compares it to a "sheaf" because he does not wish to describe the stages of a history by showing how différance imposes a graphic disorder on each text and each context; rather, he wishes to study the general system of the economy of différance: "the word *sheaf* seems to mark more appropriately that the assemblage to be proposed has the complex structure of a weaving, an interlacing which permits the different threads and different lines of meaning—or of force—to go off again in different directions, just as it is always ready to tie itself up with others" (*Margins*, p. 3).

Différance is not something that can appear in logocentric discourse (of which, no doubt, this text is an example): "*différance* is not," Derrida explains, "preceded by the originary and indivisible unity of a present possibility that I could reserve. . . . What defers presence, on the contrary, is the very basis on which presence is announced or desired in what represents it, its sign, its trace. . . ." Différance is "that which produces different things, that which differentiates, is the common root of all the oppositional concepts that mark our language . . ." (*Positions*, pp. 8–9).

Différance is neither structure nor origin, "such an alternative itself being an 'effect' of *différance*." Even so, studying the operations of différance requires that the writer use such concepts as structure and origin and "borrow the syntaxic and lexical resources of the language of metaphysics" even if the writer wishes to deconstruct this language (*Positions*, pp. 9–10).

Différance is neither absence nor presence. It is a constant movement of spacing that, by appearing nowhere, plays absence and presence against each other. It "is the systematic play of differences, of the traces of differences, of the *spacing* by means of which elements are related to each other. This spacing is the simultaneously active and passive . . . production of the intervals without which the 'full' terms would not signify, would not function" (*Positions*, p. 27; see also *Grammatology*, p. 143).

Neither, however, is différance a master term. Indeed, its very operation makes the appearance of any sort of master term impossible: "since it cannot be elevated into a master-word or a master-concept, since it blocks every relationship to theology, *différance* finds itself enmeshed in the work that pulls it through a chain of other 'concepts,' other 'words,' other textual configurations" (*Positions*, p. 40).

Différance is not an origin. Neither language nor writing originates in différance. Rather, différance allows the play of absence and presence, writing and thought, structure and force through which the question of origin comes to know itself. One cannot seek origin until it is gone. Standing in the presence of origin would be entering either a superhuman or a subhuman state, for origin must be extralinguistic: "To defer (*différer*) thus cannot mean to retard a present possibility, to postpone an act, to put off a perception already now possible. . . . To say that *différance* is originary is simultaneously to erase the myth of a present origin. Which is why 'originary' must be understood as having been *crossed out*, without which *différance* would be derived from an original plenitude" (*Writing*, p. 203; see also *Grammatology*, p. 143).

Différance is neither an activity nor an effect. In speech it is the impossibility of the silence of pure communication; in writing it is the impossibility of the implosion of marks into pure meaning; in being it is the radical impossibility of finding anything that satisfies: "What is written as *différance*, then, will be the playing movement that 'produces'—by means of something that

is not simply an activity—these differences, these effects of difference. This does not mean that the *différance* that produces
differences is somehow before them, in a simple and unmodi-
fied—in-different—present. *Différance* is the non-full, non-sim-
ple, structured and differentiating origin of differences. Thus,
the name 'origin' no longer suits it" (*Margins*, p. 11). Différance
does not imply that language does not mean. If anything, différance describes the possibility of meaning, which logocentric discourse has tried to change from a *possibility* into a fait accompli.
Again and again Derrida shows how language never finishes
meaning, for language always defers the closure of final meaning: "The possibility of distinguishing between the sign and the
nonsign, linguistic sign and nonlinguistic sign, expression and
indication, ideality and nonideality, subject and object, grammaticalness and nongrammaticalness, pure grammaticalness and
empirical grammaticalness, pure general grammaticalness and
pure logical grammaticalness, intention and intuition, etc., is
deferred *ad infinitum.*" The possibility of these distinctions is their
impossibility (*Speech*, p. 101).

Différance is not a concept that can be governed from any
position that différance itself allows: "In the delineation of *différance* everything is strategic and adventurous. Strategic because
no transcendent truth present outside the field of writing can
govern theologically the totality of the field. Adventurous because this strategy is not a simple strategy in the sense that
strategy orients tactics according to a final goal, a *telos* or theme
of domination, a mastery and ultimate reappropriation of the
development of the field" (*Margins*, p. 7).

Différance, in short, *is not:*

> It is not a present being, however excellent, unique, prin-
> cipal, or transcendent. It governs nothing, reigns over
> nothing, and nowhere exercises any authority. It is not
> announced by any capital letter. Not only is there no
> kingdom of *différance*, but *différance* instigates the subver-
> sion of every kingdom. Which makes it obviously threat-
> ening and infallibly dreaded by everything within us that
> desires a kingdom, the past or future presence of a king-
> dom. (*Margins*, p. 22)

And surely différance is not what most students expect in school.

They expect a true kingdom with a monarch, a clearly defined set of raw materials, a well-established arrangement of agriculture, manufacturing, exporting, and importing, and a clear set of geographic boundaries. Anyone who has taught composition very long has heard a frustrated student say, "I just don't know what you want. If you'd just tell me what you want, I could do it." In fact, this is a cry for authoritarian tyranny, a cry for monarchy saying, OK, you be the monarch, I'll be the subject. Then all I have to do is pay tribute and act deferential. No questions, no uncertainty, no différance. The student seeks a command. The command would offer a totalization of knowledge, a closed feat waiting to be performed.

While writing may promise such a kingdom, a kingdom where students learn to master what they "know," in fact, it leads the writer into a labyrinth, into an unending adventure. Students want writing to do all the things that différance precludes. They want it to be a governable structure whose origin in meaning remains always clear. They want it to divulge the list of master terms that will enable their writing to achieve their desired effect on knowledge, on the reader, and on themselves.

This infinite play of différance is, in my opinion, what makes writing so difficult and so interesting to teach. Students expect writing to capture and retain pure meaning. We must allow them to see that writing begins and continues forever as a movement away from pure meaning. Students expect writing to have a discrete origin in prior meaning. We must allow them to see that the operation of writing precludes both the unveiling of such an origin and the possibility of the absolute union of signifier and signified. Students expect to use writing to discover themselves and to inscribe what those "selves" think. Writing, however, as the paradigmatic signifying system, "precedes and gives rise to the very concepts of self-presence and meaning" (Allison, pp. xxxvii–xxxviii).

Getting students to conceive of writing as a weaving rather than an arresting of meaning—especially since they wish so desperately to arrest meaning and hold it in its presentation— is no mean feat. Students know intuitively that their own writing is in fact a weaving, an interlacing that permits the different threads and different lines of meaning to go off in different directions and tie themselves to other meanings. They want us to give them the skill to stop the weaving, to cut the lines that trace outwards, to break the knots where their meaning ties up with other meanings beyond their control and even beyond their comprehension.

Beginning writers, of course, think they should represent their thoughts accurately. What they don't know, and what we usually don't tell them, is that their thoughts don't exist at all until they come to differ with themselves, in which case they are already deferred. Rather than a system for capturing thought (as if thought were some entity outside language that language, like a cage or container, could hold), entry into writing begins an adventure. The last thing most students want from writing is adventure. They do not want to operate a system of strategies that always precludes foreclosing itself. They want to use writing to set truth in relief; one might almost say, they want to use writing against itself to generate the silence that any transcendental signified must be. But this does not imply that students are somehow recalcitrant, conniving malcontents. They merely bring their culture with them to the classroom, a culture that has built itself largely on the repression of writing.

Supplement

> Somewhere, parently, in the ginnandgo gap between antediluvious an annadominant the copyist must have fled with his scroll. The billy flood rose or an elk charged him or the sultrup worldwright from the excelsissimost empyrean (bolt, in sum) earthspake or the Dannamen gallous banged pan the bliddy duran. A scribicide then and there. . . .
>
> Joyce, *Finnegans Wake*

"Writing," Derrida argues, "is dangerous" from the moment it first presents itself as the replacement for what should need no replacement. Writing passes for the plenitude of speech and thought "whose deficiency and infirmity it nevertheless only *supplements.*" Writing "intervenes or insinuates itself *in-the-place-of.*" It fills the void of what should have no void. It shows that "somewhere, something can be filled up *of itself,* can accomplish itself, only by allowing itself to be filled through sign and proxy," through some sort of supplement (*Grammatology,* pp. 144–45).

Things that need supplementing are not sufficient in their own right. They lack something that they require. Most Western writers assume that writing serves as a vehicle to carry thought. But this assumption remains forever haunted by the problem that thinking (at least in the Western sense of thinking) cannot appear outside writing. Something at the core of thinking seems to be missing. Writing adds what is missing but in doing so reveals the incompleteness of the thing that needs a supplement to be itself. In other words, if writing clarifies thought, then thought needs the supplement of writing to be whole and thus thought without writing is not itself, at least not fully so (*Writing,* p. 212). This process of supplementation endangers thought because writing, rather than merely serving as an empty vehicle waiting to transport and then discharge thought whole, adds itself to and then substitutes itself for thought. What should remain outside thought insinuates itself into the inside of thought: "It breaks in as a dangerous supplement, as a *substitute* that *enfeebles, enslaves, effaces, separates, and falsifies*" (*Grammatology,* p. 215). No matter how far back the writer attempts to trace thought in order to free it from writing, supplementarity is always already there, for thought requires supplementation in order to differentiate itself from nonthought (*Grammatology,* p. 247).

In *La Vérité en peinture,* Derrida analyzes the problem of inside and outside introduced by the need for a supplement (especially pp. 53–93; see also Culler, pp. 193-96). In Greek, *parergon* means "hors d'oeuvre," "accessory," or "supplement." Derrida explains that since Plato, philosophical writing has opposed the *parergon* because it is before, beside, above, around, or against the *ergon,* the true matter. Writing gets in the way of philosophers, who seek the truth and then seek to communicate that truth. Derrida infuriates many Anglo-American philosophers by consistently showing the fundamental necessity of the *parergon* (outside) to the *ergon* (inside). In fact, without the outside, the inside cannot distinguish itself from itself; thus, in a hard-to-think way, the outside is in the inside from the beginning because the inside requires the outside in order to be an inside. But the boundaries blur. The threat "is that the operations of what should be merely a means of expression might affect or infect the meaning it is supposed to represent." The ideal, of course, would be to use absolutely transparent language as a means of contemplating thought directly. But the desire *for* an ideal exposes the attempt to escape writing and discover presence. The sequence of supplements, the forever multiplying chain of supplements and replacements, the effect of writing on thought, thought's absolute dependence on writing to know itself, all this implies that *everything* "begins through the intermediary." In writing (or in speaking for that matter) everything already operates as mediation. There simply is no stopping place or starting place. "The graphic of supplementarity is irreducible to logic, primarily because it comprehends logic as one of its *cases* and may alone produce its origin. . . . The supplement can only respond to the nonlogical logic of a game. That game is the play of the world" (*Grammatology*, p. 259; see also p. 157).

This amounts to a profound threat to reason. Reason does not wish to admit that the self-presence where reason itself operates lacks something. Nor does reason wish to acknowledge its own dependence on some sort of written or spoken language to free itself and identify itself (see *Grammatology*, p. 149). What one in fact finds at the center of "thought" as the principle by which reason operates is the movement of play: "This movement of play, permitted by the lack or absence of a center or origin, is the movement of *supplementarity*" (*Writing*, p. 289).

Absence of the supplement, the sort of fixity that would arrest thought and support reason, would be nothing more than symbolic incapacity. Combining absence of supplement with presence of fixity would mean loss of humanity. Indeed supplementarity, by escaping and always coming before what would stop the play, allows us not only to think supplementarity but to think at all, even though the thoughts, and especially the written thoughts, are always supplementations. The alternative to such endless supplementations would be silence (see *Grammatology*, pp. 241–42, 187).

The writing process spotlights the play of supplementation because writing constantly reveals itself as having no zero degree. Rather than moving toward fixity and closure, it plays in an ever-widening circle. The Western writer, however, "would like to separate originarity from supplementarity. All the rights constituted by our logos are on his side: it is unthinkable and intolerable that what has the name *origin* should be no more than a point situated within the system of supplementarity" (*Grammatology*, pp. 242–43). Most writers seek an algebraic writing in which inscription functions as an equation between the author's intended meaning and the reader's comprehension of that meaning. To their great dismay, such writers get a world of writing where the writing moves ever further from the zero degree that could exist if writing itself were not the supplement inside the very inside that should allow no supplement to penetrate. And this world of writing never ceases making itself more complex: "As a supplement, the signifier does not represent first and simply the absent signified. Rather, it is substituted for another signifier, for another type of signifier that maintains another relation with the deficient presence, one more highly valued by virtue of the play of difference" (*Speech*, p. 89). Beyond the written text "there is not a blank, virgin, empty margin, but another text, a weave of differences of forces without any present center of reference" (*Margins*, p. xxiii). "The supplement is always the supplement of a supplement. One wishes to go back *from the supplement to the source:* one must recognize that there is *a supplement at the source*" (*Grammatology*, p. 304; see also pp. 313–16, where Derrida explores the complex way the operation of supplementation allows and disallows the idea of origin).

Obviously all this is quite abstract. It does, however, serve as a cautionary warning about the way we write our texts and design our classes in writing. The process of writing is not the warm, friendly shower of blessings we frequently claim. As the student writes, writing supplements thinking thus removing it from presence. The more deeply the student becomes enmeshed in the writing process, the more surely that process places the finitude of meaning outside itself. Finally, what began as a supplement to help thought present itself becomes a replacement, a replacement that threatens the integrity of what it purports to replace. In the logic of supplementarity, plenitude must always be one remove away (see Culler, pp. 104–5).

Students want desperately to stand outside writing and operate it like an excavating machine that uncovers the meaning hidden in whatever quarry they have set out to mine. Their process of revision reveals this desire. Nancy Sommers ("Revision Strategies") and Lester Faigley and Stephen Witte ("Analyzing Revision") have shown that students carrying out unsupervised revisions tend to make only the most superficial changes: in punctuation, for example, or spelling. Rarely do they reopen the act of composing. Were they to begin writing, however, such superficial matters as punctuation and spelling would become much less important. Students usually see revision as "correctness" largely because they have been taught, *and they prefer to learn*, antiwriting (e.g., demonstrating mastery of defined rules or patterns). They can avoid writing altogether by providing shells with no interior: spelling, punctuation, sentences, paragraphs, structure, and coherence that are nothing but spelling, punctuation, sentences, paragraphs, structure, and coherence. Encouraged by the composition teacher's insistence on the framing mechanisms and usage patterns of edited prose, students attempt to construct a pure outside with no inside at all, a group of marks having nothing to do with writing and announcing themselves as correct. Thus students' "presence," never having been disturbed by writing, their interior never having been penetrated by writing, remains present, by which I mean prehuman. For the loss of presence, the entry into writing, marks the beginning of the human condition. And once in writing, no writer can ever escape the act of his or her own writing (see *La carte*, pp. 341–43, where Derrida shows how Freud fails in his attempt to escape from his own text in order to control it from the "outside").

Representation

> Shshsh! Don't start like that, you wretch! I thought ye knew all and more, ye aucthor, to explique to ones the significat of their exsystems with your nieu nivulon lead.
>
> Joyce, *Finnegans Wake*

"A theory of representation that seeks to establish foundation," Culler argues, "must take as given, must assume the presence of, that which accurate representations represent" (p. 152). Were such a foundation to exist, the test of a written text would finally have nothing to do with the writing; rather, it would work backwards from the writing, the thing that represents, to the foundation, the thing represented. In fact, however, prose does not merely and slavishly repeat thinking. Quite the contrary, in supplementing thinking so that thinking can become present, writing adds itself to thinking, thus denying it either an absolute foundation or an outside-of-writing existence.

Derrida's "La double séance" (double session, double science, double scene, double sense; see *Dissemination*, pp. 173–287) and

Miller's *Fiction and Repetition* offer the most rigorous explorations of the doubleness and repetition that forever delay the arrival of a play-stopping foundation for writing. There are, Miller explains, two forms of repetition: Platonic and Nietzschean. Each contradicts and yet requires the other. The two formulations (Miller translates Gilles Deleuze's *Logique du sens* here) amount to different readings of the world: the Platonic one "asks us to think of difference on the basis of preestablished similitude or identity"; the Nietzschean, in contrast, asks us to think of it "as the product of a fundamental disparity." In the Platonic view, the world is icon, in the Nietzschean, simulacra, if not phantasm. The Platonic model "is grounded in a solid archetypal model which is untouched by the effects of repetition." All examples are copies of this model. The Nietzschean model, on the other hand, "posits a world based on difference," a world not of copies but of similitudes or ghostly reflections. The Nietzschean examples "are ungrounded doublings which arise from differential interrelations among elements which are all on the same plane." One thing repeats another, but not exactly, there being no absolute archetype to which the representation can be compared or by which it can be judged for appropriateness. Neither form, however, negates the other. Each, in fact, "inevitably calls up the other as its shadow companion. You cannot have one without the other, though each subverts the other. The difference between one text and another from this point of view is in the varying modes of the intertwining. Anti-Platonism is present in Plato; the metaphysical antagonist is by no means expelled from Nietzsche's language." Every written text includes the voice it most wishes to silence because it required that voice in the first place in order to know itself by distinguishing itself from its opposite. However much it may wish to do otherwise, a text repeats what it works hardest at silencing (pp. 4–16).

As the analyst works backwards from repetition to repetition, deconstruction reveals a double-whammy problematic. First, writing defines itself "as the impossibility of a chain arresting itself on a signified that would not relaunch this signified, in that the signified is already in the position of the signifying substitution" (*Positions,* p. 82). Thus, writers who expect to tie thinking down in writing can only be frustrated as writing refuses to tie itself down to a founding signification. Second, as writers write, they must repeat terms that exceed their intentions. Not only do the words and syntax of the language refuse to tie themselves down to meaning, inevitably they carry freight writers do not want yet cannot get rid of. As a result, writers must write using terms that remain "under erasure" because the terms themselves carry so much excess baggage.

For Derrida, writing under erasure is a quite conscious maneuver (see Spivak and *Grammatology*, p. 60). He uses the system of Western metaphysics to mount his deconstruction simply because no other system exists. Thus, he uses the terms of this system "under erasure," thereby trying to erase the term in the moment of its use. Though less consciously, every writer faces the same situation. There are times when no exact word or syntax works; the writer must, therefore, make do the best way possible. Usually the writer uses terms very carefully, trying in an almost surgical way to slice out the part of the term's denotative and connotative chains that will work, in effect, trying to erase part, sometimes even all, of the term's history. Such a strategic use of writing, however, takes years to learn, and no one ever manages to use only those parts of writing that say exactly what he or she desires and nothing else.

Derrida's and Miller's analyses of the repetition through which writing operates require composition teachers to look again at three standard operations in the teaching of writing: invention (especially with formal heuristics), sentence combining, and exemplification. When we teach invention in our writing classes, we often leave the impression on our students that invention uncovers or discloses meaning. Thus, a student who attempts the tagmemic grid, Burke's pentad, Larson's questions for problem solving, one of the various sets of *topoi* developed from Aristotle, or even free writing *may* expect the operation of the heuristic to reveal meaning. If Derrida and Miller are right, however, any formal heuristic merely excites the play of possible signification. Instead of using a tool to uncover meaning, the students turn the polysemy of language loose. Soon they experience the same frustration Phaedrus's student in Robert Pirsig's *Zen And the Art of Motorcycle Maintenance* experiences while contemplating the bricks in the building in downtown Bozeman. Rather than simplifying writing, formal invention heuristics *can* terrify students who expect both writing and the heuristic to shut the play of possible meaning down in the presence of "what they want to say."

James Moffett's attack on sentence combining is well known (pp. vi, 167–87). Derridean analysis, however, offers a caution of a different sort against sentence combining. At its core, sentence combining stands squarely in the center of the metaphysics of presence. It assumes that meaning precedes and informs writing. Syntactic maturity, therefore, can be dissociated from semantic maturity; hence, anyone can learn to write smoother, more sophisticated sentences. Sentences themselves are merely the window dressing of thought. In fact, however, none of us believes that to be true. And having students combine sentences just to see what they will look like reshaped is apt to make them fatalistic about writing. They are tempted to retreat either into psophistry, where they can substitute their ability to persuade for their inability to know, or into antiwriting, where the purpose is nothing more than to announce sentences as mature, carefully embedded examples of themselves, divorced completely from the play of absence and presence that would occur were the student to attempt to write.

Inexperienced writers frequently offer texts that consist almost entirely of generalizations. Immediately, we demand examples or evidence to support these generalizations. Students resist as long as they can. In part, this resistance occurs because the students have recoiled in terror after seeing just a little into what the writing process may do to the security of their self-identities and their world views. They think they know what they believe, at least they hope they do. We claim that we will make their thoughts and beliefs clearer. They know just how profoundly those thoughts and beliefs are threatened, for they know that once the process of exemplification begins, their ideas have entered the arena of play. Exemplification cannot be completed, only foreclosed. And to them any thought or belief requiring infinite self-presentation is incomplete and therefore unbelievable. If they could stay at the level of pure generalization, they could avoid writing entirely. If they must exemplify their ideas and beliefs, they force those ideas and beliefs into the process of différance, for exemplification is serial, never complete, and always connected to other strands of examples.

In addition to offering new perspectives on invention, sentence combining, and exemplification, an analysis of repetition clarifies three fairly constant problems in teaching writing:

1. Students frequently accuse their writing teachers of being interested only in "the writing," and never "the content." The students believe that their writing exists to represent their thought and meaning, both of which they believe to be outside of and prior to the writing. The problem, as I have tried to show above, is that the thinking is deficient from the beginning because of its need for the supplementation of writing to be present at all. Because students know the teacher can see what they have attempted, they have considerable (and understandable) difficulty coming to grips with the deconstructions of their texts. In fact, they do not see their own texts *as texts;* they see them as presentations of meaning. Until they come to regard what they write as writing, as a text, they will continue to complain that composition teachers are interested only in "the writing" and never "the content."

2. Students know they are not the first to write, they know their texts will be evaluated against some sort of standard (however abstract) of what acceptable writing ought to be, and they know that whatever ideas they might come up with have appeared before numerous times in other people's writing; thus, they sometimes feel trapped in that they seem to have no choice but to repeat what others have repeated endlessly before them. They sense that their language is not their own, was never their own, could never be their own. In attempting to repeat what others have already repeated, they know that they cannot fully master the prior repetitions and that their essays will finally be exposed as incomplete, if not incompetent. The more the student writer tries to make a text "repeat" exactly the thought that should precede and enable it, the more this very text is haunted by the infinitely differing play between what meaning would look like if it were present and what the student's writing actually looks like as it supplements and subverts the closure of thought. In part, this explains their desire to be told what to do so that they can do it and avoid having to write.

3. Student writers are rarely sophisticated enough to know how to write "under erasure." They have not yet learned that words don't tie down to meanings; thus, they fre-

quently use diction inappropriately or use thesauruses to create the sorts of sentences that get tacked to faculty lounge bulletin boards.

Foundation

So, the truce, the old truce and nattonbuff the truce, boys. Drouth is stronger than faction.

Joyce, *Finnegans Wake*

The foundation of what the West calls "thought" depends on the assumption "that signs represent ideas and that an idea . . . can stand in semantic contrast or contradiction to another idea" (Garver, p. xiii). Language, in this assumption, founds itself on thinking. Thinking, in the standard Cartesian maneuver, simply "is." Derrida (as well as the later Wittgenstein) challenges this assumption. Chapters 4 and 7 of *Speech and Phenomena* articulate this challenge in detail. One of the principles of Western thinking, Derrida argues, has been to assume that what linguistic expressions mean is one thing; how they can be applied is another thing entirely. Such a separation, he argues, amounts to a theological conception of language. One must simply believe in the separation of meaning and expression, just as one must believe in the existence of meaning. By deconstructing the separability of meaning and expression, Derrida shows how what the West calls "thought" depends on the repression of writing, for writing reveals most clearly thought's absolute dependence on signification. Derrida's project "is a sustained argument against the possibility of anything pure and simple which can serve as the foundation for the meaning of signs" (Garver, p. xxii).

The desire for what Hartman calls "reality-mastery" (*Saving*, pp. 156–57) causes the Western tradition of splitting meaning from expression. Western thinkers wish to control not only their environment and quality of life, but also what they "think." Separating meaning and expression allows them to maintain such control, but it also requires that they degrade expression to inferior status in order to keep "thought" pure. We in the West, in other words, believe we can know what we think not only without saying it or writing it down, but also without thinking it to ourselves in a linguistic way. Deconstruction attempts to show that what presents itself as thought begins in exclusion: something must be silenced, not known, or forbidden in order for a discourse to appear as knowledge (*Speech*, pp. 30–31, 99). In other words, différance, or the play of absences, founds thought. The Cartesian *cogitato, ergo sum* is an effect of language, not an origin or foundation.

In the deconstructed hierarchy of Derridean analysis, foundation enables discourse by remaining forever absent. A true foundation would operate outside language, precluding it. Or, said better, would not "operate" at all but would simply *be*. Writing presents such a profound threat to Western thought because it reveals what must be kept hidden for Western thought to *be* thought rather than one discourse among many. As every writer knows, infinite processes of repetition, replacement, and delay found writing (*Writing*, p. 161). Obviously, therefore, ensuring that the process of writing does not affect thinking is essential; otherwise, thinking depends on writing, which it may not do if it is to remain free from the play of différance and the trace. In *Margins of Philosophy*, Derrida shows how discourse shapes inquiry, allowing inquiry to emerge and to show its results not as *a* discourse but as the revelation of meaning (pp. 175–205). For example, the linguist Benveniste explains how the grammatical functions of the verb "to be" are dispersed throughout the Ewe language. But, as Derrida points out, a linguist must look from the Indo-European perspective of language to find "to be" dispersed in another language. One must already know the need for "to be" to find this need met in a dispersed, varied way somewhere else (pp. 198–201). Finding "to be" "dispersed" in a language, I would add, resembles Columbus's "discovering" American "Indians," who presumably knew they were there all along and thus could not be "discovered" unless by the term "discovery" one means "knowledge available in the consciousness of white Europeans."

Derrida gives a similar sort of analysis in *Positions* where he explains his distrust of the concept "history" (pp. 56–59). Both history and the history of meaning in fact found themselves on themselves. One cannot trace the history of meaning without presuming that meaning has an origin and a sequence, and that meaning does not require itself to know and reveal itself. In fact, the history of meaning is the repression of writing, there being no possibility without writing either of conceiving the notion "history of meaning" or of executing such a notion. To effect a history of meaning while keeping both history and meaning intact as neutral terms needing no foundation, writing is devalued, made a tool, a secondary corrupt necessity in the service of the pure meaning that one can supposedly know. This meaning merely uses writing much the same way the soul uses the body.

Derrida's argument that the absence of any sort of foundation sets play in play, thereby opening the possibility of the human condition, offers a variety of interesting perspectives on problems associated with the teaching of writing. What follows is a catalog of those problems and my own ruminations about what a Derridean perspective means to each one.

As recently as 1981 E. D. Hirsch, Jr., and David P. Harrington ("Measuring") were constructing an entire theory of writing competence based on belief in the separability of meaning from writing. Doing this required that discourse be separated into two kinds of "traits": traits of intrinsic rhetorical and communicative effectiveness, which Hirsch and Harrington argue can be studied, and traits of intellectual and aesthetic qualities, which, they admit, cannot be studied (pp. 194–97). This method of evaluation also required belief in textual "synonymy," the possibility that two entirely different texts "say" the same thing and that the effectiveness with which they say it can be evaluated comparatively (pp. 189–94). Students who learned under the Hirsch-Harrington theory would have their papers rated on their "relative readability," the more readable the paper, the better the paper (for a more complete explanation of the idea of "relative readability," see Hirsch's *Philosophy*). The process of writing would resemble the process of tailoring clothes (my metaphor, not theirs) as the writer would ensure that the writing fit the audience (pp. 197–99) as perfectly as possible.

What founds the Hirsch-Harrington method of evaluation is the assumption that meaning and expression are separable; thus, when you change a text, you do not necessarily change what it "says." While I do not doubt than an endless series of "experiments" could be conducted to "prove" the separability of meaning from expression, I would point out that the possibility of developing such proof (indeed the possibility of thinking of such a possibility in the first place) could occur only in writing. Developing a method to generate "proof" would depend on writing; moreover, "understanding" and "explaining" this proof could happen only in writing. And I would bet a great deal that at every stage in the progress of this "proof" the writers would "write," by which I mean never get the exact words and syntax, never quite finish, never master absolutely the material to be understood and presented. While writing would in fact allow such a hypothesis to emerge, the process of writing would never stop generating "evidence" and "experiments" to "prove" and refine the hypothesis. A much more likely conception of writing, I would argue, is that rhetorical and communicative effectiveness are not separable from intellectual and aesthetic quality, nor does meaning precede and inform writing, nor is there any such thing as synonymy between two texts or among several texts. A much more likely conception of the process of writing is what Derrida calls *déclenchement* (triggering) (*Dissemination,* p. 290). The beginning of inscription triggers an operation that never plays itself out.

Derrida explains the problem of students trying to speak over the voice of their teachers. Derrida had, in his words, "the good fortune to study under Michel Foucault" (*Writing,* p. 31), yet he presumes to speak using three pages from the middle of Foucault's *Madness and Civilization* as his point of departure. He explains in detail the discomfort, the "unhappy consciousness" of the student trying to speak across, over, or through the voice of his teacher. For the student writer, this problem is magnified manyfold. However much we may try to follow Moffett's injunction against preteaching (pp. 198–200) or Peter Elbow's and Ken Macrorie's many admonitions to let students teach themselves to write, however reluctant we may be to present ourselves as the "authority who knows how to write," and however much we may try to be neutral readers, we must have some fundamental conceptions about what a text ought to look like.

Somehow, some way, our students must learn to speak through or over our voices (see Bloom, *Anxiety,* pp. 5–16). The foundation of their writing becomes a combination of the expectations of this particular teacher with those of all the other teachers whose courses they have taken. But since they can never speak with our voice absolutely, they must silence us in order to have a place to speak at all. Our discourse, what we would write if we held the pen, falls silent, allowing the student a space in which to write. Derrida writes this way all the time by writing through and even inside other texts. All of his writings (*Glas* being the most elaborate and complicated example) appear through commentary on, openings in, and shuffling among other texts. As Derrida knows all too well, what founds a written text must be some other written text or group of texts. Thus, what founds it always stands outside it, beyond its control. The student writer who naïvely believes that a text can originate within itself or that ideas generate their own expression is doomed to flee writing entirely or to labor at it only with great frustration.

Most American colleges and universities separate literature and creative writing into one place and expository writing into another even though both may, for reasons of convenience and history, be housed in the same department. This separation, as Culler explains, allows fictionality, rhetoricity, and nonseriousness to be separated from writing. It allows language to be purified from what "would disrupt it if it had not been set aside" (p. 181). Indeed, establishing a split between creative and expository writing may be the essential maneuver in establishing the possibility of serious, referential, verifiable discourse. Such a division guarantees the existing hierarchy. The really important disciplines—philosophy and math first, then history and literature—deal with ideas. The really practical disciplines—physics, biology, and chemistry first, then engineering, computer science, and business—describe the world and keep it running. The expository writing program forever serves what is "important" on the one hand and what is "practical" on the other. Composition teachers merely facilitate the tools or vessels to carry ideas, describe "reality," or administer the affairs of society.

Derridean analysis so threatens what is "important" and what is "practical" because the discourses of importance and of practicality operate on the assumption that signification can be grounded. As long as writing remains devalued, as long as it is nothing more than the vehicle to carry meaning, this ground remains firm. If, however, writing precedes *and* enables all discourse, if in fact all the humanities, the sciences, and the professions are always already writing, never free from the tertiarity and repetition of writing, then the ground of their activity is not signification, but rather play, or supplement, or différance or whichever Derridean term one chooses.

Logocentrism

Sink deep or touch not the Cartesian spring.

Joyce, *Finnegans Wake*

Logocentric is Derrida's shorthand term for any meaning that pretends to emanate from speech, logic, reason, the Word of God, or any other absolute origin that precedes and escapes the infinite play of writing. Derrida uses the term "to characterize any signifying system governed by the notion of the self-presence of meaning; i.e. any system structured by a valorization of speech over writing, immediacy over distance, identity over difference, and (self-)presence over all forms of absence, ambiguity, simulation, substitution, or negativity" (Johnson, *Dissemination*, p. 4, n. 1).

The epoch of logocentrism, which, according to Derrida, begins with Plato, allows two operations. First, logic, reason, humanity, and history can present themselves absolutely. They need no origin, but simply are. Within logocentrism it is impossible not to think them, for they constitute thinking and allow thinking to present itself as truthfulness and meaningfulness. Second, within logocentrism the one who thinks can efface the signifier, leaving nothing but "the signified in its brilliance and in its glory" (*Grammatology*, p. 286). Logocentrism always privileges speech over writing because speech seems to vanish leaving the meaning it conveys standing alone; writing, in contrast, by staying around, by remaining available for reinterpretation and misappropriation, insinuates itself into the meaning it supposedly should convey. Speech emanates from the interior, from absolute proximity to meaning; writing merely represents speaking, and corrupts it in representing it (*Speech*, pp. 75–87).

When Derrida points out the rhetorical and metaphorical nature of referential prose, when he argues that the most anarchic sorts of literary texts, such as those by Mallarmé, Ponge, Jabes, Sollers, Joyce, or Genet, inscribe themselves in the very heart of so-called straightforward, referential prose, he blurs all the lines that define such terms as "human," "thought," or "reason," revealing these terms not as neutral but as oppositions that reign only through the repression and degradation of their opponent. Derrida shows that from within logocentrism setting aside writing as a fallen supplement becomes a historical necessity, not a choice a writer might make. Writing must add nothing to what it represents because it must remain outside the pure interior of meaning. Were it to penetrate into the interior, the interior itself would already be corrupt, and meaning would be lost in the echo of play.

△

7.
CLOSING
THE
PHARMACY

Inauguration as Ending

Cells fuse, split, and proliferate; volumes grow, tissues stretch, and body fluids change rhythm, speeding up or slowing down. Within the body, growing as a graft, indomitable, there is an other. And no one is present, within that simultaneously dual and alien space, to signify what is going on.

Julia Kristeva, *Desire in Language*

Derrida's status as the reigning French intellectual guru, abetted by the fear and trembling he causes among those literature scholars most hostile to the teaching of writing, tempts one to stop before allowing Platonism to reassert itself or deconstruction to undermine itself. After all, the Derridean canon offers a powerful theoretical matrix within which to conceive and to teach writing, a matrix in which the never-finished process of inscription is itself the truth of all things. Such a move would, however, create three problems: first, it would oversimplify the power of Platonism by attempting to silence its most profound question; second, it would betray part of the sophistication of deconstruction, which automatically calls itself into question; and third, it would leave composition studies locked inside philosophy, a fate almost as bad as remaining under Plato's curse of inferiority. As a result, Plato must have his say, and deconstruction must fall prey to the self-reflexive scrutiny it demands.

After this, perhaps there will be space for a new rhetoric of writing, a new sophistry (without the *p!*).

Not surprisingly, giving in to deconstruction's demand to review itself and giving Plato his final say turn out to be the same act. It is an act Derrida frequently calls "solicitation." In *Writing and Difference*, Derrida offers this definition: ". . . (from the Latin) *soliciting*. In other words, *shaking* in a way related to the *whole* (from *sollus*, in archaic Latin 'the whole,' and from *citare*, 'to put in motion')." Soliciting any text endangers that text, for solicitation "concentrates our vision on the keystone . . . the stone which encapsulates both the possibility and fragility of its existence." Threatening any structure allows the reader to comprehend that structure by revealing "not only its supports but also that secret place in which it is neither construction nor ruin but lability" (p. 6). In *Of Grammatology*, Derrida uses *solicitation* more broadly as the name for deconstructing the theological belief in the existence of meaning outside of and prior to signification: "This reference to the meaning of a signified thinkable and possible outside of all signifiers remains dependent upon the onto-theo-teleology that I have just evoked. It is thus the idea of the sign that must be deconstructed through a meditation upon writing which would merge, as it must, with the undoing [*solicitation*] of ontotheology, fully repeating it in its *totality* and *making* it insecure in its most assured evidences" (p. 73).

Then, in *Dissemination* (pp. 357–62) and *Margins of Philosophy* (pp. 133–36), Derrida expands his use of the term even more. It comes to mean (1) "shaking up a whole culture," (2) questioning the ideology of both reader and writer by threatening any possible position from which to mount the closure of a text, (3) causing every Western concept, including the concept of Being, to "tremble," (4) showing how everything, including human beings, is a grapheme in general, and (5) reducing meaning itself (as opposed to a Husserlian reduction *to* meaning). In *Margins*, Derrida claims to have shown how writing in general inscribes itself in and before everything, making everything, including human beings, a grapheme in general. This demonstration, Derrida believes, threatens the security of what is nearest the human being, making it tremble: "That is, the co-belonging and co-propriety of the name of man and the name of Being, such as this co-propriety inhabits, and is inhabited by, the language of the West . . . such as it is inscribed and forgotten according to the history of metaphysics, and such as it is awakened also by the deconstruction of ontotheology. . . . But this trembling—which can only come from a certain outside—was already requisite within the very structure that it solicits" (p. 133). In sum, as he tries to explain in *Positions*, Derrida's solicitation of Western logocentrism requires reevaluation "of the general text and what was believed to be, in the form of reality (history, politics, economics, sexuality, etc.) the simple, referable exterior of language or writing, the belief that this exterior could operate from the simple position of cause or accident" (p. 91).

Derrida himself, of course, also writes texts. They too are liable to solicitation. Even I can claim to "solicit" them, which I do in this chapter. To do so, however, I must find the keystone, the place where Derrida's system of reading (and however cagey he may be about that system, it is a system) remains liable, where its possibility and fragility lie exposed, where they can be threatened and made to tremble. When Derrida threatens Plato, he focuses his attention on the pharmakon; when he threatens Rousseau, he focuses his attention on the supplement; his own writing process remains liable at its beginning point, at its inauguration.

I. In Auguration

The term *inauguration* appears frequently in Derrida's books, especially those written before 1972. It seems to be a term particularly suited to the Derridean lexicon, so much so that those who know his texts best find it where it appears only in its absence. Culler, for example, translates the clauses "ce qui *ouvre* le sens et le langage, c'est cette écriture comme disparition de la présence naturelle" (*Grammatology*, p. 228/159)[1] as "what *inaugurates* meaning and language is writing as the disappearance of natural presence" (p. 106) (both italics mine). Culler's translation differs from Gayatri C. Spivak's only in that Spivak translates *ouvre* as "opens" (the obvious English cognate), rather than as "inaugurates," which Culler apparently finds closer to the Derridean strategy for describing writing than the more mundane "opens" (French-English dictionaries do not list *inaugurate* as an English equivalent of the French verb *ouvrir*; they do, however, list *open* as a cognate for the French *inaugurer*). Perhaps

Culler chose *inaugurates* because the term appears so frequently elsewhere in *Of Grammatology* as well as in Derrida's other books.[2]

As he claims to deconstruct the chain of displacements that allows the West to present itself, Derrida uses the term *inaugurate* in each of his maneuvers. It appears at the first moment of deconstruction when Derrida overturns the opposition between speech and writing as he deconstructs the Western belief in self-presence. The power that inaugurates speech, he argues, also dislocates the speaker it creates, thereby preventing that speaker from ever joining fully with any of his or her signs: "cette puissance qui, inaugurant la parole, disloque le sujet qu'elle construit, l'empêche d'être présent à ses signes, travaille son langage de toute une écriture. . . ." ("this power which, inaugurating speech, dislocates the subject that it constructs, prevents it from being present to its signs, torments its language with a complete writing. . . .") (*Grammatology*, p. 204/141). Thus, speech, the action that institutes the Western speaker as a meaningful being, at the same instant deconstitutes the presence of whatever that meaningful being might mean.

Having overturned the speech-writing opposition, Derrida turns to the notion of self-presence itself, which, he argues, inaugurates metaphysics by serving as the location for the opposition between form and matter:

> La présence a toujours été et sera toujours, à l'infini, la forme dans laquelle, on peut le dire apodictiquement, se produira la diversité infinie des contenus. L'opposition— inaugurale de la métaphysique—entre forme et matière, trouve dans l'idéalité concrète du présent vivant son ultime et radicale justification.

> (Presence has always been and will always, forever, be the form in which, we can say apodictically, the infinite diversity of contents is produced. The opposition between form and matter—which inaugurates metaphysics—finds in the concrete ideality of the living present its ultimate and radical justification.) (*Speech*, p. 5/6)

Having deconstructed presence, he turns to origins and beginnings. The possibility of thinking "origin" he argues, occurs only after the play of signification has begun, but the play of signification inaugurates the concept of an origin by forbidding its appearance: "Le concept d'origine, ou de signifié fondamental, est-il autre chose qu'une fonction, indispensable mais située, inscrite, dans le système de signification inauguré par l'interdit?" ("Is the concept of origin, or of the fundamental signified, anything but a function, indispensable but situated, inscribed, within the system of signification inaugurated by the interdict?") (*Grammatology*, p. 376/266). As a result, any sort of beginning is fictional, a "violent, arbitrary cut." Rather than some sort of inaugural act, such a cut occurs in the first place because there was never a pure event that was not already some sort of repetition that referred back to some other beginning, which in turn referred back ad infinitum:

> Commencement toujours fictif et la coupure, loin d'être inaugurale, est imposée par l'absence, sauf illusion à décompter, de tout commencement décisoire, d'évènement pur qui ne se divise, ne se répète et ne renvoie déjà à un autre "commencement," à un autre "évènement," la singularité de l'évènement étant plus que jamais mythique dans l'ordre du discours.

> (It is of course a beginning that is forever fictional, and the scission, far from being an inaugural act, is dictated by the absence—unless there exists some illusion to discount—of any decisive beginning, any pure event that would not divide and repeat itself and already refer back to some other "beginning," some other "event," the singularity of the event being more mythical than ever in the order of discourse.) (*Dissemination*, pp. 333-34/300)

Next, Derrida shows that everything in the West that attempts to escape and precede writing is in fact writing-in-general, which inaugurates not only repetition, signification, and living speech, but also idealization and even death by making them possibilities whose actuality remains forever excluded by the openness of writing:

> En quoi l'écriture—nom courant de signes qui fonctionnent malgré l'absence totale du sujet, par (delà) sa mort—est-elle impliquée dans le mouvement même de la sig-

nification en général, en particulier de la parole dite "vive"? En quoi inaugure-t-elle et achève-t-elle l'idéalisation, n'é- tant elle-meme ni réelle ni idéale? En quoi enfin la mort, l'idéalisation, la répétition, la signification ne sont-elles pensables, en leur pure possibilité, qu'à partir d'une seule et même ouverture?

(How is writing—the common name for signs which func- tion despite the total absence of the subject because of (beyond) his death—involved in the very act of signifi- cation in general and, in particular, in what is called "liv- ing" speech? How does writing inaugurate and complete idealization when it itself is neither real nor ideal? And why, finally, are death, idealization, repetition, and sig- nification intelligible, as pure possibilities, only on the basis of one and the same openness?) (*Speech*, p. 104/93)

By suspending life, however, writing *inaugurates* life as some- thing one can own and control. But one must give life up to write, unless, of course, one agrees to accept writing *as* life: "La mort par l'écriture inaugure aussi la vie" ("Death by writing also inaugurates life") (*Grammatology*, p. 205/143).

The most important claim in Derrida's elaborate set of expla- nations of what inaugurates what and what gets inaugurated how is that his own analysis inaugurates nothing; rather, it in- augurates what he calls the "solicitation" of everything that pre- sents itself as original. Constantly showing the difference and deferral through which meaning forever plays (Derrida calls such showing "the very demand of writing"[3]) keeps any such thing as meaning from appearing in its own right; at the same time, such a showing constantly calls attention to the operations of form, theme, and rhetoric on which it depends and from which even the showing itself cannot escape:

Si la dissémination est sans préface, ce n'est pas pour ouvrir à quelque production inaugurale, à quelque prés- entation de soi, bien au contraire, c'est parce qu'elle mar- que les limites essentielles et communes de la rhétorique, du formalisme, et du thématisme, comme du système de leur échange.

(If dissemination is without a preface, this is not in order that some sort of inaugural production, some self-presentation can be opened up; quite the contrary, it is because dissemination marks the essential limits shared by rhetoric, formalism, and thematicism, as well as those of the system of their exchange.) (*Dissemination*, p. 42/35)

These places where Derrida uses the term *inaugurate* to inaugurate his theory of writing, a theory that in fact turns out to be a theory of the origin of everything, force his followers (and I do consider myself one), however persuaded they may be, to see that this theory is itself "inaugurated" by a series of oversimplifications. One need do no more than listen to Derrida's idea of the history of Western thought and his reading of *Phaedrus* to see the stark flimsiness of some of these oversimplifications. What emerges is nothing more than a cryptically presented, charismatic set of dogmas that depend on what Derrida condescendingly calls logocentrism for their existence and that never in any way escape such logocentrism except by using it to declare a new faith in which one must finally believe.

II. How the West Was Augured

Derrida begins his history of Western thought by offering assumptions over which few would quibble. Then he gradually moves toward assertions that are really quite shocking because they are so oversimplified. The terms *augur/inaugurate* play throughout this movement that claims neither to begin nor to allow beginning.[4]

Step one: "Platonism," Derrida argues, "sets up the whole of Western metaphysics in its conceptuality" (*Dissemination*, p. 76). While historians of philosophy might rush to point out Plato's place in a sequence that includes not only Socrates and the pre-Socratics but also Pythagoreanism, sophistics, and a host of other philosophical movements before Plato, most of us are willing to let the all-of-philosophy-is-but-a-series-of-footnotes-to-Plato cliché pass. Even step two most of us will be willing to grant: "The difference between signifier and signified is no doubt the governing pattern within which Platonism institutes itself and determines its opposition to sophistics. In being inaugurated in this manner, philosophy and dialectics are determined in the act of determining their other" (*Dissemination*, p. 112). While the jargon ("signifier," "signified," and "difference") seems particularly French, one can see how it relates to Plato's soul-body, Bed-bed divisions. The third step, however, begins to stretch credulity: if writing is not debased and speech valorized, Derrida contends, logic no longer works. Because Platonic writing is a pharmakon and because a pharmakon is both poison and remedy, a sort of absolute and inseparable mixture of two antithetical moments of the same thing, writing must forever remain outside. Should it penetrate to the inside, it would poison that inside. Speech, however, can remain inside, which explains why speech is valued and writing depreciated:

> Such are the relations between the writing supplement and the *logos-zōon*. In order to cure the latter of the *pharmakon* and rid it of the parasite, it is thus necessary to put the outside back in its place. To keep the outside out. This is the inaugural gesture of "logic" itself, of good "sense" insofar as it accords with the self-identity of *that which is:* being is what it is, the outside is outside and the inside inside. Writing must thus return to being what it *should never have ceased to be:* an accessory, an accident, an excess. (*Dissemination*, p. 128)

The fourth step completes the theory. Derrida sees Plato's depreciation of writing in *Phaedrus* and the "Seventh Letter" as the inaugural move in the entire history of Western metaphysics, and he sees Rousseau and Saussure as the key thinkers who confirm that move when they, too, depreciate writing. This seems odd on the face of it. In particular, it elevates Rousseau and Saussure to a position in the history of Western thought far more important than almost anyone outside France would be willing to grant them, and it makes *Phaedrus*, however significant that text may be, much more important than anyone other than Derrida has ever thought it to be. Though the claim about *Phaedrus* appears frequently in Derrida's texts and receives the most detailed attention in *Dissemination* (with which I deal below), it appears in its starkest form at the end of *Margins of Philosophy:* "This essential drifting, due to writing as an iterative structure cut off from all absolute responsibility, from *consciousness* as the authority of the last analysis, writing orphaned, and separated at birth from the assistance of its father, is indeed what Plato condemned in *Phaedrus*. If Plato's gesture is, as I believe, the philosophical movement par excellence, one realizes what is at stake here" (pp. 316–17).

The Plato-Rousseau-Saussure theory appears frequently in Derrida's various deconstructions. In *Of Grammatology*, he says the exclusion of writing is "the exclusion by which it [the Western world] has constituted and recognized itself, from the *Phaedrus* to the *Course in General Linguistics*" (p. 103; see also p. 33, and pp. 97–98, where nearly the same claim appears). What "seems to inaugurate itself in Western literature with Plato," he says in *Dissemination*,

> will not fail to re-edit itself at least in Rousseau, and then in Saussure. In these three cases, in these three "eras" of the repetition of Platonism, which give us a new thread to follow and other knots to recognize in the history of *philosophia* or the *epistēmē*, the exclusion and the devaluation of writing must somehow, in their very affirmation, come to terms with:
> 1. a generalized sort of writing and, along with it,
> 2. a "contradiction": the written proposal of logocentrism; the simultaneous affirmation of the being-outside of the outside and of its injurious intrusion into the inside;
> 3. the construction of a "literary" work. Before Saussure's *Anagrams*, there were Rousseau's; and Plato's work, outside and independent of its logocentric "content," which is then only one of its inscribed "functions," can be read in its anagrammatical texture.
>
> Thus it is that the "linguistics" elaborated by Plato, Rousseau, and Saussure must both put writing out of the question and yet nevertheless borrow from it, for fundamental reasons, all its demonstrative and theoretical resources. (p. 158)

Earlier in *Dissemination* Derrida had already said that "just as Rousseau and Saussure will do in response to the same necessity . . . Plato maintains *both* the exteriority of writing *and* its power of maleficent penetration, its ability to affect or infect what lies deepest inside." Indeed, Derrida then adds, the manner in which Plato, Rousseau, and Saussure "try in vain to master" writing by excluding it resembles what Freud, while illustrating the logic of dreams, calls "Kettle-logic" (pp. 110–11). In *Writing and Difference*, this time writing about Freud directly, Derrida reaffirms his belief in a twenty-three-hundred-year conspiracy to exclude writing:

> Thus are perhaps augured, in the Freudian breakthrough, a beyond and a beneath of the closure we might term "Platonic." In that moment of world history "subsumed" by the name of Freud, by means of an unbelievable mythology . . . a relationship to itself of the historico-transcendental stage of writing was spoken without being said, thought without being thought: was written and simultaneously erased, metaphorized; designating itself while indicating intraworldly relations, it *was represented*. (pp. 228–29)

Given the outlandishness of Derrida's thesis (and however much he may hedge his arguments, it *is* a thesis) that Plato's *Phaedrus* institutes the West by excluding writing, an exclusion kept strategically in place at key moments in the last two centuries by Rousseau and Saussure, how might one go about refuting it? When, for example, Derrida argues that the "fallen writing" instituted by *Phaedrus* excludes itself, thereby allowing Western thought to begin (*Grammatology*, p. 15), what is one to do? Derrida himself gives precious little "evidence" apart from the Plato-Saussure-Rousseau triad, plus occasional brief notes from the works of Lévi-Strauss and Freud and a chapter from Curtius. And while it is true that Rousseau and Saussure do spend some time excluding writing, Plato spends very little time doing so.

In mounting a refutation of Derrida, does it suffice that hardly anyone in the history of Western letters has thought much about the possibility that Western thought depends on the exclusion of writing? Or does that in fact prove the deep urgency of keeping the exclusion repressed? Is the truth of writing such a deep, terrible secret that all Western thinkers have either agreed to participate in the exclusion or been duped into using a medium that in fact used them? Must such writers keep the maneuver absolutely buried in order to write at all? To refute Derrida, would one have to read all extant Western texts in order to show that virtually none of them exclude writing? Could he then respond by arguing that since fewer than a dozen thinkers in the last twenty-three hundred years have excluded writing, Plato obviously succeeded in his attempt? And might he buttress his thesis by pointing out that at the only two moments when the exclusion might have been revealed, at the end of the eighteenth century and at the beginning of this century, Rousseau and Saussure came along to keep it excluded? How could anyone hope to prove that these weren't the only possible moments when this exclusion could have been revealed?

Wouldn't a theory that the West depends on the exclusion of writing depend on "evidence," evidence that in turn would depend on a hypothesis that it could serve as evidence for?[5] And wouldn't such a process as formation of a hypothesis, discovery of evidence, and presentation of argument in writing be logocentrism of the most banal sort? Or could one merely *believe* such a theory in order to set one's system in motion, believe, perhaps, in a way similar to the way Plato's Socrates agrees to "believe" in the myths of his time in order to get his study of himself underway (*Phaedrus*, sec. 229c)?

Before trying to answer those question, I'd like to look at Derrida's reading of *Phaedrus* itself. For *Phaedrus*, Derrida would have us believe, is the single most important text ever written because it contains the exclusion of writing, the exclusion that inaugurates the West and tends its intellectual life.

III. How the West Was Unaugured

Derrida's reading of *Phaedrus* is, in fact, profoundly troublesome to anyone even slightly persuaded by his theories. This reading unfolds in two stages. First he explains it generally in *Of Grammatology* as he describes what he calls the inauguration of the West. Then he offers an extended reading of *Phaedrus* in "Plato's Pharmacy" (*Dissemination*, pp. 61–171).

The problems are apparent even in *Of Grammatology*, where Derrida repeatedly reads *Phaedrus* at face value. The possibility that Plato *may* be playing, may in fact be toying with the play of meaning himself, never seems to cross Derrida's mind. Derrida reads *Phaedrus* exactly the same way he reads Saussure. "The contamination by writing," he says, the fact or the threat of it, are denounced in the accents of the moralist or preacher by the linguist from Geneva. The tone counts; it is as if, at the moment when the modern science of the logos would come into its autonomy and its scientificity, it became necessary again to attack a heresy. This tone began to make itself heard when, at the moment of already tying the *epistémè* and the *logos* within the same possibility, the *Phaedrus* denounced writing as the intrusion of an artful technique, a forced entry of a totally original sort, an archetypal violence. . . . (*Grammatology*, p. 34)

In other words, the condemnations of writing made by Ammon and Socrates in *Phaedrus* merely repeat exactly what Plato "meant to say," with no possibility of play, deceit, or ambiguity clouding what Plato "meant to say." And this sort of face-value reading of *Phaedrus* persists throughout *Of Grammatology*. "The *Phaedrus*," Derrida argues a few pages later, "condemned writing precisely as play—*paidia*—and opposed such childishness to the adult gravity [*spoudè*] of speech" (p. 50).

After he reads *Phaedrus* and *The Course in General Linguistics* as the univocal voice of the condemnation of writing, Derrida reads Rousseau into the triad. Rousseau, he contends, excludes writing in order to exclude the possibility of the play of meaning. Meaning must *be*; hence, it cannot depend on chance or play: "By this last gesture and by all that it commands in Rousseau's thought, meaning is put out of play. As in all onto-theological metaphysics, as already in Plato" (p. 260). Finally, Derrida apparently thinks one can in fact "know" what Plato "says" without any possibility that Plato says more than one has found or even something different from what one has found. "It is not by chance," he concludes at the end of *Of Grammatology*, "that in mythology, the Egyptian in particular, the god of sciences and technologies is also the god of writing; and that it is he whom Rousseau incriminates in the *Discourse on the Arts and Sciences*. (Plato had already denounced his invention of writing at the end of the *Phaedrus*.)" (p. 313). Such a parenthetical statement, in its off-the-cuff manner, bluntly assumes that one can assert Plato's meaning and that the meaning is absolutely and exactly what it appears on first reading. Were this an isolated parenthetical comment, one might overlook it, but it appears again and again and indeed forms the basis for (one might almost say "inaugurates") the whole Derridean system.

Derrida's close reading of *Phaedrus* itself in *Dissemination* is even more disappointing than the oversimplified history of meaning he offers in *Of Grammatology*. In effect, he demonstrates the following about *Phaedrus*:

1. One cannot translate *Phaedrus* into French. Plato's term *pharmakon*, which plays a key role in *Phaedrus*, demonstrates this impossibility. No French word that carries all the significations associated with the Greek word *pharmakon* exists; thus, whatever partial cognate the translator chooses leaves something important out.

2. Plato cannot write "from scratch." He must borrow arguments from the sophists and repeat words and ideas that have been stated and repeated before him.

3. Plato must use terms whose possible meanings and history of meanings always exceed what Plato himself would like to use the terms for. Since Plato can never reach back to the origin of his vocabulary, that very vocabulary always operates a little beyond either his control or his intention.

4. Plato cannot use his text to present unmediated meaning. Whatever meaning may emerge must forever remain locked inside the play of signification associated with each written signifier.

5. The "owner" of any idea or any expression remains forever in doubt. One can neither show the absolute origin of a thought nor reveal a thought that does not depend on something that came before it.

6. Since Plato did not know "the truth," working backwards to the purest possible understanding of what Plato "meant to say" would not place a reader nearer "truth."

7. The concept "truth" in *Phaedrus* is in fact a journey dependent on an endless series of metaphors, each of which would exceed any possible absolute definition.

8. Since "truth" must be gone for someone to seek it, Plato's text depends for its existence on the absence of the divine vision that would be available were the lovers capable of seeing their god and traveling in his sphere.

Having demonstrated these "problems" in *Phaedrus*, Derrida considers it "deconstructed," and he then announces the effects of this "deconstruction": (1) The most rigorous, canny sort of reader can deconstruct *Phaedrus* and catch Plato being used *by* writing rather than using it himself. (2) After such a rigorous deconstruction, the reader of the deconstructor's text sees that Plato lost control of *Phaedrus* and sees *Phaedrus* disintegrate under the deconstructor's careful, solicitous gaze. (3) Plato tries to save the logos by privileging it. To do this, he must make the logos a purified form of writing; thus, Plato is caught out in his own game because the logos is always already writing.

What's really surprising about all this is that it isn't very surprising. The first eight points aren't much of an accomplishment. Surely no one who has written and read much can be too shocked upon learning that translations never quite succeed, or that the overdetermined, tautological process of vocabulary definitions proceeds infinitely, or that Plato did not know "the truth," or that a reader who managed to gather all and only that meaning Plato "meant to write" would not know "the truth," or that the history of ideas extends forever both synchronically and diachronically, or that the absence of pure "truth" allowed the play of signification to start in the first place. As for the three points in which *Phaedrus* is supposedly deconstructed, the first two indicate a kind of smug self-congratulation that simply isn't justified. Derrida has not reduced Plato to the sort of helpless frustration described on the last four pages of "Plato's Pharmacy." If one grants, as I would be willing to do, that Derrida's first eight points can be demonstrated, by no means does that "prove" the last three. Indeed, the first eight points, rather than "deconstructing" *Phaedrus* and demonstrating its inability to speak itself, merely begin the reading process by opening the dialectic that plays throughout all of Plato's texts. It almost seems that because Derrida cannot extrapolate the closed, pure finality of "truth" from *Phaedrus*, he wishes to expose it as a failure. Were Derrida's name not one to conjure with these days, one might almost accuse him of naïveté about how to deal with and what to expect from a complex text.

The third deconstructive claim, the one about the exclusion of writing and valorizing of speech, is even stranger than the other two. Leaving aside the problem of authorial intention introduced by the fact that Plato does not speak directly anywhere in *Phaedrus*, one can turn to Socrates' statements about true and false writing and, to keep the reading simple, pretend that Socrates merely speaks Plato's meaning. The two key passages read as follows:

[1.] SOCRATES: Now can we distinguish another kind of communication which is the legitimate brother of written speech and see how it comes into being and how much better and more effective it is?

PHAEDRUS: What do you mean and how does it come about?

SOCRATES: I mean the kind that is written on the soul of the hearer together with understanding; that knows how to defend itself, and can distinguish between those it should address and those in whose presence it should be silent.

PHAEDRUS: You mean the living and animate speech of a man with knowledge, of which written speech might fairly be called a kind of shadow.

SOCRATES: Exactly. . . . (sec. 276a–b)

[2.] SOCRATES: To believe, on the other hand, that a written composition on any subject must be to a large extent the creation of fancy; that nothing worth serious attention has ever been written in prose or verse—or spoken for that matter, if by speaking one means the kind of recitation that aims merely at creating belief, without any attempt at instruction by question and answer; that even the best of such compositions can do no more than help the memory of those who already know; whereas lucidity and finality and serious importance are to be found only in words spoken by way of instruction or, to use a truer phrase, written on the soul of the hearer to enable him to learn about the right, the beautiful and the good; finally, to realize that such

> spoken truths are to be reckoned a man's legitimate
> sons, primarily if they originate within himself, but
> to a secondary degree if what we may call their
> children and kindred come to birth, as they should,
> in the minds of others—to believe this, I say, and
> to let all else go is to be the sort of man, Phaedrus,
> that you and I might well pray that we may both
> become. (secs. 277e–288a)

Derrida would have us believe that these passages constitute the
gesture that founded the West. The gesture accomplishes, according to Derrida, two purposes crucial to what has come to
be the tradition of Western metaphysics. First, by valorizing
speech and excluding writing, the gesture keeps self-presence
intact. Even though every Western thinker's thoughts require
writing, excluding writing keeps the infinitely deferred play of
writing from contaminating the absolute existence of those
thoughts. Second, the gesture protects the possibility of truth
by allowing it to live in presence, which, of course, remains
intact through the exclusion of writing.

Derrida thinks he has caught Plato because when Plato wishes
to describe the medium spoken in pure self-presence, the medium in which truth appears, he compares that medium to writing; thus, Derrida claims to have revealed speech as always
already writing. His conclusion is that neither pure self-presence
nor the so-called truth it protects exists. What exists instead is
infinite play. This conclusion raises a variety of interesting requirements. First, it requires a Plato quite naïve about the metaphorical, playing nature of language. According to Derrida,
there is no possibility at all that Plato knew he was doubling
and perhaps confusing his metaphors and doing so intentionally
when he elevated speech over writing and then in order to
"clarify" what sort of speech he meant, turned it back into a type
of writing.

Second, Derrida's conclusion requires a Plato who wishes to
protect some sort of closed truth. But doesn't Plato at every point
constantly remind his reader of the complexity of both his texts
and their meaning? Does anything in any of his dialogues imply
that Plato himself has figured out the truth and then inscribed,
or perhaps spoken, it to the reader? In the passage above, Plato's
Socrates already says he is not the sort of person who can write

on the soul. This, in fact, is the sort of person that Plato's Socrates wishes to *become*. And as this same Socrates makes quite clear, the end of such a process of becoming is the end of the human condition. Hasn't Derrida (1) merely repeated *Phaedrus* by showing that it begins an endless search and then (2) claimed to have deconstructed it because the search it begins is endless? More importantly, hasn't Derrida shown that Plato must (1) use metaphors to speak at all and then claimed (2) that Plato's text finally wrote Plato because metaphors don't repeat exactly what they supposedly stand for? Does Derrida think Plato didn't know that? Surely Socrates' description of the soul makes clear the impossibility of any human being's having the power whether in speaking or writing, simply to *present* meaning: "This must suffice concerning soul's immortality; concerning its nature we must give the following account. To describe it as it is would require a long exposition of which only a god is capable; but it is within the power of man to say in shorter compass what it resembles. Let us adopt this method, and compare the soul to a winged charioteer and his team acting together" (sec. 246a). Still leaving aside the complication that Plato himself does not speak this directly, a hedge at least as canny as any of Derrida's hedges of deconstruction, clearly Socrates admits that he can only represent what he as a mortal cannot know. And it does not take tremendous insight to see that he represents this impossible knowledge with a metaphor that in and of itself no human can know: a winged charioteer.

By showing that truth exists only in its absence, that metaphors operate both by representing inexactly and by playing infinitely, in short, by showing the problems that language creates, Derrida hasn't deconstructed *Phaedrus*. At best, he has (1) merely outlined some of the complexities that Plato obviously knew he had to deal with, (2) destroyed the ground on which a naïve reading that seeks the closure of truth in *Phaedrus* could be built, and thus (3) described the ever-open dialectical nature of the process of reading *Phaedrus*, a process that surely would not have surprised Plato, this consummate writer who hid himself everywhere in his texts.

If Derrida's conclusions about *Phaedrus* are, finally, disappointing, a close look at the methods he uses to reach those conclusions shows why. For example, though he claims to have shown how Plato's text exceeds Plato's control, Derrida himself appears calmly in control of his own text, almost to the point of complacency. Admittedly, Derrida begins his deconstruction with his usual hedges about a text's ability to speak its own meaning, and admittedly he claims only to tell the truth of Plato's text whereas Plato, according to Derrida, attempts to tell the truth of the truth. Nevertheless, throughout "Plato's Pharmacy" Derrida places markers that show he believes his own essay knows where it is going, has its own meaning present at every point in its saying, retains full control over itself, and believes itself capable of asserting control over Plato's text.

At the beginning of chapter 2 of "Plato's Pharmacy," as he demonstrates the impossibility of translating the term *pharmakon* into French, Derrida says, "according to a necessity that will not cease to become clearer to us from now on, the *logoi* are the children" (p. 78). Thus, even at the beginning of his own text, Derrida knows where his text is going and knows that he will gradually reveal both the laws of and the failures of Plato's text. At the end of this same chapter, Derrida's certainty about his ability to control his own text while at the same time revealing Plato's inability to control *Phaedrus* appears again, this time as Derrida turns away from his study of the term "logos" and begins a study of mythological gods of writing: "We will let these yarns of suns and sons spin on for a while. Up to now we have only followed this line so as to move from *logos* to the father, so as to tie speech to the *kurios*, the master, the lord, another name given in the *Republic* to the good-sun-capital-father (508a). Later, within the same tissue, within the same texts, we will draw on other filial filaments, pull the same strings once more, and witness the weaving or unraveling of other designs" (p. 84). Derrida clearly knows what his text is going to say. He expects no surprises (though, no doubt, he expects us to be surprised) as he presents the controlled meaning that is everywhere present and under control in his own essay.

In chapter 4, as he shows how Plato tries to control the opposing forces that contend on the site of the term *pharmakon*, Derrida reveals both that he knows already what he will gradually show us and that he can in fact show us what he knows with no danger that his own showing will tangle itself and disintegrate as *Phaedrus* does: "It could be shown, and we will try to do so when the time comes, that this blockage of the passage of opposing values is itself already an effect of 'Platonism,' the consequence of something already at work in the translated text, in the relation between 'Plato' and his 'language'" (p. 98). On two occasions later in chapter 4, Derrida's self-assured confidence in his own text's ability to escape the sort of disintegration it reveals in other texts appears again. In the first instance, he claims the ability both to "understand Plato" and to displace the entire tradition of writing that extends from Plato to Saussure: "To come to an understanding with Plato, as it is sketched out in this [Derrida's] text, is already to slip away from the recognized models of commentary. . . . If the reader has any doubt, he is invited to reread the preceding paragraph. Every model of classical reading is exceeded there at some point. . . ." (p. 104). In the second instance, Derrida feels confident enough of his control of Plato to generalize about what Plato wanted desperately and could not have: "What Plato *dreams* of is a memory with no sign" (p. 109).

Thus, Derrida's text, which he compares to a military campaign through Plato's territory (p. 96), claims throughout to manifest what Hartman calls totalization, the ability of the meaning a text carries to be everywhere present and under control in every part of the text. Yet Derrida uses this totalization to reveal the inability of all other writers to achieve such totalization. Derrida's belief that he can totalize and control in *his* text the ways other writers fail to totalize and control *their* texts operates as a sort of theology, almost a dogma. For example, after tracing out a brief summary of mythological gods of writing, Derrida begins to trace out the play of meaning associated with the term *pharmakon*. Between the two tracings, he announces the assumption that sets those tracings in motion:

> Let us return to the text of Plato, assuming we have ever really left it. The word *pharmakon* is caught in a chain of significations. The play of that chain seems systematic. But the system here is not, simply, that of the intentions of an author who goes by the name of Plato. The system is not primarily that of what someone *meant-to-say*. Finely regulated communications are established, through the play of language, among diverse functions of the word and, within it, among diverse strata or regions of culture. These communications or corridors of meaning can sometimes be declared or clarified by Plato when he plays upon

them "voluntarily," a word we put in quotation marks because what it designates, to content ourselves with remaining within the closure of these oppositions, is only a mode of "submission" to the necessities of a given "language." (pp. 95–96)

Thirty-five pages later, having shown how the word *pharmakos* appears in *Phaedrus* even though it is a word that Plato not only did not write in *Phaedrus* but never wrote anywhere, Derrida goes beyond mere assumption to belief:

> In a word, we do not believe that there exists, in all rigor, a Platonic text, closed upon itself, complete with its inside and its outside. Not that one must then consider that it is leaking on all sides and can be drowned confusedly in the undifferentiated generality of its element. Rather, provided the articulations are rigorously and prudently recognized, one should simply be able to untangle the hidden forces of attraction linking a present word with an absent word in the text of Plato. Some such force, given the *system* of the language, cannot *not* have acted upon the writing and the reading of this text. (p. 130).

Even if one leaves aside quibbles over the possible meanings of Derrida's own words (e.g., "believe," "exist," "all rigor," and "prudently"), quibbles that seem insignificant given the revelation Derrida claims to offer, this passage clearly reveals that Derrida's *belief* sets his reading in motion. And Derrida can no more prove this belief than Plato can present the truth. One must either accept it or reject it theologically. If one rejects the belief, then one is apt to believe that words an author never wrote do not appear in that author's texts. If one accepts the belief, then one is apt to find numerous words never actually written and to discover that those that were actually written turn out to operate in ways the author not only did not intend but in fact tried mightily to prevent.

By assuming the beliefs that the system of signification always exceeds and defeats whatever a writer "meant to say" and that no text closed upon itself is possible, Derrida himself escapes the implications of both beliefs, and thus he can matter-of-factly say what Plato tried to say and could not say. In other words,

Derrida both discovers authorial intention and shows how no system in which authorial intention can occur exists. He can show us what is not there by showing us how what is not there cannot be there.

Look, for example, at what Derrida's *belief* allows him to write. It allows him to write down Plato's intention: "Plato is bent on presenting writing as an occult, and therefore suspect, power" (p. 97). It allows him to expose both the skeleton in Plato's closet and the inaugural role played by that skeleton as the paradigm for all post-Platonic Western thought: "Writing appears to Plato (and after him to all of philosophy, which is as such constituted in this gesture) as that process of redoubling in which we are fatally (en)trained: the supplement of a supplement, the signifier, the representative of a representative" (p. 109). Derrida's belief gives him a point of view from which to control the absolute operation of Plato's text by comprehending that operation: "The *pharmakon*, without being anything in itself, always exceeds them [the contradictions and pairs of opposites that finally undo *Phaedrus*] in constituting their bottomless fund. It keeps itself forever in reserve even though it has no fundamental profundity nor ultimate locality. We will watch it infinitely promise itself and endlessly vanish through concealed doorways that shine like mirrors and open onto a labyrinth" (pp. 127–28).

Finally, the belief allows Derrida to believe he has mastered Plato and presented that mastery in "Plato's Pharmacy." On the last four pages, as he claims to have caught Plato by showing Plato's inability to control the significations of *Phaedrus*, Derrida thinks he has reduced Plato to an impotent analyst bending over farther and farther, stopping his ears to avoid utter confusion as he attempts to separate two repetitions of the same (different) thing(s) he is trying to write down.

IV. Consequences, Or Truth?

Of course, there is no way to explain what leads Derrida to attempt showing that Plato, rather than using language, got caught being used *by* language. My hunch, however, is that Derrida suffers from a radically oversimplified, even nostalgic, conception of what Plato, and other thinkers since his time, considered truth to be. Derrida betrays this conception in several places. For example, in showing that Thoth, Plato's Egyptian god of writing, prevents the closure of dialectics by mimicking it, Derrida argues that this very capability of mimicking prevents the final disclosure of truth. Thoth, Derrida contends, "would be the mediating movement of dialectics if he did not also mimic it, indefinitely preventing it, through this ironic doubling, from reaching some final fulfillment or eschatological reappropriation. Thoth is never present. Nowhere does he appear in person. No being-there can properly be *his own*" (p. 93). Derrida clearly believes that the dialectic Plato's Socrates advocates will never achieve final fulfillment. Nothing in *Phaedrus*, however, ever suggests it will, as I tried to show in chapter 4 above. The dialectic Socrates describes for humans merely begins a journey, a journey that no human could ever complete.

Derrida proves that the human condition, the linguistic condition, precludes absolute truth, and as a result he thinks he has overturned Plato. In fact, however, the forever out-of-place, displaced text that Plato left never for a moment claims to be the closure of truth. And even if one accepts Socrates' second speech in *Phaedrus* and his dicta on truth, rhetoric, and writing that come after that speech as an exact transcription of what Plato "meant to say," a reading that I find hopelessly naïve and simplistic, even if one accepts such a reading, those speeches and those dicta present truth as a possibility unavailable to humans. Truth is a journey as two lovers begin to explore the play of meaning in order to see where it goes and how it works. This journey requires a lifetime of trying to know and come near the right, the beautiful, and the good—concepts that never pretend to be other than metaphors, concepts that *present* themselves as incomplete and inexact replacements for what humans can neither know nor say. And if one reads Plato's text as a truly complex weaving of the play of meaning, any sort of closed explanation of *Phaedrus* would immediately call itself into question. Plato was a writer every bit as (p)sophisticated as Derrida. He understood both the forever-playing nature of the search for meaning *and* the danger that writing presents in its ability to seem to end that play. Derrida can't master Plato's text by showing its inability to close down in truth. What Derrida can do is reveal his own oversimplified conception of the complex metaphor Plato uses and names truth, a metaphor Plato uses without ever expecting anyone to work that metaphor back to some final and complete rending of the veil.

Derrida's oversimplified conception of truth appears in its starkest form at the end of "Plato's Pharmacy," where he begins his claim to have deconstructed *Phaedrus*, which, since he believes *Phaedrus* is the gesture that inaugurates the West, is the same as claiming to have deconstructed the West. He states his triumph over both by claiming to have shown that there is no difference between grammar and ontology. I quote Derrida's conclusion at length:

> What distinguishes dialectics from grammar appears twofold: on the one hand, the linguistic units it is concerned with are larger than the word . . . ; on the other, dialectics is always guided by an intention of *truth*. It can only be satisfied by the presence of the *eidos*, which is here both the signified and the referent: the thing itself. The distinction between grammar and dialectics can thus only in all rigor be established at the point where truth is fully present and fills the logos. But what the parricide in the *Sophist* establishes is not only that any *full, absolute* presence of what *is* is impossible; not only that any full intuition of truth, any truth-filled intuition, is impossible; but that the very condition of discourse—true or false— is the diacritical principle of the *sumplokē*. If truth is the presence of the *eidos*, it must always, on pain of mortal blinding by the sun's fires, come to terms with relation, nonpresence, and thus nontruth. It then follows that the absolute precondition for a rigorous difference between grammar and dialectics (or ontology) cannot in principle be fulfilled. (p. 166)

Derrida's conclusion, then, is that Plato cannot simply present the truth in *Phaedrus*, or anywhere else for that matter. Having shown the richness of the play of meaning in *Phaedrus*, Derrida somehow jumps to the conclusion that he has deconstructed it, leaving Plato baffled as his own text escapes him. Is it possible that anyone who has read much of Plato and thought about the ways Plato presents his discourses—always out of time, always out of the mouths of others, always using discourse he has borrowed, always calling attention to the writing in which he is caught, always pointing out the impossibility of saying "what he means," always keeping the movement of dialectics open as the characteristic of being human—is it possible that someone can come along in the twentieth century after two and a half millennia of constant reinterpretation of the Platonic canon and think he has discovered something when he claims to show that Plato's texts do not vanish in the presence of truth and that truth itself is what humans by definition cannot know? Is that possible?

V. Inauguration

Derrida's most persistent claim in all his texts, and especially in those written before 1974, is that no origin exists. If one tries to work backwards from language to the meaning that language means, what one finds is language. But Derrida catches himself in his own trap with his own word. When he argues, as he does in almost every text before 1974, that Plato "inaugurates" the West, and that *Phaedrus* contains the gesture by which this inauguration occurs, in fact Derrida sets his own discourse up on an origin: the origin of Plato. He argues that Plato could not say the truth; he could only talk about it in its absence. Thus, Plato keeps truth alive by locating it in speech. This, according to Derrida, allows Plato to retain truth in its absence while using writing as the medium that merely serves speech and represents truth. Derrida, in contrast, *really* knows the truth, and the truth *is* writing: recursive, repetitious, never finished, never present; in short, an eternal différance. Hasn't Derrida in fact merely described the operation of *Phaedrus,* the operation of dialectic in general, and then claimed to have defeated it? Hasn't Derrida himself merely repeated Plato and then claimed to have shown Plato something not only that Plato already knew but also that Plato said better in every way?

But in repeating Plato, in showing that the play of language opens the human condition by precluding the appearance of truth, hasn't Derrida also omitted something? In seeking the right, the beautiful, and the good, in thinking of truth as possibility, Plato's Socrates inaugurates a method that forever holds everything open to question. No system, no belief, no action can escape Socrates' dialectical scrutiny. The difference between the scrutiny inaugurated by Plato's Socrates and that inaugurated by Derrida is that Derrida removed the metaphors right, beautiful, and good, and then defined the truth of the truth as *impossibility*. Since belief activates both these moments of repetition, the question that remains is which version to choose: Truth as possibility, or its Other. Surely the difference between Plato and Derrida is that Plato demands that we decide what to do now that we know we are human; Derrida, on the other hand, demands that we continue infinitely to prove that we *are* human.

△

8.
WEAK DISCOURSE
AND STRONG
DISCOURSE

"Sophistês" originally meant "skilled craftsman" or "wise
man." The specialized meaning "professional teacher" did not
come into use until the end of the fifth century B.C., the period
of the travelling teachers. The bad sense of the word
developed almost immediately; Aristotle summed up the
Sophist's art as "the appearance, not the reality, of wisdom",
and the Sophist as one who makes money out of this
pretence.
     The title was nevertheless used in Roman Imperial times for
"professor" of rhetoric, or prose writer, without any bad
meaning.
                    Kathleen Freeman, *Ancilla to the Pre-Socratic Philosophers*

When Plato's Socrates demands that truth precede speaking or writing and when Derrida shows the deconstructability
of every metaphysical position, including his own, each in his
own way forecloses on the possibility that writing can present
and justify a conclusion. I recognize, therefore, that in ending
this book with a theory for composition studies, I defy both Plato
and Derrida by inviting Platonists to show that I did not know
the truth before I wrote and Derrideans to show the deconstructability of my claim. Undeniably, each of those acts of reading can be performed on my text. My purpose in working through
the long struggle that precedes this chapter has been to clear a
space in which composition studies finally can be liberated from
philosophy. Plato lays a curse on rhetoric and writing by requiring the rhetor to know the truth before attempting persuasion and by claiming that truth, by definition, cannot occur in

writing. Derrida lays a curse on the entire tradition of Western metaphysics *since* Plato by showing that philosophy never for one moment escapes writing or rhetoric. Thus, from the perspective of rhetoric and writing, Plato and Derrida are two moments of the same maneuver. One argues that truth is a possibility and then sets out on a quest whose destination is the end of the human condition. The other shows that any sort of claim to truth conceals not only from its reader but also from itself the process of différance that forever prevents truth either from appearing (which would be the transcendental signified) or from having a place in which to appear (which would be pure self-presence).

Liberating composition studies from philosophy does not, of course, obviate philosophy, nor is it meant to; rather, it prevents philosophy from occupying any position that would allow it to judge rhetoric and writing. Even after liberation, writers need the Platonic ideal, the notion of the forever-absent truth toward which discourse moves. At the same time, writers need deconstructive strategy to prevent any discourse from presenting itself *as* the truth. What exempts rhetoric and writing from any condemnation by philosophy is that all philosophy, including Platonism and deconstruction, is both written and rhetorical. Rhetoric, as the sophists tried to explain so many years ago, is the prior medium in which the possibility and impossibility of truth play out an endless struggle.

Operating in this prior medium—that is, operating like sophists and as rhetoricians—is far from easy. Writers who remain rhetoricians must resist the urge to give in either to Plato or to Derrida. Writers who give in to Plato in effect cease to be writers and become philosophers on a quest that will never produce any inscription at all, a quest that requires writers constantly to admit abashedly that they do not know the truth. Writers who give in to Derrida become philosophers who never finish unworking all those discourses that conceal or remain ignorant of their own written rhetoricity; such writers feel obligated always to work backwards in order to show that what would be required to begin a discourse is already gone. Writers who remain rhetoricians, in contrast, keep both Plato and Derrida at work at all times during the composing process, but forever subordinate them to that process so that neither the Platonic search for truth nor the Derridean strategy of deconstruction overwhelms the process.

In this volume's first four chapters, I try to show that Plato's philosophical attempt to judge rhetoric and writing traps itself in endless impossibilities and self-contradictions. After trying to "represent" Derridean analysis as persuasively as I can in chapters 5 and 6 (a "representation" I think necessary given the way Derrida and his followers usually write and the hostility Derridean texts often generate), I try to show in chapter 7 that Derrida's attempt to clear away philosophical tradition in order to begin philosophy anew collapses as the tradition from which it grows reasserts itself. Throughout all this, my strategy has been to allow philosophy, the discourse that would like to privilege itself at the expense of rhetoric and writing, to cancel itself, leaving an opening for rhetoric and writing where they are neither prejudged as inferior nor locked permanently inside their own forever-unfinished process. Plato, who will settle for nothing less than truth, cancels Derrida, who in turn cancels Plato by writing so as to show the impossibility of other writers. What keeps both alive, what makes both available, what makes both possible are rhetoric and writing. Because my own position, which is essentially sophistical, is so much closer to Derrida's than to Plato's, it is, however, important to reassert that Derrida has only half the system of rhetoric. As he shows the written rhetoricity of every text, he himself uses rhetoric, which immediately calls his own writing into question. At the same time, he bases his operation on the Platonic idea that the truth of the truth is written rhetoricity. In other words, Derrida knows, in quite a Platonic way, what the truth of the truth in fact is.

Not surprisingly, nothing in this chapter is new either to the world, given that Protagoras and Gorgias have been around for better than two millennia, or to recent discourse, given Richard Weaver's demonstration of the sermonic, audience-centered nature of all discourse and Richard Lanham's argument that the rhetorical nature of all intellectual discourse should place rhetoric at the center of the university curriculum. Nevertheless, I would like to advance the following idea in hopes of providing a frame for debate about the meaning of composition studies. Some of the words I will use are, I think, new to that field, if not to the world.

Statements like the following have come down through the ages as manifestations of the corrupt, nihilistic evil of sophistry. "Of all things," writes Protagoras, "the measure is Man, of the things that are, that they are, and of the things that are not, that they are not." "About the gods," he writes elsewhere, "I am not able to know whether they exist or do not exist, nor what they are like in form; for the factors preventing knowledge are many: the obscurity of the subject, and the shortness of human life." Protagoras anticipated much of poststructural analysis when, according to Diogenes Laertius, he said any argument carries its contradiction with it (Freeman, pp. 125–26).

According to both Isocrates and Sextus, passages in Gorgias's no-longer-extant texts argue that nothing exists. If anything did exist, no one would be able to comprehend it. And if someone could comprehend it, that person would be unable to communicate the comprehension. "Being," the extant canon says, "is unrecognizable unless it succeeds in seeming, and seeming is weak unless it succeeds in being." Perhaps most damning of all, Gorgias's last two arguments in his oration defending Helen seem to exempt people from responsibility for their actions. Those persuaded by the clever, he contends, should be held blameless for their actions because the bewitching, hypnotic power of persuasion overcomes everyone sometime. By like token, those seduced by the passion of love, because they have fallen under the power of the god of love and because the need to love is a human frailty, should at worst be pitied; they are the victims of fate merely obeying the compulsion of love, not free individuals with the strength of will to make a choice.

And if one moves away from such overriding issues as the existence of god, the nature of being, and the possibility of morality to so mundane an issue as pedagogy, again the sophists are damned: first, because they taught by requiring their students to imitate models slavishly; second, because they made no effort to distinguish what one ought to say from what one could say, preferring rather to show students how to make the worse case seem the better.

Rejecting Protagoras, Gorgias, and all their followers as relativistic nihilists whose ideas would lead to social decay, sexual perversity, and anarchy creates a comfortable certainty for Western thought. By rejecting sophistry, Western thought can play itself out as a history in which truth, after much tribulation, triumphs through its own self-righteous virtue and then remains available in the West forever. In this history, the True, the Beautiful, and the Good come under bitter attack by the sophists, who believe, or at least dupe their students into believing, that the True doesn't exist, and if it did no one could know it, and if anyone knew it, what that person knew would be incommunicable. On the other side, there are the philosophers, particularly Socrates, his student Plato, and then his student Aristotle. Right away, everyone can tell the good guys, who suffer poverty and even execution in defense of Truth, from the bad guys, who become affluent by flattering and deluding those with power and money. But in the end, the innate superiority of philosophy over sophistry (and over sophistry's minions, rhetoric and writing) becomes apparent, and the West begins its inexorable journey toward Truth. This Truth forever exerts its power in the form Plato gave it, that is, the form of an absence. Thus, the West can move toward the True and never have to answer as to its whereabouts on the journey because the truth of the True is that one never gets there. In this history, science discovers the truth of nature, social science discovers the truth of humanity, literature and philosophy express the profound understanding of great souls, and so forth. In this history, the sophists are absolutely necessary; they must be defeated and then remain forever available in that defeat. Their silent, marginalized defeat keeps the Platonic quest in motion.

But what would happen if one were to attempt to articulate some principles of the sophistry worked out by Protagoras and Gorgias, that is, the principles of sophistry instead of those of *p*sophistry? What might those principles be? There are, I think, six that permeate the limited extant work of Protagoras and Gorgias:

1. If permanent (or divine) truth exists, humans by definition cannot know it, nor can any of their systems of communication convey it. Thus, humans must deal in probabilities, which, though never the closure of truth, allow arguments not only to be made but also to be evaluated, evaluated using criteria freely available to everyone. To a sophist, therefore, rhetoric becomes crucially important, for rhetoric, and the powerful discourse it generates, becomes one of the keys to discovering the probable. In contrast to Plato, who will accept nothing but permanent truth freed from any temporal circumstances, the sophists offer a rhetoric for the *kairos* (situation) by taking into

account all the possibilities and limitations any given situation creates. In contrast to Derrida, who keeps the operation of deconstruction in motion, the sophists allow themselves to be persuaded by an argument while never forgetting the inadequate, deceitful foundation that enabled the argument.

2. Sophistry is a way to make choices in a world of probability. This process of choice-making occurs both privately, as one uses the power of rhetoric and writing to persuade oneself, and publicly, as one attempts to persuade others. In other words, sophistry, in conjunction with rhetoric and writing, is the process whereby the individual develops an ethical self.

3. The language of persuasive power generated by rhetoric and writing compensates for the unknowability of truth. While all language suffers from obscurities and deficiencies, these very limitations liberate human beings and generate possibilities for being human.

4. Language has the power to fabricate what seem to be realities and to generate belief. Without such a persuasive language (*peithô*), people would become incapacitated. All people must be willing to be persuaded both by themselves and by others. The deception and self-deception of rhetoric and writing allow societies to emerge and to sustain themselves. They also allow individuals to choose how to live their lives. But well-trained sophists know exactly how any decision or action emerged. They also know both how to undermine such decisions and actions and how to explain their effect on others.

5. Sophistry teaches us how to speak so as to push understanding beyond its current limits.

6. Sophistry teaches us to see how any argument can be pursued not only to an extreme but also to a paradoxical conclusion.

No, these principles don't seem so radical after all, especially in the wake of poststructural analysis. Once they are extricated from philosophical condemnation, they merely describe the foundation for any democratic society. Both the idea and the operation of democracy, after all, depend on rhetoric and writing. Just as Protagoras's sophistry throve in Periclean Athens, it thrives in any democracy. Democracy, one might say (and I confess to believing), always allows sophistry because the opinion of the majority makes the government. More than allowing sophistry, however, democracy renders sophistry necessary for there must be some effective means of generating opinion in a majority of the population.

In spite of popular conceptions, the sophistry of Protagoras and Gorgias does not require cynical pandering to the base, flattery-prone, ignorant masses. While both Protagoras and Gorgias clearly believed that humans were not likely to be other than human (yes, that belief depends on *probability*, not truth, but it is a probability with a long history of successful prediction), and while they believed strongly in the power of rhetoric to shape all human things, they also believed that humans could make better and worse choices and that the value of rhetoric, in spite of its capability of being misused, was to make the better choice prevail. Though each admits that rhetoric can never lead to an absolute best choice, each shows how rhetoric can lead to a best choice at a given time, in a given place, with a given set of circumstances. It is in the interest of such choice making that Protagoras separates discourse into what Gilbert Romeyer-Dherbey calls strong discourse and weak discourse (pp. 22–28).

Any purely private discourse, Romeyer-Dherbey summarizes Protagoras as saying, remains weak because it remains untested in the arena of public life. In contrast, any discourse that has been expressed publicly and found adherents becomes strong, deriving its strength from its ability to withstand the scrutiny of public life. The most important aspect of strong discourse, however, is its tolerance for, even encouragement of, other discourses. Protagoras clearly saw that any strong discourse generates not only its opposite, but also a host of other strong competitors. The strength of sophistry (dare one say the strength of democracy) lies first in the sophists' awareness of how rhetoric and writing create belief and action; second in the sophists' willingness to hold all belief permanently in question (without disbelieving); and third in the sophists' ability to take action only when that action can support itself with a strong discourse, a discourse whose history of general persuasiveness is long and whose opposite has been given every opportunity to be heard. Strong discourse can exist, therefore, only in a cacophonous plurality of other voices, many of which are also strong. Only weak discourse seeks to silence that cacophony. Strong discourse never succeeds in silencing all its competitors, for no discourse can remain strong without being surrounded by competitors. One must not, however, underestimate the attraction of weak discourse, for it always presents itself in the guise of the messiah or the philosopher-king—the one who claims to offer truth but in fact supplies only the silence that must occur when rhetoric, persuasion, writing, and sophistry, those most human of things, have been precluded.

Strong discourse, in spite of its democratic nature, does not imply that all opinions reveal wisdom; quite the contrary, it presumes that those with the best opinions will find a way to propose those opinions persuasively to others. Implicit in the idea of strong discourse is the belief that wisdom consists in knowing how in persuasion and argumentation to replace personal discourse with global discourse by replacing a weak conception with a rich one. Strong discourse cannot, of course, protect against brief periods of dominance by weak discourse masquerading as strong. The frailty of weak discourse becomes apparent, however, as soon as the weak discourse attempts to silence its competitors for fear they will expose its weakness. Strong discourse remains persuasive, but it never becomes tyrannical or terrorist, and it *never* exists alone.

Of course the only truth available in strong discourse is that made by humans, and this "made" truth is critical truth, not closed truth. It always asks what value a discourse has, yet it never forgets that the act of posing the question What value do you have? raises the question What is the value of value? Strong discourse, in short, encompasses Plato's dialectic by putting all received notions in question and then seeking constantly for a better truth; at the same time, it encompasses Derrida's deconstruction by remaining constantly aware of the process of différance through which apparent or probable truth becomes itself. While it is certainly true that a sophist knows how to make the worse case appear the better, it is also true that those with a sophistical education know how to recognize that trick when someone else tries to pull it. A society with enough sophists, therefore, is fairly well insulated against the worse case presenting itself as strong discourse and getting away with the trick.

In short, the purpose of this book (however infra dig it may be to write a book with so banal a thing as a purpose) is to argue that the teaching of writing should help students learn to seek strong discourse. Such an argument is admittedly mere sophistry. I believe, however, that such an argument can be made once the deception of Plato's written, psophistical, rhetoric has been exposed. I also believe that Derrida is essential to composition studies, for without him, we lack the reading strategy to reveal Plato's self-deconstructing psophistry. But in spite of our need for Derrida, I believe those of us who work in composition studies cannot stop with him; if we do, we run the risk of becoming philosophers just like him. Our true theoretical source is Derrida's predecessors, those voices that Platonism and the Western quest for Truth have kept silent all these years, the voices of Protagoras and Gorgias. Perhaps more to the point, Derrida remains necessary only as long as someone tries to play the role of philosopher-king, the know-it-all who has seen the True and come to tell us about it.

The direction composition studies have taken over the last twenty years has, in my opinion, been clearly sophistical. As we have moved farther and farther from neo-Platonic notions that good writing comes from some sort of divine inspiration toward notions that good writing can be, even must be, *learned;* as we have made the writing classroom increasingly collaborative where the teacher plays the role of philosopher-king less and less and the role of discourse facilitator more and more, we have moved toward the time when strong discourse can actually occur in the writing classroom. Strong discourse in the classroom, like strong discourse anywhere else, will, of course, derive its strength from its ability to persuade adherents, not from its ability to satisfy the opinion of one teacher, who finally plays the role of tyrant. Strong discourse will also require a kind of pluralism that makes the teacher-centered classroom difficult, if not impossible. Clearly most of us have some distance to go before we discover a way to allow strong discourse to occur in our classes, but merely recognizing that any *single* discourse, even the teacher's, must be weak discourse is an accomplishment given the prejudices against sophistry that dominate both Plato's academy and society at large.

Having watched the chaos that erupted so frequently as Athens, Thebes, and Sparta each struggled in turn to establish hegemony over its neighbors, Isocrates warns against following those who believe they have exact knowledge of how society ought to be arranged (*Isocrates*, vol. 2, sec. 8). Later he explains the conception of human knowledge that supports his educational system: "Since it is not in the nature of man to attain a science by the possession of which we can know positively what we should do or what we should say, in the next resort I hold that man to be wise who is able by his powers of conjecture to arrive generally at the best course, and I hold that man to be a philosopher who occupies himself with the studies from which he will most quickly gain that kind of insight" (*Isocrates*, vol. 2, sec. 271).

For Isocrates, as well as for his teacher Gorgias and his predecessor Protagoras, rhetoric and writing belong at the center of the curriculum because rhetoric and writing are the ways to make choices in a world of probability. Sophistical rhetoric, therefore, is both a study of how to make choices and a study of how choices form character and make good citizens. From the sophists, I believe, one learns how to seek and how to value strong discourse. And strong discourse is the lifeblood of democracy. In short, we do not want our students to write like Plato and we do not want them to write like Derrida, but we may need to use a good bit of Derrida against Plato and then a little Plato against Derrida to liberate ourselves from philosophy and enable ourselves to begin teaching like Protagoras, Gorgias, and Isocrates. It would, after all, be far from a bad thing to be called Professor of Rhetoric and Prose Writer.

NOTES
WORKS CITED
INDEX

NOTES

1. Plato's (Soul) Writing

1. Most of the quotations from *Phaedrus* and the "Seventh Letter" are from the Hamilton translations, listed in the Works Cited. Citations from these translations will include only the section numbers and letters. For quotations from the Hackforth or Jowett translations, the translator's last name as well as the section number(s) and letter(s) will be cited.

2. Two recent books attest to the importance of Plato's attacks on writing to the composition field: *Essays on Classical Rhetoric and Modern Discourse* (Conners, Ede, and Lunsford) and *The Rhetorical Tradition and Modern Writing* (Murphy). Both books contain essay-length studies on the importance of *Phaedrus*, and allusions to *Phaedrus* crop up in many of the other essays in these books. Also, in 1981 an entire issue of *Rhetoric Society Quarterly* (vol. 9), which included nine articles, was dedicated to *Phaedrus*. See also Walter.

3. There are many, many such defenses. The two most recent are Burger (pp. 13, 90–109) and Swearingen (pp. 298–300).

4. In *Gorgias*, Socrates calls rhetoric a "knack" like cookery and flattery (secs. 462e–463b).

5. I have followed Hackforth (p. 8) and De Vries (p. 7) in setting the dramatic date at 410. One of the points to this chapter is to demonstrate the power of writing to "make" (create, remake, and so forth) history. I have followed De Vries, who summarizes all the problems of the task, in setting the date of composition at 367 (pp. 7–11).

6. I realize no proof of Plato's importance needs to be given. Even so, it is worth quoting part of a paragraph written in 1965 on Plato as a writer:

> The study of philosophy in our tradition may well begin with Plato, but, strangely enough, it never seems to leave him behind. Starting with the first generation after him—with Aristotle—

philosophers have been praising Plato for his magnificent insights and at the same time undertaking to refute him, showing that his system is unclear, his arguments weak, and his conclusions fallacious. No other philosopher has been so widely praised and blamed by his successors but more to the point, no other philosopher has remained so persistently vital in philosophical debate. The continuing relevance of Plato is as evident in our time as it has ever been, and can be seen in various forms in such diverse thinkers as Heidegger, Whitehead, and the modern linguistic analysts. For professionals as well as amateurs, philosophy begins with Plato. (Sinaiko, p. 1)

The point I will make below is that everything about the Platonic strategy of (not)writing was calculated to bring about just such a state of affairs.

7. For an introduction to reading theories that explain why readers cannot read texts whose behavior is entirely unpredictable or whose nature does not fit into a preexisting scheme, see Smith (*Understanding*); Goodman; Gibson and Levin; Schank and Abelson; Adams and Collins; and Bleich.

8. At the beginning of the *Rhetoric*, Aristotle defines rhetoric, in Cooper's translation, as "the counterpart of Dialectic" (p. 1) and "as the faculty of discovering in the particular case what are the available means of persuasion" (p. 7). In effect, he has abandoned any attempt to argue with Plato's elevation of dialectic and set out to write a practical manual for the practical world. Virginia Steinhoff makes essentially the same point I am making (pp. 31–33). For a historical survey of the Platonic (idealistic) and Aristotelian (pragmatic) influences on rhetorical theory, see Nan Johnson (pp. 98–114).

9. My idea of meaning floating out of a dialogue, or at least appearing always in retrospect, comes from Jacques Lacan (*Écrits*). In particular, Lacan compares meaning to the anchoring tacks in an upholstered chair, and suggests that sentences work backwards:

Ce point de capiton, trouvez-en la fonction diachronique dans la phrase, pour autant qu'elle ne boucle sa signification qu'avec son dernier terme, chaque terme étant anticipé dans la construction des autres, et inversement scellant leur sens par son effet rétroactif. (p. 805)

(This stitch in the padding has the same effect as the diachronic function in a sentence insofar as it completes its meaning only with its last word, each word being anticipated during construction of the others, and, inversely, sealing their meaning with its retroactive effect.) (my translation)

See also Neel ("Reading and Writing," p. 162).

10. The drawing itself is in the Bodleian. Derrida intersperses it throughout his text (on the front cover, in the last page, in color

facing page 266, in miniature on page 268), and he discusses the drawing throughout *La carte postale;* see particularly pp. 25, 256.

11. Derrida, *Of Grammatology,* p. 6; this is Spivak's translation of Derrida's epigram from Nietzsche's "Aus dem Gedankenkreise der Geburt der Tragodie." Cicero also describes piquantly Socrates' unwillingness to write: "The genius and varied discourses of Socrates have been immortally enshrined in the compositions of Plato, Socrates himself not having left a single scrap of writing" (2:49).

12. Plato's claims never to have written are surely one of the oddest phenomena in Western thought. I offer my explanation of this oddity below. Anyone interested in pursuing other interpretations should start with these three ideas: (1) Plato never completed his philosophy and thus *could not* write it down (Taylor, p. 23); (2) Plato's philosophy was finally mysticism and thus was outside the possibility of writing (Grene, chap. 9); (3) the core of Platonic thought is a set of "unwritten doctrines," and therefore *Phaedrus* and the "Seventh Letter" should be taken at face value when they depreciate writing (Cherniss, *Aristotle's* and *Riddle;* Rowe, pp. 197–200). Sinaiko offers yet another possibility: "Because of the rigorously dramatic form of the dialogues, nothing that is said in them can be directly ascribed to Plato. Though he is their author, never once in his works does he speak to the reader in his own proper person." Thus what Plato says in the "Seventh Letter" "is quite literally true: Plato in his own person never did commit his philosophical ideas to writing" (p. 4).

13. Hamilton calls it a "fanciful etymology of a kind of which Plato is fond" (p. 36); Hackforth, rather petulantly, calls it "one of those etymological jests in which Plato often, and sometimes rather pointlessly, indulges" (p. 36); De Vries, citing other sources, calls it a "fiction of inspiration," "etymological play," and "strained" (p. 82).

14. The authenticity of Lysias's speech is, of course, open to question. De Vries, who finally decides Plato wrote Lysias's speech, offers a good summary of the debate extending back to Diogenes Laertius and Hermias (pp. 11–14), as does Hackforth, who also concludes that Plato wrote the speech (pp. 16–18). Hamilton is one of the few recent scholars to suggest that Plato incorporated an authentic speech by Lysias (pp. 12–14). When Hackforth wrote in 1952, he called himself "siding with the minority" in attributing the speech to Plato. Since midcentury, however, a shift has occurred. By the time Burger argued in 1980 that Plato was the author (p. 21), those favoring Plato were in a clear majority. No doubt, Robin (p. lxiii) and Shorey ("*EROTIKOS,*" p. 131) were right in arguing that the issue can never be settled finally and conclusively, though Shorey argues persuasively that Plato wrote the speech. It will be obvious from what follows that I think Plato wrote the speech. My case, however, stands even if he did not because when Plato took the speech over, he made it his own. In the unlikely event

that Lysias did write the speech, the moment it was incorporated into Plato's text it was perverted to Plato's purposes.

15. Socrates explains at sections 235c–236a that if he competes with Lysias he will have to use most of the same arguments Lysias has used because the subject has many unavoidable commonplaces. This echoes (copies?) Isocrates' "Helen":

> Such compositions follow one set road and this road is neither difficult to find, nor to learn, nor to imitate. On the other hand, discourses that are of general import, those that are trustworthy, and all of similar nature, are devised and expressed through the medium of a variety of forms and occasions of discourse whose opportune use is hard to learn, and their composition is more difficult as it is more arduous to practice dignity than buffoonery and seriousness than levity. . . . For it does not belong to the same mentality to do justice to both kinds of subjects; on the contrary, while it is easy by eloquence to overdo the trivial themes, it is difficult to reach the heights of greatness of the others; and while on famous subjects one rarely finds thoughts which no one has previously uttered, yet on trifling and insignificant topics whatever the speaker may chance to say is entirely original. (3:66–67)

16. In explaining the differing rhetorical theories of Plato, Isocrates, and Aristotle, Kinneavy says that Isocrates' use of exemplary models for imitation make him "the father of western humanism" ("Translating," p. 75).

17. Walter Ong tells (writes the telling of!) the following story:

> I was recently interviewed for . . . a talked book. The supervisor of the book . . . there is no author in any earlier sense of this word . . . brought a tape recorder to the interview and taped my answers. . . . Then he slept on the tape . . . and came back the next morning with supplementary questions for a fill-in interview, which he also taped. He took all the tape back to Brooklyn and had it transcribed. Of course the stenographer edited the tape a bit in transcribing it. The supervisor . . . edited the transcription some more, after which he sent it to me for further editing. When I had reworked it and sent it back to him, he called me in St. Louis by long distance telephone from New York and once again, this time over the telephone, taped my answers to additional questions which had occurred to him after the two or three revisions. Then he had these additional questions transcribed, edited them, fed them back into the revised manuscript, and sent the whole to me for further revisions. When the book comes out, what do we have? . . . We were

talking to make edited or printed matter sound as though it were not edited or printed, knowing that the only way to do this was to edit it very carefully before printing it. (*Interfaces*, pp. 83–85)

18. De Vries points out many of the allusions to and parodies of Isocrates, as well as Isocrates' "irritated" replies (pp. 15–18). Van Hook and Burger show how Plato entered the dispute between Isocrates and Alcidamus over the value of writing. Burger provides a catalog of Alcidamus's arguments against Isocrates that also appear in *Phaedrus* (p. 152), though there is no way to date Alcidamus and assign provenience to one of the two writers.

19. As with almost everything about *Phaedrus*, this too is disputed. In the *Orator*, for example, Cicero calls the ending a compliment, and in this century modern scholars have agreed (Jaeger, p. 190; Hamilton, pp. 15–16; and Taylor, p. 318).

20. The point I make here remains even if Plato did not forge the speech by Lysias. In that case, Plato's text begins even before I think it does, and it begins with the pen in Lysias's hand, thus making *Phaedrus* even more derivative from and dependent on sophistry to know itself than I have argued.

21. Or merely steals.

2. The Structure of Origin and the Origin of Structure

1. No part of this chapter could have been written without Derrida's essays "Force and Signification" and "'Genesis and Structure' and Phenomenology," (*Writing*, pp. 3–30, 154–68). The second "vignette" is nothing more than a distillation of the ideas I generated as a result of these two essays.

2. See Taylor (p. 299, n. 2) and Jaeger (p. 330, n. 2). Jaeger, however, thinks Diogenes Laertius, whom he calls "that great ignoramus," mistranslates the adjective meaning youthful and that Olympidorous did not mean Plato was himself young when he wrote *Phaedrus*.

3. Robin (p. 25) and Jaeger (p. 182) trace the history of Schleiermacher's effect on the construction of Plato's canon. Schleiermacher saw *Phaedrus* as the first work and the initial program of all Plato's thought, which then was developed in the later dialogues. "Dans ce dialogue est enveloppé tout ce que développera systématiquement la suite entière des autres dialogues" ("This dialogue contains everything that will develop systematically throughout the entire sequence of the other dialogues"), Robin summarizes Schleiermacher as saying (p. 25; my translation). Schleiermacher even thought *Phaedrus* was the program for the Academy.

4. Surely the most elaborate explanation of structure is by Her-

man Sinaiko (pp. 26–118). In places, however, the structure Sinaiko discovers is so complex I wonder whether it isn't structure to the point of disintegration. On pages 40-41, for example, Sinaiko outlines Socrates' second speech, which turns out to develop to nineteen levels. The idea that the lovers become like the gods they follow is the nineteenth level. I reproduce just the numbers and letters leading up to this nineteeth level to show the complexity of the structure Sinaiko finds:

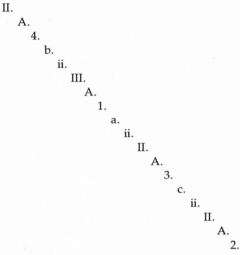

II.
  A.
    4.
      b.
        ii.
          III.
            A.
              1.
                a.
                  ii.
                    II.
                      A.
                        3.
                          c.
                            ii.
                              II.
                                A.
                                2.
                                  a. "in the process they become themselves more like the god they follow"

Does anyone outline to this degree, even as a reader? And this is merely an outline of *part* of *Phaedrus*! What would an outline of the whole thing look like? (I can't resist referring to Janet Emig's famous expose of the whole idea of outlines, and I'll bet not even Professor Sinaiko thinks Plato ever had an outline this complicated.)

    5. I do not take this as an indication that *Phaedrus* does in fact meet its own criteria for structure, but rather as a manifestation of the reigning orthodoxy of the New Criticism, with its concomitant rage for organic wholeness. See Brooks and Warren (pp. 16–20). I cannot resist pointing out that even Derrida enters the fray—on the side of those who find organic wholeness (*Dissemination*, pp. 66–67).

    6. The closest Plato comes to discussing "thinking" is his explanation of division and collection, which, he says, enable him "to speak and to think" (sec. 266b). Plato seems to have known intuitively what happens to any word once attention is focused on it. My own idea comes indirectly from Saussure (pp. 111–34). See Barthes (*Elements*,

pp. 58–88) and especially Lemaire (pp. 68-75), who explains how words enter discourse: "La selection est le choix d'un terme parmi d'autres possibles et elle implique la possibilité d'une association que l'on peut faire entre les mots, sur base de quelconques similitudes" ("The selection is the choice of one term among other possible terms, and it implies the possibility of a relationship that one can make between the words on the basis of whatever similarities") (p. 69; my translation). Lemaire gives the following scheme of linguistic operation:

a	b	c	d	horizontal dimension = contiguity, syntagm,
a'	b'	c'	d'	and metonomy
a"	b"	c"	d"	vertical dimension = similarity, system,
a'''	b'''	c'''	d'''	and metaphor

"Chaque unité linguistique," Lemaire continues,

> est semblable à la colonne d'un édifice antique. Cette colonne est dans un rapport de contiguïté avec d'autres parties de l'édifice: l'architrave par example. . . . Mais, d'autre part, cette colonne, dorique, par example, rappelle en nous d'autres styles architecturaux; l'ionique et le corinthien. (p. 70)

> (Each linguistic unit resembles a column on an antique building. This column is in contiguous rapport with the other parts of the building: with the architrave, for example. . . . But in addition, this column, Doric for example, reminds us of other architectural styles, such as Ionic or Corinthian. (my translation)

For an explanation of Plato's idea of dividing and classifying as the organizing principle of exploratory discourse, see Kinneavy (*Theory*, pp. 162–66).

7. This quotation is from Jean Rousset's *Forme et Signification: Essais sur les structures litteraires de Corneille à Claudel* (Paris: Jose Corti, 1962), p. xiii. The translation is by Barbara Johnson in Derrida's *Dissemination* (p. 24).

8. For a quite different analysis of Plato that also concludes he was "creating thinking," see Havelock (pp. 13, 40–47, 138, 146–59, 165–90, 224–30, 235–48) and Jaynes.

9. Plato uses this strategy of Socrates as poor speaker frequently. See particularly the beginning of the *Apology*, where Socrates denies he is a clever speaker and claims only to know how to tell the truth (secs. 17c–18c). Of course, Plato is exercising his brilliance as a writer here too in the rhetorical ploy of the plain-speaking person so honest as to be incapable of rhetoric. Plato knows it would be impossible to claim that role for himself so he claims it through his displacement, his Socrates.

10. Pythagoreanism is enormously difficult for modern scholars to know much about because of the oral, esoteric transmission of all its

early doctrines (*hieroi logoi*). Jaynes says the Pythagoreans "practiced mathematics, vegetarianism, and a firm illiteracy—to write things down was a source of error" (p. 290).

11. This paragraph and the next depend in part on Culler's explanation of writing and logocentrism (pp. 85–110).

12. For those who share, or at least flirt with, Conley's position, see Enos and Gage.

13. While his purpose is nothing like mine, Corbett also points out the ironic, sophistical position in which Plato places himself (p. 597).

3. "Physician, Heal Thyself"

1. See notes 14 and 20 for chapter 1 above.

2. See, for example, Palmer's attempt (pp. 41–51).

3. For a discussion of a word as an absent place, see Spivak (pp. xiiii–xx, lxxx–lxxxii).

4. Anyone unfamiliar with the jargon in this sentence should see Lindemann (pp. 86–94); Winterowd (pp. 35–163); Raymond (pp. 15–51, 415–28); and Young, Becker, and Pike.

5. See the story of the composition student contemplating the brick in Pirsig (pp. 170–73).

6. Sinaiko makes a telling observation on the actual nature of dialectic in Plato's canon: "Although Plato unquestionably considered dialectic of paramount importance in his written works he never explicitly presents us with a genuine example of the activity or an adequate account of it. It is hardly surprising, therefore, that those who write about Plato should experience difficulties in explaining what he meant by dialectic or that they should differ sharply among themselves" (p. 19). Sinaiko calls this paradoxical and then goes on to summarize the disputes over what exactly Platonic dialectic is.

I would respond to this dilemma with the explanation that Plato couldn't explain what he meant by dialectic without revealing its written nature. He could give it only by always delaying and replacing it in writing.

7. De Vries surveys the use of the word *play* in Plato's works especially in *Phaedrus* (pp. 18–22). See also Jaeger's book-length study of "paidia" in Greek culture.

8. See Hackforth (pp. 165–66, n. 2). "Euphorion and Panaetius," says Diogenes Laertius, "relate that the beginning of the *Republic* was found several times revised and rewritten, and the *Republic* itself Aristoxenus declares to have been nearly all of it included in the *Controversies* of Protagoras" (p. 311).

9. For a list of the places outside *Phaedrus* where Plato plays

on "the ambivalent nature (or absence of nature) of the *pharmakon*," see Burger (p. 147, n. 35).

10. On the relationship between text and critic, Hartman says,

> We have entered an era that can challenge even the priority of literary to literary-critical texts. Longinus is studied as seriously as the sublime texts he comments on; Jacques Derrida on Rousseau almost as interestingly as Rousseau. This is not as perverse as it sounds: most of us know Milton better than the Bible, or have read the latter again by way of Milton.
>
> The fading distinction between primary and secondary texts argues a renewed loss of innocence, like eating once more from the tree of knowledge. (*Fate*, p. 17)

11. Sinaiko goes even further, giving Plato the writer a level of consciousness and a superiority over the reader so great that whatever the reader finds, whatever the reader learns, whatever the text is perceived to include was planned by Plato:

> To be seen for what they are, the diaologues require that the philosophically serious reader respond to them with intelligence, patience, and a genuine desire for understanding. Despite all initial appearances to the contrary, the dialogues will then gradually take their place among the most carefully written, tightly structured, and perfectly organized dramatic works in Western literature, works containing nothing accidental, irrelevant, or unnecessary. Every detail—good arguments and bad, dramatic settings, personal qualities of the characters, digressions, comic interludes, poetic flights of the imagination—is deliberate, intentional, and philosophically relevant. (p. 21)

12. The second part of the translation from *Phaedo* appears in Flew (p. 139).

13. For other explanations, see Bass (Preface, p. xvi), Barbara Johnson (p. 5, n. 3), Spivak, and *Margins* (pp. 3–27).

4. *Pharmakon* and *Pharmakos*: Drugs, Scapegoats, and Writing

1. All quotations from "Plato's Pharmacy" are from Barbara Johnson's translation, which appears in *Dissemination*, pp. 61–171. Future citings will be given by inserting the page numbers of Johnson's translation into my text. References to Derrida's other works will include the title of the appropriate work in parenthesis.

2. Oddly enough, such students have not retreated to nihilism. They have made themselves into something like Chamberlain and Etter's computer writer program, Racter. Racter uses its twenty-four

hundred-word vocabulary to construct apparent sentences (e.g., "The policeman's beard is half-constructed."), dialogues, limericks, short stories, and other modes that resemble writing. Racter does everything but intend to mean.

3. I have already given a detailed study of the vigor with which the first members of the Modern Language Association tried to separate English departments from the teaching of rhetoric and composition; see my "Vicissitudo Non Est," *CEA Forum* 7 (1977): 1–5.

5. "The Most Improbable Signature": A Derridean Theory of Writing

1. See, for example, the *New York Times Sunday Magazine* (9 Feb. 1986), p. 20; the *New Republic* (25 Apr. 1983), p. 27; even *Newsweek* (22 June 1981).

2. Most references to Derrida's works will be cited in the text by using the first significant word in the title followed by the page numbers.

3. Unquestionably, the texts Derrida has published since 1974 (beginning with the publication of *Glas*) have a less threatening tone than those published before 1974. In particular, *La carte postale* (1980) and *D'un ton apocalyptique adopté naguère en philosophie (1982)* make for delightful reading, unlike the six books published in 1967 (the original French editions of *Of Grammatology, Speech and Phenomena*, and *Writing and Difference*) and 1972 (the French editions of *Positions, Dissemination*, and *Margins of Philosophy*), which, whatever else they may be, are not delightful reading. In the early pages of *D'un ton*, Derrida softens the idea of the word *apocalypse* by showing its etymologial roots in the Hebrew word *gala*, which appears more than one hundred times in the Hebrew Bible (p. 13). The title of Derrida's *D'un ton* comes from, as he says it, a parodic, distorting deportation of Guillermit's translation of Kant's *Von einem neuerdings erhobenen Vornehmen Ton in der Philosophie*, translated into French as *D'un ton grand seigneur adopté naguère en philosophie* (p. 17). In the last fifteen pages of Derrida's *D'un ton*, he makes clear, as he plays with the word *come*, which appears frequently throughout the Revelation of St. John, that whatever apocalypse is coming, has come: "Il y a l'apocalypse *sans apocalypse*" ("There is the apocalypse, *without apocalypse*") (p. 96; my translation); "L'apocalypse, c'est fini, je te le dis, voilá ce qui arrive" ("The apocalypse, it's finished, I tell you, here is what is coming") (p. 98; my translation).

4. This explanation appears on the last three pages of the essay "Différance," which appears as the last chapter of *Speech* and the first chapter of *Margins*.

5. A number of people have begun to advocate deconstruction as a mode of teaching writing. See particularly Atkins and Johnson (p.

4), Kaufer and Waller, Crowley, Northam, and Comley, all in Atkins and Johnson, *Writing and Reading Differently.*

6. Husserl goes to great lengths to separate meaning into two modes: expression and indication. Any system of communication dependent on external symbols—whether spoken, written, gestural, or some other form—depends on indication, which ultimately debases meaning. At the core of "solitary mental life," however, pure expression can occur. The phenomenological reduction leads to that pure expression of solitary mental life. Derrida's deconstruction of phenomenology shows at length that expression never escapes its need for indication (*Writing*, pp. 154–68, and *Margins*, pp. 155–75). At no point does Husserl succeed in working back before language to pure meaning.

7. For places where Derrida explains his need for Western metaphysics in order to deconstruct Western metaphysics, see *Writing*, p. 282, where Derrida explains how he uses a discourse "which borrows from a heritage itself"; *Grammatology*, p. 24, where he explains that the operation of deconstruction can only occur from within, never from outside the system being deconstructed; *Dissemination*, p. 5, where he describes the process of using a discourse while trying to escape from it; and *Margins*, p. xiii, where he asks, "In order effectively, practically to transform what one decries (tympanizes), must one still be heard and understood within it, henceforth subjecting oneself to the law of the inner hammer?"

8. That Derrida's analysis is powerful cannot, in my opinion, be denied. It has begun to play a role even among bibliographers—*even in Australia!* See Love, who, though he ends up siding with Ong, nevertheless admits that bibliographers must take Derrida into account in some way.

9. Given the disastrous reception of Hirsch's *Philosophy of Composition*, I recognize what serious ground I tread on in offering a "philosophy of composition." As I hope I make clear, however, this "philosophy" runs parallel to, not at cross purposes with, the received wisdom of the discipline.

10. Perhaps the clearest statement of a program of deconstructive reading appears in *Writing*, where Derrida sets out his program of reading Husserl's treatment of philosophies of structure (particularly Diltheyism and gestaltism). First, Derrida sets out to show the debate within the concepts Husserl uses, a debate that constantly unbalances those concepts thus requiring endless attempts to reduce the discourse to its "founding" meaning and endless explications of the concepts themselves. Second, Derrida attempts to show how the debate within Husserl's own concepts finally undermines the philosophical system of phenomenology Husserl attempts to set up (pp. 156–57).

For Miller's explanation of how the deconstructive reader seeks out the patterns of repetition in a text whereby the argument the text advances carries with it its opposite, see *Fiction*, pp. 3–9. For a series of short definitions of deconstructive reading, see Atkins and Johnson, pp. 1–2.

11. In a long footnote to *Grammatology*, Derrida quotes Leroi-Gourhan at length. Leroi-Gourhan's language verges, at least in my opinion, on science fiction. In effect, he argues that books and even reading are passing from Western civilization, to be replaced with powerful systems of electronic communications. He argues that linear writing is passing away even more rapidly than books and reading. He expects a new, as of yet unknowable system of pluridimensional thought to replace what now operates under the rubric of linear reading and writing. I find the whole quotation naïve, even trivial, but in order to let it stand on its own, I do as Derrida did—quote it in a note:

> As to the long-term consequences in terms of the forms of reasoning, and a return to diffuse and multidimensional thought, they cannot be now foreseen. Scientific thought is rather hampered by the necessity of drawing itself out in typographical channels and it is certain that if some procedure would permit the presentation of books in such a way that the materials of the different chapters are presented simultaneously in all their aspects, authors and their users would find a considerable advantage. It is absolutely certain that if scientific reasoning has clearly nothing to lose with the disappearance of writing, philosophy and literature will definitely see their forms evolve. This is not particularly regrettable since printing will conserve the curiously archaic forms of thought that men will have used during the period of alphabetic graphism; as to the new forms, they will be to the old ones as steel to flint, not only a sharper but a more flexible instrument. Writing will pass into the infrastructure without altering the functioning of intelligence, as a transition which will have some centuries of primacy. (*Grammatology*, p. 332, n. 35)

12. For a brief introduction to theories of the reader, see Culler, pp. 33–36. For an extended introduction, see Neel, "Reading and Writing."

13. For Derrida's play with the concept parasite, see *La carte*, p. 15, and *Dissemination*, p. 128.

14. "I believe," Derrida explains, "that generalized writing [e.g., writing-in-general or arche-writing] is not just the idea of a system to be invented, an hypothetical characteristic or a future possibility. I think on the contrary that oral language already belongs to this writing. But that presupposes a modification of the concept of writing that we for the moment merely anticipate" (*Grammatology*, p. 55).

15. Searle's review of Culler's *On Deconstruction*, "Word Turned

Upside Down," depends in part for its rhetorical effect on the assumption that all he needs to do to ridicule the idea of deconstruction is to explain that Derrida, and hence his followers, actually believe writing precedes speaking.

16. In part 1 of *Grammatology*, Derrida explains that Saussure cannot show how speaking is the true subject of linguistics without using writing both to uncover his idea and to present it. In fact, writing allows the invention of linguistics as the study of spoken language and also provides the medium for such an invention to work. In particular, see pp. 43–44.

17. Two quotations from *Margins* show my point in "Derrida's" words:

[1.] Since every sign, as much in the "language of action" as in articulated language (even before the invention of writing in the classical sense), supposes a certain absence (to be determined), it must be because absence in the field of writing is of an original kind if any specificity whatsoever of the written sign is to be acknowleged.

. . . If, perchance, the predicate thus assumed to characterize the absence proper to writing were itself found to suit every species of sign and communication, there would follow a general displacement: writing no longer would be a species of communication, and all the concepts to whose generality writing was subordinated (the concept itself as meaning, idea, or grasp of meaning and idea, the concept of communication, of sign, etc.) would appear as noncritical, illformed concepts, or rather concepts destined to ensure the authority and force of a certain historic discourse. (pp. 314–15)

[2.] This is the possibility on which I wish to insist: the possibility of extraction and of citational grafting which belongs to the structure of every mark, spoken or written, and which constitutes every mark as writing even before and outside every horizon of semiolinguistic communication; as writing, that is, as a possibility of functioning cut off . . . from its "original" meaning and from its belonging to a saturable and constraining context. Every sign, linguistic or nonlinguistic, spoken or written . . . as a small or large unity can be cited, put between quotation marks; thereby it can break with every given context, and engender infinitely new contexts in an absolutely nonsaturable fashion. This does not suppose that the mark is valid outside its context, but on the contrary that there are only contexts without any center of absolute anchoring. This citationality, duplication, or duplicity, this iterability of the mark is not an accident or an anomaly, but is that (normal/abnormal) without which a mark could no longer even have a so-called "normal" functioning. What would a mark be that one could not cite? And whose origin could not be lost on the way?" (pp. 320–21)

18. Even Richard Nixon's spoken words undid him, both those that were recorded and those that were merely "repeated" by his various staff members.

19. Derrida explains that the word *iter* comes from the Sanskrit *itara*, meaning other. Thus, from the beginning the origin of the concept, repetition, is already linked at least as much to otherness as to sameness.

20. Jacques Lacan uses the metaphor of "anchoring points" in language, where meaning, though nowhere present, floats out. See chapter 1, note 9 above. For an introduction to the debate between Lacan and Derrida, see *La carte*, pp. 439–524, which has been translated by Domingo et al. as "The Purveyor of Truth." See also "The Frame of Reference" in Johnson's *The Critical Difference*.

21. Culler offers a longer explanation of how cause-effect gets reversed in deconstruction (pp. 86–88), and Searle responds in his review.

22. Derrida considers two other issues in carrying out his analysis of the relationship between speech and writing: the possibility of illiteracy and the relationship between writing and violence. Because writing in general, or arche-writing, opens not only speech but also humanity, it is ethnocentric to "deny" writing to "preliterate" cultures. In fact, "peoples said to be 'without writing' lack only a certain type of writing" (*Grammatology*, pp. 83–84; see also 123–25, 127–29). In effect, any society capable of producing proper names has writing, for the production of proper names is already writing-in-general. The submission of the self to the signifier both opens the possibility of "self" in the Western sense and forecloses the possibility of full self, which would never allow itself to be named, repeated, represented endlessly: "All societies capable of producing, that is to say of obliterating, their proper names, and of bringing classificatory difference into play, practice writing in general. No reality or concept would therefore correspond to the expression 'society without writing.' . . . The scorn for writing, let us note in passing, accords quite happily with the ethnocentrism" (*Grammatology*, p. 109).

Because writing obliterates both the proper name and the person proper, it is an act of violence, setting infinite play in motion. Whereas both Rousseau and Lévi-Strauss argue that writing in the narrow, linear sense is an act of violent social control, Derrida shows how "violence did not wait for the appearance of writing in the narrow sense, that writing has always begun in language" (*Grammatology*, pp. 134–35). As Derrida explains near the end of *Grammatology*, the belief that linear, phonetic writing introduced systematic tyranny and terrorism to the world "is at once to ignore the appeal of substitution and to think evil as a surprising, exterior, irrational, accidental and therefore effaceable addition" (p. 294). In fact, as he explains in "Outwork" to *Dissemination*, writing is the name of the operation that wrenches apart the hierarchy between speech and writing, good and evil, body and soul, revealing the dance of opposites that each requires in order to know itself (p. 4). Just as the speaking of pure presence would be the silence of God *after* the end of humanity, the speaking of peace would have been the silence of God *before* writing opened the play of infinity that allowed humanity to know itself by differing from itself.

23. Culler explains how Rousseau tries to restore plenitude to speech through writing only to reveal that speech was inadequate from the beginning or it would not have needed writing (p. 103).

24. Sharon Crowley, another long-time composition teacher who has been influenced by Derrida, also argues that composition studies have long been dominated by the metaphysics of presence, which "postulates a reality, a truth, which exists outside the perceiving consciousness of man and which is unmoved, essentially unchanged, by his perception of it." Thus, "students are taught to use writing in good metaphysical style: don't let the written words get between the idea and the reader; words should be transparent, like glass" ("Of Gorgias," pp. 279–84).

25. Rousseau intends to show how culture opposes and undermines nature, leaving unhappiness instead of happiness, harmony instead of melody, writing instead of speech. Derrida, however, shows how what Rousseau calls culture and wishes to define as secondary to and a deterioration of nature, already existed in nature and was in fact the operation through which nature came to be known. Reading, Derrida explains in his deconstruction of Rousseau's nature/culture opposition, "must always aim at a certain relationship, unperceived by the writer, between what he commands and what he does not command of the patterns of the language that he uses" (*Grammatology*, p. 158).

26. See *Grammatology*, where Derrida explains his theory that the subordination of writing guarantees speech and meaning (pp. 6–9) and where he deconstructs the hierarchy of speech to writing that Saussure tries to construct (pp. 52–53). See also Hartman, *Saving*, for an explanation of the relationship in Derrida's texts between writing and nonbeing (p. xix) and Culler's summary of Derrida's reversal of the hierarchy of speech over writing (pp. 100–101).

27. The problem for philosophy, indeed for all metaphysical discourse, is that writing is the replacement of what thinking would be if thinking could occur outside writing. Writing, which should be exterior to and the servant of thinking, turns out to be what must replace thinking for thinking to be absent and sought in the first place. Writing is the place where thinking differs from itself in order to know itself.

Without writing, thinking would be indifferent, blinding, inaudible absence. Writing, in short, "designates the place of unease, or the regulated incoherence within conceptuality" (*Grammatology,* pp. 237–38).

"To see writing as silent speech," Hartman argues "is already to misunderstand it and to reduce its force. Writing . . . undoes the illusion of the simple location of meaning or self-presence: an illusion fostered by what is nearest ourselves, our body, but particularly our voice. . ." (*Saving,* p. xx). The implications of foregrounding writing expand infinitely. Such foregrounding destroys the possibility of a "simple voice" saying "what it means," and it destabilizes words. To see the degree of destabilization, one need do no more than look at what Derrida does with *ancre* (anchor) and *encre* (ink); or with the circumflex of *être,* which becomes *ester* and *reste* in *Spurs;* or even at the appearance in Plato's *Phaedrus* of the word *pharmakos,* a word that appears there by being expelled.

28. Hartman argues that every text is haunted by what it cannot exclude (*Saving,* p. xxiii).

29. Barthes makes much the same point at the end of his analysis of Balzac's "Sarasine" (S/Z, pp. 214–17). In her Introduction to *Dissemination,* Johnson explains how Derrida "puts in question the classical mentalist, expressionist presuppositions and procedures of the act of reading itself" (p. xxix). In *Positions,* Derrida argues that reading does not "seek out a finished signified beneath a textual surface." Reading is transformational. While this transformation "cannot be executed however one wishes," while "it requires protocols of reading," no reader is likely to find a closed set of protocols that satisfy both the reader and the text at hand. As a further result, the reader does not finish by answering "yes" or "no" to the text (p. 63; see also 52).

30. The play in "Envois" ranges from what Derrida and his friends do during a stay at Oxford University to such things as the syngrammatic and anagrammatic play in the name of the Biblical Esther, the authenticity of "Plato's Letters," and the playing around in *Finnegans Wake.*

31. For an interesting study of how the system defines a reader's role, see Gibson.

32. Derrida describes the attending discourse as follows: "It is not an 'author,' a 'narrator,' or a 'deus ex machina,' it is an 'I' that is both part of the spectacle and part of the audience; an 'I' that, a bit like 'you,' attends (undergoes) its own incessant, violent reinscription within the arithmetical machinery; an 'I' that, functioning as a pure passageway for operations of substitution, is not some singular and irreplaceable existence, some subject or 'life,' but only, moving between life and death, reality and fiction, etc., a mere function or phantom. A term and

a germ, a term that disseminates itself, a germ that carries its own term within it" (*Dissemination*, p. 324).

33. Derrida compares this oscillation of "I" and "you" in the writing process to a darkroom where there are nothing but negatives. The "I" of the inscription demands the use of "you"; at the same moment, it depends absolutely on the supplementation of itself that a necessary "you" cannot avoid adding: "While it is feigning to speak to you, to assist you, the 'I' that passes through requires, as a surface vacant of itself, that something supplement it, and this in that very simulacrum of attendance" (*Dissemination*, p. 327).

34. Both Hartman and Derrida explore the way naming opens play rather than signifying secure, self-contained identity. Being named already places one in a system of signifiers where all the names belong to others, where all the names depend on all the *other* names for their signifying value rather than standing outside those names and founding a separate, whole identity. In writing, and if writing in general describes all thinking and speaking, then in "Being," "there is no ultimate recognition scene." The operation of writing "keeps us looking in a glass, darkly. It disenchants the hope it expresses by playing language against itself, by dividing, spacing, splitting, joycing, tachygraphing, equivocating, reversing its charged words" (Hartman, *Saving*, p. 62). Moreover, a proper name can never be "proper"—either in the sense of "referring to one individual only" or in the sense of being suitable, right, and appropriate. A proper name displaces the individual, inscribing him or her, making him or her a grapheme in general—even if this particular individual's name only gets inscribed in speaking. What must be lost at the moment of naming is absolute presence, for naming makes the individual a signifier, sharing that role with all the other signifiers and at the same time depending on them to have any "role" at all (see *Grammatology*, p. 109). A "proper" name, I would add, rather than naming an identity, names a problem, and writing reveals the complex nature of that problem.

35. Derrida describes his "interpretation" of *Numbers* as follows:

> We will hence be inscribing—simultaneously—in the angles and corners of these *Numbers*, within them and outside them, upon the stone that awaits *you*, certain questions that touch upon "this" text "here," the status of its relation to *Numbers*, what it pretends to add to "that" text in order to mime its presentation and re-presentation, in order to seem to be offering some sort of review or account of it. For if *Numbers* offers an account of *itself*, then "this" text—and all that touches it—is already or still "that" text. Just as *Numbers* calculates and feigns self-presentation and inscribes presence in a certain play, so too does what

could still with certain irony be called "this" text mime the presentation, commentary, interpretation, review, account, or inventory of *Numbers*. As a generalized simulacrum, this writing circulates "here" in the intertext of two fictions, between a so-called primary text and its so-called commentary. . . . (*Dissemination*, p. 294)

36. Derrida's canon is filled with texts that appear inside or parallel to other texts. As but a few examples: *Glas* occurs inside and parallel to texts by Genet and Hegel; "Tympan," the first section of *Margins*, is written parallel to Michel Leiris's *Biffures*; chapters 3 and 11 of *Writing* occur in the spaces of the works of Edmond Jabes; and "Living On · Border Lines," in addition to studying Shelley's *Triumph of Life*, carries a text written parallel to itself.

37. Especially at the end of *Glas* and in those essays after it, dissemination moves to the fore of Derrida's thinking. All these essays question the strategies for textual interpretation that have dominated English departments for fifty years. Derrida compares reading for the theme or the thesis to a police action. The reader does exactly the same thing to the play of meaning that a police state does to its citizens, whose movements are restricted and whose locations are constantly monitored. The only difference is that police states can, at least to a degree, control their citizens; readers, on the other hand, cannot control meaning, however much they may try: "Ce serait arrêter une fois de plus, et au nom de la loi, de la vérité, de l'ordre symbolique, la marche d'une inconnue: son glas, ce qui s'agit ici" ("This would have stopped yet again, and in the name of the law, of truth, of the symbolic order, the movement of an unknown person: his or her death knell is what is questioned here") (*Glas*, p. 36; my translation).

38. Walter Ong most clearly explains the position opposite Derrida's, the position in which speech is in fact prior to and purer than writing. "With writing," Ong says, "the earlier noetic state undergoes a kind of cleavage, separating the knower from the external universe and then from himself." Though writing allows for art and science, "it does so at the price of splitting up the original unity of consciousness and in this sense alienating man from himself and his original lifeworld." The "real word," according to Ong, is the spoken word. "Writing and print, despite their intrinsic value, have obscured the nature of the word and of thought itself, for they have sequestered the essentially participatory word . . . from its natural habitat, sound, and assimilated it to a mark on a surface, where a real word cannot exist at all." Writing, Ong argues, is unreal; only speech is real. See *Interfaces*, pp. 21–22, 197–214.

39. Derrida's analysis seems so radical because he argues that what opens knowledge in the West—writing—must never be scruti-

nized. Because of the process of writing itself, it is crucial that the *process* of writing not infect the *product* (*Dissemination*, pp. 15, 31, 33–38). Otherwise, everything Western becomes the play of writing, which plays endlessly. "The situation of writing within the history of metaphysics," Derrida argues, is "a debased, lateralized, repressed, displaced theme, yet exercising a permanent and obsessive pressure from the place where it remains held in check" (*Grammatology*, p. 270). And writing must remain repressed in order for what it reveals to be "truth" rather than merely one discourse violently silencing other discourses.

40. The student's problem resembles Tristram Shandy's as he tries to tell his life story. He ends up going in the opposite direction, as his life goes much faster than his ability to write it down. Indeed, Tristram's "diagram" of the process of his first five books may more nearly describe the writing process than anything else in print (Sterne, pp. 358–61).

41. Derrida later changes the word *impossible* to *resistance* and then to a word he coins in French, *restance*, a neologism that Johnson describes as "meaning" "the fact or act of remaining or of being left over" (*Dissemination*, p. 8, n. 9). The sentences in French read as follows:

> Si l'on était en effet justifié à le faire, il faudrait, dès maintenant, avencer que l'une des thèses—il y en a plus d'une—inscrites dans la dissémination, c'est justement l'impossibilité de réduire un texte comme tel à ses effets de sens, de contenu, de thèse ou de thème. Non pas l'impossibilité, peut-être, puisque *cela se fait* couramment, mais la résistance—nous dirons la *restance*—d'une écriture que ne s'y fait pas plus qu'elle ne se laisse faire. (*La dissémination*, p. 13)

> (Indeed, if such a thing were justifiable, we would have to assert right now that one of the theses—there is more than one—inscribed within dissemination is precisely the impossibility of reducing a text as such to its effects of meaning, content, thesis, or theme. Not the impossibility, perhaps, since *it is commonly done*, but the resistance—we shall call it the *restance*—of a sort of writing that can neither adapt nor adopt such a reduction.) (*Dissemination*, pp. 7–8)

42. For a discussion of how a writing assignment can be a problem in and of itself instead of a mode of exploring and solving other problems, see Young, "Problems."

43. Geoffrey Hartman coined the word *boa-deconstructor* (*Deconstruction and Criticism*, p. ix).

44. Critical theorists who attack the Derridean position are, of course, legion. For a general introduction to their arguments, see Hirsch's *Validity in Interpretation* and *The Aims of Interpretation*, Graff's *Literature*

Against Itself, Lentricchia's *After the New Criticism*, White's "The Absurdist Moment in Contemporary Literary Theory," Abrams's "The Deconstructing Angel," and Searle's "Word Turned Upside Down."

45. In my opinion, the best explanations of how to respond to student writing are Moffett (pp. 188–210), Lindemann (pp. 212–35), and Murray (pp. 138–215). Though none of the three considers himself or herself a "deconstructor," the methods of evaluating writing they advocate imply (in my opinion) a tacit acceptance of Derrida's theories of the writing process.

46. See the readings of *Phaedrus* (*Dissemination*, pp. 61–173), *Madness and Civilization* (*Writing*, pp. 196–231), Freud (*La carte*, pp. 275–438), Jabes's texts (*Writing*, pp. 64–79, 294–300), and *Numbers* (*Dissemination*, pp. 287–366).

47. Reading, Miller contends, "is itself a kind of writing, or writing is a trope for the act of reading. Every act of writing is an act of reading an interpretation of some part of the totality of what is" ("Composition," p. 9).

48. Derrida argues that no absolutely justifiable beginning place for reading a text exists. The reader must make the first incision at the most likely juncture, realizing fully that this is only one juncture. A different incision will surely reveal a different text (*Grammatology*, p. 162). Any writing teacher, I would add, must decide where to begin responding to the student's paper. There are almost always many possible beginning points, but whichever one the teacher chooses will orient and direct the entire reading.

49. For an introduction to the operation of *Glas*, see Hartman's "Monsieur Text" (*Saving*, pp. 1–32).

50. Writing, Derrida argues again and again, names the operation of différance, the movement of supplement, the process of dissemination, the infinite deferral of presence, the forever-open opening where meaning can promise itself yet never appear. And, once in, there is no escape from writing. Even to mount a deconstruction of writing requires writing: "The movements of deconstruction do not destroy structures from the outside. They are not possible and effective, nor can they take accurate aim, except by inhabiting those structures. . . . Operating necessarily from the inside, borrowing all the strategic and economic resources of subversion from the old structure . . . the enterprise of deconstruction always . . . falls prey to its own work" (*Grammatology*, p. 24; see also *Margins*, pp. xii–xiii).

7. Closing the Pharmacy: Inauguration as Ending

1. The first number in parenthesis after each quotation gives the page number in the French edition from which the quotation is

taken; the second gives the page in a published translation if one is available (otherwise, I have supplied my own translation). Because my point is to show the frequent use of the terms *auger/inaugurate,* the quotations in the early part of this chapter are given in French as well as in English in order to show that the terms *auger/inaugurate* appear in Derrida's own texts and do not belong to his translators.

2. The terms *auger/inaugurate* are among Derrida's favorite. In addition to the places cited in my text, they appear, among many, many other instances, in the following situations in Derrida's texts: In *Grammatology,* Derrida says that imagination "inaugurates liberty and perfectibility because sensibility, as well as intellectual reason, filled and satisfied by the presence of the perceived, is exhausted by a fixist concept" (p. 183) and then that imagination "inaugurates the perversion whose possibility is itself inscribed in the notion of perfectibility" (p. 184). He also says that "Rousseau's entire text *describes* origin as the beginning of the end, as the inaugural decadence" (p. 199) and that everything in Rousseau's texts "proceeds from this inaugural distinction: 'It seems then that need dictated the first gestures, while the passions wrung forth the first words'" (p. 195). In *Dissemination,* Derrida quotes Mallarmé as saying the blank space on the page inaugurates the page (p. 178); Mallarmé, I would add, seems to imply that the blank space inaugurates reading itself. In *Margins,* Derrida says Saussure is the "inaugurator" of "most of the semiological or linguistic researches that dominate the field of thought today" (p. 10). Later in *Margins,* in deconstructing Husserl's attempt to separate expression from indication, Derrida says, "The order of the concept is inaugurated by expression, but this inauguration is the redoubling of a preexisting conceptuality, since it first will have had to imprint itself on the naked page of meaning" (p. 164).

3. The French text reads as follows: "La raison pour laquelle Hegel disqualifie la préface . . . comment ne pas y reconnaître la requête même de l'écriture, telle que nous la lisons ici?" (*La dissemination,* p. 41). The word *requête,* which I have translated as "demand," Johnson translates as "question" (*Dissemination,* p. 35).

4. At this point, having presented sufficient quotations from French to show that *augur/inaugurate* are terms that appear both orthographically and chirographically (if not holographically) in Derrida's texts, I will revert to the practice of quoting him from the various standard translations.

5. Alan Bass, in *Positions,* explains that "in the history of philosophy, terms with double meanings are the ones that have been used to disqualify writing" (p. 100, n. 5). He makes this statement as if it is certain (beyond any possibility of question) that "the history of philosophy" has a clear and established pattern of disqualifying writing. But

the only examples he gives are the same ones that Derrida gives—from Plato (*pharmakon*) and Rousseau (*supplement*). While it may be true that such a history of disqualification through double terms exists, such a possibility is, in my opinion, far from proven, and the burden of proof lies on those who believe such a disqualification has taken place.

WORKS CITED

Primary

Plato. *The Dialogues of Plato.* Translated by Benjamin Jowett. 2 vols. New York: Random House, 1892.

———. *Phaedrus.* Translated by Reginald Hackforth. Indianapolis: Bobbs-Merrill, 1952.

———. *Phaedrus and the Seventh and Eighth Letters.* Translated by Walter Hamilton. New York: Penguin, 1973.

Derrida, Jacques. *De la grammatologie.* Paris: Les Editions de Minuit, 1967.

———. *La voix et le phénomène: Introduction au problème du signe dans la phénoménologie de Husserl.* Paris: Presses Universitaires de France, 1967.

———. *La dissémination.* Paris: Editions du Seuil, 1972.

———. *Positions.* Paris: Les Editions de Minuit, 1972.

———. *Speech and Phenomena.* Translated by David B. Allison. Evanston, Ill.: Northwestern Univ. Press, 1973.

———. *Glas.* Paris: Editions Galilée, 1974.

———. *Of Grammatology.* Translated by Gayatri Chakravorty Spivak. Baltimore: Johns Hopkins Univ. Press, 1974.

———. "The Purveyor of Truth." Translated by Willis Domingo, James Hulbert, Moshe Ron, and M.-R. L. *Yale French Studies* 52 (1975): 31–114.

———. *Spurs: Nietzsche's Styles/Eperons: Les styles de Nietzsche.* Bilingual edition. Translated by Barbara Harlow. Chicago: Univ. of Chicago Press, 1978.

———. *La vérité en peinture.* Paris: Flammarion, 1978.

──────. *Writing and Difference*. Translated by Alan Bass. Chicago: Univ. of Chicago Press, 1978.

──────. "Living On · Border Lines." In *Deconstruction and Criticism*, by Harold Bloom, Jacques Derrida, Paul de Man, Geoffrey Hartman, and J. Hillis Miller, pp. 75–176. New York: Seabury Press, 1979.

──────. *La carte postale: De Socrate à Freud et au-delà*. Paris: Flammarion, 1980.

──────. *Dissemination*. Translated by Barbara Johnson. Chicago: Univ. of Chicago Press, 1981.

──────. *Positions*. Translated by Alan Bass. Chicago: Univ. of Chicago Press, 1981.

──────. *Margins of Philosophy*. Translated by Alan Bass. Chicago: Univ. of Chicago Press, 1982.

──────. *D'un ton apocalyptique adopté naugère en philosophie*. Paris: Editions Galilée, 1982.

Secondary

Abrams, Meyer H. "The Deconstructing Angel." *Critical Inquiry* 3 (1977): 425–39.

Adams, Marilyn J., and Allan Collins. *A Schema Theoretic View of Reading*. Urbana, Ill.: Center for the Study of Reading, 1977.

Allison, David B. Translator's Introduction to *Speech and Phenomena*, by Jacques Derrida, pp. xxxi–xlii. Evanston, Ill.: Northwestern Univ. Press, 1973.

Aristotle. *The Complete Works of Aristotle*. Edited by Jonathan Barnes. 3 vols. Princeton: Princeton Univ. Press, 1984.

──────. *The Rhetoric of Aristotle*. Translated by Lane Cooper. Englewood Cliffs, N.J.: Prentice-Hall, 1932.

Atkins, G. Douglas, and Michael L. Johnson, eds. *Writing and Reading Differently: Deconstruction and the Teaching of Composition and Literature*. Lawrence: Univ. Press of Kansas, 1985.

Barthes, Roland. *Elements of Semiology*. Translated by Annette Lavers and Colin Smith. New York: Hill and Wang, 1968.

──────. *S/Z*. Translated by Richard Miller. New York: Hill and Wang, 1974.

──────. *Writing Degree Zero*. Translated by Annette Lavers and Colin Smith. New York: Hill and Wang, 1967.

Bass, Alan. Translator's Preface to *Writing and Difference*, by

Jacques Derrida, pp. ix–xx. Chicago: Univ. of Chicago Press, 1978.

The Bedford Bibliography for Teachers of Writing. Prepared by Robert Gorrell, Patricia Bizzell, and Bruce Herzberg. Boston: St. Martin's, 1984.

Bleich, David. *Subjective Criticism.* Baltimore: Johns Hopkins Univ. Press, 1978.

Bloom, Harold. *The Anxiety of Influence.* New York: Oxford Univ. Press, 1973.

Booth, Wayne C. *The Rhetoric of Fiction.* Chicago: Univ. of Chicago Press, 1961.

Britton, James, Tony Burgess, Nancy Martin, Alex McLeod, and Harold Rosen. *The Development of Writing Abilities (11–18).* London: Schools Council Research Studies, 1975.

Broadhead, Glenn J., and Richard C. Freed. *The Variables of Composition: Process and Product in a Business Setting.* Carbondale: Southern Illinois Univ. Press, 1986.

Brooks, Cleanth, and Robert Penn Warren. *Understanding Poetry.* New York: Holt, Rinehart, and Winston, 1938.

Burger, Ronna. *Plato's* Phaedrus: *A Defense of a Philosophic Art of Writing.* University: Univ. of Alabama Press, 1980.

Chamberlain, William, and Thomas Etter. *The Policeman's Beard Is Half Constructed.* New York: Warner Books, 1986.

Cherniss, Harold. *Aristotle's Criticism of Plato and the Early Academy.* Baltimore: Johns Hopkins Univ. Press, 1944.

————. *The Riddle of the Early Academy.* 1945. Reprint. New York: Russel and Russel, 1962.

Cicero. *De Oratore.* 3 vols. Loeb Classical Library. Cambridge: Harvard Univ. Press, 1942.

Comley, Nancy R. "A Release from Weak Specifications: Liberating the Student Reader." In *Writing and Reading Differently,* edited by G. Douglas Atkins and Michael L. Johnson, pp. 129–39. Lawrence: Univ. Press of Kansas, 1985.

Conley, Thomas. "*Phaedrus* 259e ff." *Rhetoric Society Quarterly* 11 (1981): 11–15.

Connors, Robert J., Lisa S. Ede, and Andrea A. Lunsford, eds. *Essays on Classical Rhetoric and Modern Discourse.* Carbondale: Southern Illinois Univ. Press, 1984.

Corbett, Edward P. J. *Classical Rhetoric for the Modern Student.* 2d ed. New York: Oxford Univ. Press, 1971.

Crowley, Sharon. "Of Gorgias and Grammatology." *College Composition and Communication* 30 (1979): 278–85.

————. "writing and Writing." In *Writing and Reading Differently,* edited by G. Douglas Atkins and Michael L. Johnson, pp. 93–100. Lawrence: Univ. Press of Kansas, 1985.

Culler, Jonathan. *On Deconstruction: Theory and Criticism After Structuralism*. Ithaca: Cornell Univ. Press, 1982.

de Man, Paul. *Allegories of Reading: Figural Language in Rousseau, Nietzsche, Rilke and Proust*. New Haven: Yale Univ. Press, 1979.

———. *Blindness and Insight: Essays in the Rhetoric of Contemporary Criticism*. New York: Oxford Univ. Press, 1971.

Descartes, René. *Discourse on Method*. Translated by Laurence J. Lafleur. New York: Liberal Arts Press, 1950.

De Vogel, C. J. *Pythagoras and Early Pythagoreanism*. Assen, Netherlands: Royal Van Gorcum, 1966.

De Vries, Gerrit J. *A Commentary on the* Phaedrus *of Plato*. Amsterdam: Hakkert, 1969.

Diogenes Laertius. *Lives of Eminent Philosophers*. Translated by R. D. Hicks. Loeb Classical Library. Cambridge: Harvard Univ. Press, 1925.

Elbow, Peter. *Writing Without Teachers*. New York: Oxford Univ. Press, 1973.

Emig, Janet. *The Composing Process of Twelfth Graders*. Urbana, Ill.: NCTE Press, 1971.

Enos, Richard L. "The Most Significant Passage in Plato's *Phaedrus:* A Personal Nomination." *Rhetoric Society Quarterly* 11 (1981): 16–18.

Faigley, Lester. "Competing Theories of Process: A Critique and a Proposal." *College English* 48 (1986): 527–42.

Faigley, Lester, and Stephen Witte. "Analyzing Revision." *College Composition and Communication* 32 (1981): 400–414.

Fish, Stanley E. "How Ordinary Is Ordinary Language?" *New Literary History* 5 (1973): 41–54.

———. "Normal Circumstances, Literal Language, Direct Speech Acts, the Ordinary, the Everyday, the Obvious, What Goes Without Saying, and Other Special Cases." *Critical Inquiry* 4 (1978): 625–44.

Flew, Antony. "Immortality." In *The Encyclopedia of Philosophy*, Paul Edwards (Editor in Chief). 4: 139–50. New York: Macmillan, 1967.

Freeman, Kathleen. *Ancilla to the Pre-Socratic Philosophers*. Cambridge: Harvard Univ. Press, 1966.

Gage, John. "A New Way into the *Phaedrus* and Composition: A Review [of *Plato's* Phaedrus, by Ronna Burger]." *Rhetoric Society Quarterly* 11 (1981): 29–34.

Garver, Newton. Preface to *Speech and Phenomena*, by Jacques Derrida, pp. iii–xxvii. Evanston, Ill.: Northwestern Univ. Press, 1973.

Gibson, Eleanor J., and Harry Levin. *The Psychology of Reading.* Cambridge: MIT Press, 1975.

Gibson, Walker. "Authors, Speakers, Readers and Mock Readers." *College English* 11 (1950): 265–69.

Golden, James L. "Plato Revisited: A Theory of Discourse for All Seasons." In *Essays on Classical Rhetoric and Modern Discourse,* edited by Robert J. Conners, Lisa S. Ede, and Andrea A. Lunsford, pp. 16–36. Carbondale: Southern Illinois Univ. Press, 1984.

Goodman, Kenneth. *The Psycholinguistic Nature of the Reading Process.* Detroit: Wayne State Univ. Press, 1968.

Gorman, Peter. *Pythagoras: A Life.* London: Routledge and Kegan Paul, 1979.

Graff, Gerald. *Literature Against Itself: Literary Ideas in Modern Society.* Chicago: Univ. of Chicago Press, 1979.

Grene, David. *Man in His Pride.* Chicago: Univ. of Chicago Press, 1950.

Guthrie, W. K. C. *A History of Greek Philosophy.* 3 vols. Cambridge: Cambridge Univ. Press, 1967.

Hackforth, Reginald. Introduction to *Phaedrus,* by Plato, pp. 3–20. Indianapolis: Bobbs-Merrill, 1952.

Hamilton, Walter. Introduction to *Phaedrus and the Seventh and Eighth Letters,* by Plato, pp. 7–18. New York: Penguin, 1973.

Hart, James Morgan. "The College Course in English Literature." *TMLA* 1 (1884): 79–86.

Hartman, Geoffrey. *The Fate of Reading.* Chicago: Univ. of Chicago Press, 1975.

———. *Saving the Text: Literature, Derrida, Philosophy.* Baltimore: Johns Hopkins Univ. Press, 1981.

Havelock, Eric. *Preface to Plato.* Cambridge: Harvard Univ. Press, 1963.

Hirsch, E. D., Jr. *The Aims of Interpretation.* Chicago: Univ. of Chicago Press, 1976.

———. *The Philosophy of Composition.* Chicago: Univ. of Chicago Press, 1977.

———. *Validity in Interpretation.* New Haven: Yale Univ. Press, 1967.

Hirsch, E. D., Jr., and David P. Harrington. "Measuring the Communicative Effectiveness of Prose." In *Writing: Process, Development, and Communication,* edited by Carl H. Frederickson and Joseph F. Dominic, pp. 189–207. Hillsdale, N.J.: Erlbaum, 1981.

Isocrates. *Isocrates in Three Volumes.* Volumes 1 and 2 translated by George Norlin; volume 3 translated by Larue Van Hook.

Loeb Classical Library. Cambridge: Harvard Univ. Press, 1968.

Iversen, Erik. "The Hieroglyphic Tradition." In *The Legacy of Egypt*, 2d ed., edited by J. R. Harris, pp. 170–96. Oxford: Clarendon Press, 1971.

Jaeger, Werner. *Paideia: The Ideals of Greek Culture*. 3 vols. Translated by Gilbert Highet. Oxford: Blackwell, 1947.

Jarrett, James L., Ed. *The Educational Theories of the Sophists*. New York: Teacher's College Press, 1969.

Jaynes, Julian. *The Origin of Consciousness in the Breakdown of the Bicameral Mind*. Boston: Houghton Mifflin, 1976.

Johnson, Barbara. *The Critical Difference: Essays in the Contemporary Rhetoric of Reading*. Baltimore: Johns Hopkins Univ. Press, 1980.

Johnson, Nan. "Ethos and the Aims of Rhetoric." In *Essays on Classical Rhetoric and Modern Discourse*, edited by Robert J. Conners, Lisa S. Ede, and Andrea A. Lunsford, pp. 98–114. Carbondale: Southern Illinois Univ. Press, 1984.

Kane, Thomas S. *The Oxford Guide to Writing*. New York: Oxford Univ. Press, 1983.

Kaufer, David, and Gary Waller. "To Write Is to Read Is to Write, Right?" In *Writing and Reading Differently*, edited by G. Douglas Atkins and Michael L. Johnson, pp. 66–92. Lawrence: Univ. Press of Kansas, 1985.

Kerford, G. B. *The Sophistic Movement*. Cambridge: Cambridge Univ. Press, 1981.

Kermode, Frank. "Sensing Endings." *Nineteenth Century Fiction* 33 (1978): 144–58.

Kinneavy, James L. *A Theory of Discourse*. 1971. Reprint. New York: Norton, 1980.

———. "Translating Theory into Practice in Teaching Composition." In *Essays on Classical Rhetoric and Modern Discourse*, edited by Robert J. Conners, Lisa S. Ede, and Andrea A. Lunsford, pp. 69–81. Carbondale: Southern Illinois Univ. Press, 1984.

Knoblauch, C. H., and Lil Brannon. *Rhetorical Traditions and the Teaching of Writing*. Montclair, N.J.: Boynton/Cook, 1984.

Kristeva, Julia. *Desire in Language: A Semiotic Approach to Literature and Art*. London: Basil Blackwell, 1981.

Lacan, Jacques. *Écrits*. Paris: Editions du Seuil, 1966.

Lanham, Richard. *Literacy and the Survival of Humanism*. New Haven: Yale Univ. Press, 1983.

———. "The Rhetorical Paideia: The Curriculum as a Work of Art." *College English* 48 (1986): 132–41.

Lauer, Janice. "Issues in Rhetorical Invention." In *Essays on Classical Rhetoric and Modern Discourse*, edited by Robert J. Connors, Lisa S. Ede, and Andrea A. Lunsford, pp. 127–39. Carbondale: Southern Illinois Univ. Press, 1984.

Lauer, Janice, Gene Montague, Andrea Lunsford, and Janet Emig. *Four Worlds of Writing*. 2d ed. New York: Harper and Row, 1985.

Leitch, Vincent B. "Deconstruction and Pedagogy." In *Writing and Reading Differently*, edited by G. Douglas Atkins and Michael L. Johnson, pp. 16–27. Lawrence: Univ. Press of Kansas, 1985.

Lemaire, Anika. *Jacques Lacan*. 5th ed. Brussels: Pierre Maidaga, 1977.

Lentricchia, Frank. *After the New Criticism*. Chicago: Univ. of Chicago Press, 1980.

Lindemann, Erika. *A Rhetoric for Writing Teachers*. New York: Oxford Univ. Press, 1982.

Love, Harold. "Manuscript Versus Print in the Transmission of English Literature, 1600–1700." *Bulletin of the Bibliographical Society of Australia and New Zealand* 9 (1985): 95–106.

Macrorie, Ken. *Uptaught*. Rochelle Park, N.J.: Hayden, 1970.

Miller, J. Hillis. "Composition and Decomposition." In *Composition and Literature: Bridging the Gap*, edited by Winifred Bryan Horner, pp. 40–57. Chicago: Univ. of Chicago Press, 1983.

———. *Fiction and Repetition: Seven English Novels*. Cambridge: Harvard Univ. Press, 1982.

———. "The Figure in the Carpet." *Poetics Today* 1 (1980): 107–18.

———. "The Function of Rhetorical Study at the Present Time." *ADE Bulletin* 62 (1979): 10–18.

———. "Stevens' Rock and Criticism as Cure." *Georgia Review* 30 (1976): 5–33, 330–48.

———. "The Two Rhetorics: George Elliot's Bestiary." In *Writing and Reading Differently*, edited by G. Douglas Atkins and Michael L. Johnson, pp. 101–14. Lawrence: Univ. Press of Kansas, 1985.

———. "*Wuthering Heights* and the Ellipses of Interpretation." *Notre Dame English Journal* (1980): 85–100.

Moffett, James. *Teaching the Universe of Discourse*. Boston: Houghton Mifflin, 1968.

Murphy, James J., ed. *The Rhetorical Tradition and Modern Writing*. New York: Modern Language Association, 1982.

Murray, Donald M. *A Writer Teaches Writing*. 2d ed. Boston: Houghton Mifflin, 1985.

Neel, Jasper. "Reading and Writing: A Survey of the Questions About Texts." In *Research in Composition and Rhetoric: A Bibliographic Sourcebook,* edited by Michael G. Moran and Ronald F. Lunsford, pp. 153–90. Westport, Conn.: Greenwood Press, 1984.

————. "Vicissitudo Non Est." *CEA Forum* 7 (1977): 1–5.

Ong, Walter J. *Interfaces of the Word: Studies in the Evolution of Consciousness and Culture.* Ithaca: Cornell Univ. Press, 1977.

————. *Rhetoric, Romance, and Technology: Studies in the Interaction of Expression and Culture.* Ithaca: Cornell Univ. Press, 1971.

Palmer, Frank. *Grammar.* New York: Penguin, 1971.

Philip, J. A. *Pythagoras and Early Pythagoreanism.* Toronto: Univ. of Toronto Press, 1966.

Pirsig, Robert M. *Zen and the Art of Motorcycle Maintenance.* New York: Bantam, 1974.

Raeder, Hans. *Platons Philosophische Entwicklung.* Leipzig: Verlag and Druck, 1920.

Raymond, James C. *Writing (Is an Unnatural Act).* New York: Harper and Row, 1980.

Robin, Léon. *Platon.* 1935. Reprint. Paris: Presses Universitaires de France, 1968.

Romeyer-Dherbey, Gilbert. *Les Sophists.* Paris: Presses Universitaires de France, 1985.

Rorty, Richard. "Philosophy as a Kind of Writing: An Essay on Derrida." *New Literary History* 10 (1978): 141–60.

Ross, Sir David. *Plato's Theory of Ideas.* Oxford: Clarendon Press, 1951.

Rowe, Christopher, J. *Plato.* Brighton, England: Harvester Press, 1984.

Said, Edward W. *Beginnings: Intention and Method.* New York: Basic Books, 1975.

Saussure, Ferdinand de. *Course in General Linguistics.* Translated by Wade Baskin. 1959. Reprint. New York: McGraw-Hill, 1966.

Schank, Roger, and Robert Abelson. *Scripts, Plans, Goals, and Understanding: An Inquiry into Human Knowledge Structures.* Hillsdale, N.J.: Erlbaum, 1977.

Schleiermacher, F. *Platons Worke.* Berlin: Realschulbuchhandlung, 1804.

Searle, John. "Word Turned Upside Down." *New York Review of Books,* 27 Oct. 1983: 74–79.

Shorey, Paul. "On the *EROTIKOS* of Lysias in Plato's *Phaedrus.*" *Classical Philology* 28 (1933): 131–32.

————. "Platonism and the History of Science." *Proceeding of the American Philosophical Society* 66 (1927): 174–81.

————. "Review of *Sprachliche Forschungen.*" *Classical Philology* 7 (1912): 49D–92.

————. *The Unity of Plato's Thought.* Chicago: Univ. of Chicago Press, 1903.

————. *What Plato Said.* Chicago: Univ. of Chicago Press, 1933.

Sinaiko, Herman L. *Love, Knowledge, and Discourse in Plato: Dialogue and Dialectic in* Phaedrus, Republic, Parmenides. Chicago: Univ. of Chicago Press, 1965.

Smith, Frank. *Psycholinguistics and Reading.* New York: Holt, Rinehart, and Winston, 1973.

————. *Understanding Reading: A Psycholinguistic Analysis of Reading and Learning to Read.* New York: Holt, Rinehart, and Winston, 1971.

Sommers, Nancy. "Revision Strategies of Student Writers and Experienced Writers." *College Composition and Communication* 31 (1980): 378–88.

Spivak, Gayatri Chakravorty. Translator's Preface to *Of Grammatology,* by Jacques Derrida, pp. ix–lxxxvii. Baltimore: Johns Hopkins Univ. Press, 1974.

Steinhoff, Virginia N. "The *Phaedrus* Idyll as Ethical Play: The Platonic Stance." In *The Rhetorical Tradition and Modern Writing,* edited by James J. Murphy, pp. 31–45. New York: Modern Language Association, 1982.

Sterne, Laurence. *The Life and Opinions of Tristram Shandy, Gentleman.* Boston: Houghton Mifflin, 1965.

Stewart, Donald C. "The Continuing Relevance of Plato's *Phaedrus.*" In *Essays on Classical Rhetoric and Modern Discourse,* edited by Robert J. Conners, Lisa S. Ede, and Andrea A. Lunsford, pp. 115–26. Carbondale: Southern Illinois Univ. Press, 1984.

Swearingen, C. Jan. "The Rhetor as Eiron: Plato's Defense of Dialogues." *Pre/Text* 3 (1982): 289–336.

Taylor, Alfred E. *Plato: The Man and His Work.* London: Methuen, 1926.

Trimmer, Joseph F., and Nancy I. Sommers. *Writing with a Purpose.* 8th ed. Boston: Houghton Mifflin, 1984.

Ulmer, Gregory L. *Applied Grammatology: Poste(e)-Pedagogy from Jacques Derrida to Joseph Beuys.* Baltimore: Johns Hopkins Univ. Press, 1985.

Van Hook, LaRue. "Alcidamus Versus Isocrates: The Spoken Versus the Written Word." *Classical Weekly* 12 (1919): 89–94.

Walter, Otis M. "Plato's Idea of Rhetoric for Contemporary Students: Theory and Composition Assignments." *College Composition and Communication* 25 (1984): 20–30.

Weaver, Richard. "Language Is Sermonic." In *Language Is Sermonic: Richard M. Weaver on the Nature of Rhetoric* edited by Richard Johannesen, Rennard Strickland, and Ralph Eubanks, pp. 165–79. Baton Rouge: Louisiana State Univ. Press, 1970.

White, Hayden. "The Absurdist Moment in Contemporary Literary Theory." In *Directions for Criticism: Structuralism and Its Alternatives*, edited by Murray Krieger and L. S. Dembo, pp. 85–110. Madison: Univ. of Wisconsin Press, 1977.

Winterowd, W. Ross. *Composition/Rhetoric: A Synthesis*. Carbondale: Southern Illinois Univ. Press, 1986.

————. *Contemporary Rhetoric: A Conceptual Background with Readings*. New York: Harcourt Brace Jovanovich, 1975.

Young, Richard. "Problems and the Composing Process." In *Writing: Process, Development, and Communication*, edited by Carl H. Frederikson and Joseph F. Dominic, pp. 59–65. Hillsdale, N.J.: Erlbaum, 1981.

Young, Richard, Alton L. Becker, and Kenneth L. Pike. *Rhetoric: Discovery and Change*. New York: Harcourt, Brace and World, 1970.

Young, Richard, and Patricia Sullivan. "Why Write? A Reconsideration." In *Essays on Classical Rhetoric and Modern Discourse*, edited by Robert J. Connors, Lisa S. Ede, and Andrea A. Lunsford, pp. 215–25. Carbondale: Southern Illinois Univ. Press, 1984.

INDEX

Jasper Neel, who received his degrees from Mississippi College and the University of Tennessee, Knoxville, was the Director of English Programs for the Modern Language Association from 1976 to 1979 and Chair of the English Department at Francis Marion College from 1979 to 1984. He has edited a number of books for the MLA Press and published several essays on the relationship between literary theory and composition theory. Professor Neel is currently a member of the English faculty at Northern Illinois University.